What happened in the Sixties? The "Now" generation back "Then." Page R-1

Dacron's VanHusen Corp. makes twin mobility twice as affordable Page M-5

This week's *Newscast in Print*: "Negroes-The Problem That Won't Go Away" Page P-2

TODAY'S WEATHER QUALITY:
ACCEPTABLE
Data from Ohio State Weather Service
O.S.W.S. DEPT. OF WEATHER

DACRON Republican-Democrat
One Of America's Newspapers

OHIO
LUCKY BUCKEYE
Daily Lottery
4 6 1969
WINNING NUMBER

Section A | DACRON, OHIO, SUNDAY, FEB. 12, 1978 | ©1978 South Central Ohio Coal, Gas, Electricity, Telephone & Telegraph Communications Group | TWENTY CENTS

Powder Room Prowler Strikes Anew

Photo by Rep.-Dem Staff Photographer Prissy VanHusen
Hank's Shell Station on Dacron's West Side
...aftermath scene of the latest prowler attack as onlookers look on.

By LARRY MICKLE
Rep.-Dem. Staff Writer

Dacron's "Powder Room Prowler" has struck terror into the ladies room for the sixth time this year, yesterday. His latest victim, Miss Belinda Heinke, was returning from a shopping trip to the Corngate Plaza shopping center when she stopped to freshen up at a Shell station on the corner of Monroe Street and Secor Ave. It was there that the Prowler was apparently lying in wait, concealed within the Shell station's women's comfort facilities.

According to police, Miss Heinke entered a stall inside the comfort facility and had seated herself there when the Prowler dropped onto her head from a crouched position which he had been maintaining on top of the stall's partition, and forced her to be assaulted in a disgusting manner.

Henry Cobble, owner of the service station, which is known as Hank's Shell Station, was alerted to the assault by loud yelling and screams of indignation. He rushed to the women's room door but was unable to gain entrance because of Miss Heike's having fastened a
Continued on Page A2

AN OPEN LETTER TO THE POWDER ROOM PROWLER
From DONOVAN GROAT
Rep.-Dem. Senior Feature Writer

Dear Prowler,
Your recent attack, the sixth this year, was the most appalling attack by a powder room prowler I have ever seen color slides of. It may be senseless to appeal to your reason, you may have no more of that than the bag you wear over your head. It may be the act of an idiot with bungs in his ears to appeal to your compassion; likely you have no more of that than a fist-handed Nazi with innocent dead bodies on his hands and a million Jews on his breath . . . but all I can do is try.
Continued on Page A19

Two Dacron Women Feared Missing in Volcanic Disaster

Japan Destroyed

CLEVELAND, Feb. 11 (Combined Sources)—Possible tragedy has marred the vacation plans of Miss Frances Bundle and her mother Olive as volcanoes destroyed Japan early today.

Rep.-Dem. Archives
The Eastern Hemisphere
...where Japan was formerly located.

Miss Bundle and her mother departed Friday for Cleveland, where they joined other members of the East Ohio Presbyterian Women's Auxiliary Association on a one-week group tour of the Orient leaving from that city. The Presbyterian charter group was to arrive in Tokyo today, but it is not known whether they did so. The Bundles were driven to Cleveland by Miss Bundle's brother-in-law, Ed.

Photo by Mrs. Bundle's sister Grace
Miss Francis Bundle (left) and her mother
...before leaving for Cleveland on Friday.

Miss Bundle and her mother had been looking forward to their Oriental tour for more than a year and a half, according to Rev. Elliot Dotter, pastor of the N. Melville Ave. Presbyterian Church. The charter excursion was available to members of the East Ohio Presbyterian women's group at a special rate of $540 per person, which included hotel accommodations and breakfast, and the Bundles had been saving diligently for some time in order to take advantage of this travel opportunity.

The Bundle family has long been prominent in Dacron church circles. Until his death in 1959, the late Mr. William Bundle, a retired assistant sales director at MacAdam, Ins., had served for years as a deacon at Melville Ave. Presbyterian.
Cont. Sec. G, Page 12

Plan to Sell Soviet Jews

MOSCOW, Feb. 10 (OPI)—The Soviet news agency Tass has reported that Kremlin officials are debating a program to sell the U.S.S.R.'s Jewish population on the world market. The plan would reportedly be designed to reduce world criticism of the treatment of Soviet Jews and bring an estimated criticism of the treatment of Soviet Jews and bring an estimated $50,000,000 in hard currency into the Soviet economy.

"The Soviet peoples are fair and just," Tass said. "We would give discounts for quantity purchases. Maybe even arrange for lay-away plans."

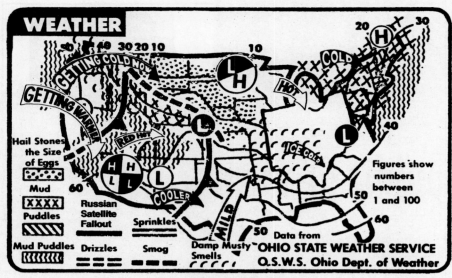

Real Cold

DACRON—Clear and very cold tonight. Low in the low-to-mid to possibly upper 20's or 30's. Partly cloudy. Winds north or southeasterly, 5 to 60 miles per hour. Barometric pressure is kind of low.

OHIO—Cold.

3-DAY OUTLOOK FOR OHIO—Cold.

EXTENDED FORECAST—Cold this winter. Turning warmer in the spring. Then hot and humid all summer. A period of cooling will follow in autumn. Then cold and wintry next winter.

WORLD TEMPERATURES

Paris	51	Tokyo	48	Moscow	12
Akron	30	Youngstown	30	Dayton	29
Rome	64	London	37	Madrid	63
Sandusky	28	Columbus	29	Cincinnati	31

METEOROLOGICAL DATA
Saturday February 11, 1978

Degree days this week	14
Degree weeks this month	56
Degree months	11
Degree years	6
Degree holidays & weekends	14
Humidity count	1
Pollen pressure	44
Warm factor	60
Sunset today	yes
Barom. precip. temp	81
Precip. temp. barom. deg.	2x8
Deg. temp. precip	72
Temp. precip. deficit PM	27
Time Celsius EST	11:00

LAKE ERIE TIDES
Hi/none   Lo/none

YESTERDAY'S POLLUTION INDEX
256 at 4PM

TODAY'S POLLUTION FORECAST
200-250

0-100	alert
100-200	precaution
200-300	caution
300-400	warning
400-500	caution
500-600	alert

TODAY'S ALMANAC
Bushy tails on female gray squirrels in February means two more years of winter.
Rotate your refrigerator goods—6:45 PM

Powder Room Prowler Strikes Anew
Continued from page A1

hook on the inside.

Police Called

"I don't know how this could have happened," said Mr. Cobble in a later interview. "The rest rooms are for customers only." Mr. Cobble called the police and returned to the women's room, prepared to pry the door open with a large screwdriver when, before the police were able to arrive, the "Powder Room Prowler" rushed from the powder room, struck Mr. Cobble in the face with Miss Heinke's purse, and made his escape.

Witnesses say he was wearing bag over his head at the time.

Miss Heinke was treated at Forest Lawn Memorial

Hospital for "stomach trouble" and released, and Mr. Cobble was also treated for getting slapped in the face with a purse. Police say that Miss Heinke was not able to give a very complete description of the "Powder Room Prowler" partly because she was still having a lot of stomach troubles, but that they did get some more valuable clues such as, that the Prowler was wearing unusual high-heeled shoes.

Investigation to Be Led

Assistant Police Chief Carl Leper, who has been assigned to lead a special Powder Room investigative team, said he hoped the Prowler case would be solved "as soon as we find

out who did it."

Miss Heinke could not be reached, but her mother, Mrs. Gustav Heinke of 2344 Ranchwagon Rd., Dacron Dales, said the whole incident was "awful," and expressed wishes that the "Powder Room Prowler" be quickly caught before "other people's daughters get as embarrassed as mine is."

Miss Heinke, 31, who lives at home, is an ex-Dacron High School honor student who attended the University of California at Los Angeles and the Massachusetts Institute of Technology in Massachusetts and graduated with two Ph.D.s in chemistry and physics. She now teaches second grade.

Kidnapped To Venus

By JERRY BURGER
Rep.-Dem. Staff Writer

SATURDAY, Feb. 11—A 31-year-old Dacron librarian who was found early this morning wandering nude in Wright Brother Park claims that she 'was "abducted by Venusians" last Wednesday evening and taken to "the back of the moon" where she was "implanted with outer-space semen" and then returned to earth.

Police found Miss Penelope Cuntz of 1304 Van Wert St. walking naked down a park bridle path at 4 A.M. She identified herself but was at first unable to give any account of why she was there or where her clothes were. Miss Cuntz was taken to Forrest Lawn Memorial Hospital where she later told doctors of the supposed kidnapping.

According to her account, she was walking home from her job at the VanHusen branch of the Dacron Public Library at about 6 P.M. Wednesday night when she decided to take a shortcut through Wright Brother Park. Halfway across the park she was confronted by six "tiny green, men" who forced her to accompany them to their "atomic saucer" parked in a vacant lot on West Truman St. Shortly thereafter, Miss Cuntz said she found herself on the back of the moon. Later, the Venusians returned her to the vacant lot.

Hospital spokesmen said an examination showed evidence of physical trauma and sexual tampering. Doctors at Forrest Lawn believe Miss Cuntz is suffering from severe exposure and shock. Police theorize that she was attacked and left for dead in some park shelter and did not regain consciousness until two days later. She had not been to work since Wednesday, and library supervisors said she had not called in sick

Suspicions were, raised that Miss Cuntz might be another victim of the "Powder Room Prowler" but police were quick to point out that her condition showed none of the usual marks of "that perpetrator's particular problem."

Rites Held For Crossword Editor's Wife

Hermwood Litmajor, the *Republican-Democrat*'s crossword editor, said farewell to his wife of 28 years Friday in private services. Evelynn Litmajor, 56, was stabbed 985 times Wednesday evening by a one-armed man who forced his way into the Litmajor home. Mr. Litmajor suffered scratch marks on his face and arms and was forced to witness the slaughter of his beloved wife. No motive has been determined, and police are without a suspect. Mr. Litmajor will continue his weekly crossword puzzle despite the tragedy.

Bring Suit in Wild Dog Pack Case

The Greater Dacron A.S.P.C.A., honored by Mayor Pilegravey last fall for capturing a pack of 30 wild dogs which were later gassed at the city dog pound, will now have a lawsuit brought against it for that action, says Dacron Estates Hunt Club Master of Foxhounds Edward Duffy. Duffy, who has been searching since last October for the Hunt Club's lost pack of 30 foxhounds, claims that the city
Cont. Sec. H. Page 5

Bloody Knife Found in Park

DACRON, Feb. 11— Two cub scouts discovered a bloody knife in a clump of bushes in Gullett Park. The knife was wrapped in a handkerchief bearing the monogram HL. The youths were tracking sparrow when they made the discovery. A police spokesman said that the. knife was examined. "It's just a knife with some blood on it. An ice fisherman probably dropped it." The knife and hanky will be held at the Hoover St. police station until next Friday. If it is not claimed by then, it will be given to the Goodwill.

NATIONAL LAMPOON · 10850 WILSHIRE BOULEVARD · LOS ANGELES · CA 90024 · USA

RUGGED LAND · 401 WEST STREET · SECOND FLOOR · NEW YORK CITY · NY 10014 · USA

RuggedLand

Published by Rugged Land, LLC

401 WEST STREET • SECOND FLOOR • NEW YORK CITY • NY 10014 • USA
RUGGED LAND and colophon are trademarks of Rugged Land, LLC.
NATIONAL LAMPOON and colophon are trademarks of National Lampoon.

PUBLISHER'S CATALOGING-IN-PUBLICATION DATA
(Provided by Quality Books, Inc.)

National lampoon's Sunday newspaper parody : The Dacron,
Ohio Republican-Democrat / edited by P.J. O'Rourke and
John Hughes. --1st ed.
p. cm.
ISBN 159071037-1

1. Newspapers--Humor. 2. American wit and humor.
I. O'Rourke, P. J. II. Hughes, John, 1950- III. Title:
Dacron, Ohio Republican-Democrat. IV. Title: National lampoon.

PN6231.N63N38 2004   081
                           QBI04-800042

RUGGED LAND WEBSITE ADDRESS:WWW.RUGGEDLAND.COM
COPYRIGHT NATIONAL LAMPOON © 2004

SEPTEMBER 2005
1   3   5   7   9   10   8   6   4   2

Today's Log

Births

Forrest Lawn Memorial Hospital

Mr. and Mrs. Ed Glawn, 677 Partypack Rd., Dacron Dells, boy, Friday
Mr. and Mrs. Dan Salnight, 75 Highfence Pkwy., Dacron Estates, girl, Saturday

Calvary General Hospital

Mr. And Mrs. Skipp Rent, 708 Emerson, boy, Friday
Ivy and Mrs. Carey Hodd, 2122 1/2 N. Flat. Ave., girl, Friday
Miss Penelope Cuntz, 1304 Van Wert, green thing that glows in the dark, Saturday
Mr. and Mrs. Stew Meet, 4506 N. Smalltree, boy, Saturday

Our Lady of Affliction Hospital

Mr. and Mrs. Thatsa Pollock, 858 E. Taft, 2 girls, Friday
Mrs. and Mrs. Passa DiPizza, 1202 E. Polk, 2 boys, Friday
Mrs. and Mrs. Hunky Surname, 200 1/4 E. Hoover, boy, Friday
Mr. and Mrs. Bludgeon O'Hooligan, 1106 Shackallev, 3 boys and 2 girls, Friday, Saturday and early this morning

Scarsview General Hospital

Miss Mazola Roosevelt, 200 S. Shakespeare, boy, Friday
Miss Gemstone Brown, 108 Public Housing Cir., girl, Friday
Miss Lucite Jones, 318 MacAdams Houses, girl, Friday
Miss Pantela Johnson, 210 S. Irvine, girl, Friday
Miss Audio Wilson, 4404 Urban Renewal Sq., girl, Saturday

Abortions

Forrest Lawn Memorial Hospital

Teena Popper, 15, 947 Carport St., Dacron Dells, girl
Bitsy Jeanwear, 16, 2422 Patio Pl., Dacron Glens, girl
Suzi Testorsnift, 14, 1761 Ownphone Dr., West Dacron, too early to tell

Deaths

Ethel Bell, 86, of 4855 Elmlight Rd., tripped over a pattern in the linoleum.
Alton Bierly, 51, of Port Coal, Ohio, smoking.
Timothy Adams, 8, of 1046 Bosco Pkwy., running with a popsicle stick in mouth.
Stanislas Slovoki, 25, of Hamtramck Mich., drowning, freezing and decomposition.
Loraine Metz, 18, of 665 Lawnroller Dr., Dacron Dells, hymeneal hemorrhage.
Omarr Reilly, 58, of 312 Gingko, middle age.
Ralph Pescador, 78, of 188 W. Coco Cr., long painful illness.
Olga Florence, 3 days, of 3629 Sherbert, was dropped.
Gloria Grant, 81, of 667 Curtsey, poor rescue squad training.
Knute Aukschtenz, 31, of 222 Villa de Manzana, radiation poisoning.
Nora Gorman, 54, of 819 Maildrop, secret drinking.
Mary Doel, 0, of no permanent address, spontaneously aborted self.
Helen Blinkers, 60, of 1658 White Pine, cancer of the car.

Divorces Granted

Week of Feb. 6 thru 12

Phillips, Joyce from James. Grounds: Incompatibility.
Mitzner, Julie from Rudolph. Grounds: Compatibility with other people.
Wolfe, Julio from Donald. Grounds: Abuse.
Collin Elaine from Eddy. Grounds: Self-abuse.
Marshall, Kathleen from Jerry. Grounds: Pet swapping.
Olmstead Harold from Connie. Grounds: Childery.
Reese, Susan from Daniel. Grounds: Tired of each other.
Richardson, Dorthea from Douglas. Grounds: She met a cute Latin type.
Grainger, Ellen from John. Grounds: He snores.
Long, Patricia from Andrew. Grounds: Her mother.
Wynn, Florence from Henry. Grounds: His friends.
Martin, Diana from Harold. Grounds: Both drink.
Filch, Donna from Douglas. Grounds: She puts things away where he can never find them.
Miller, Joyce from James. Grounds: Kids got on his nerves.
Conley, Terri from Joseph. Grounds: Argument over who's going to do the dishes.
Raymond, Margaret from Otis: Grounds: Can't find an apartment.
Richer, Donna from Richard. Grounds: Smelly feet.
Samples, Marsha from William. Grounds: Her dog ate his slippers.
Stover, Patricia from Andy. Grounds: He farts and says "mmm ... Kiss me again!"
Tressler, Noomi from Hugh. Grounds: The house is a mess.
Stone, Laurie from Stephen: Grounds: Garage needs painting.

Fire Alarms

Friday

10:10 P.M.—Dacron Shaft and Flue Factory, 1650 Flatcar, fire in parking lot, three parking spaces damaged.
11:19 P.M.—5860 World War Way, house of Leonard Snadden family Bible fire from spontaneous combustion of prom mums, $15 loss.
11:52 P.M.—Corner of E. Grant and Burger St., explosion in National Socialist Party of America bookstore, 26 Afrika Corps campaign hats and a real Iron Cross lost.

Saturday

1:01 A.M.—Corner of S. Melville and 11th, false alarm.
1:05 A.M.—Corner of S. Melville and 11th, false alarm.
1:09 A.M.—Corner of S. Melville and 11th, false alarm.
1:15 A.M.—Corner of S. Melville and 11th, false alarm.
1:18 A.M.—Corner of S. Melville and 11th, false alarm.
1:26 A.M.—Corner of S. Melville and 11th, false alarm.
4:56 A.M.—VanHusen. Mfg. Co., 600 E. Polk, faulty insurance coverage, $50,000 loss.
10:22 A.M.—232 Religion Blvd., house of Art Dodge, wanted out-of-town guests to view fire engine.
10:48 A.M.—Dacron North Side Rest Home, 3323 N. Emerson, 11 elderly persons rescued from clothes hamper chute.
12:22 P.M.—C. Estes Kefauver High School, 3301 Upton Ave., fire in school office, loss of student records, $65 petty cash.
5:19 P.M.—Corner of Hoover and Longfellow, man dropped lit cigarette onto auto seat under crotch, loss of pants, seat cover.
7:25 P.M.—1604 Versailles, house of Filbert Petterson, flaming bag of dog excrement on porch, nail in doorbell, no loss.
9:43 P.M.—1556 Rakeleaf, Marijuana in rec room, $10 loss.
10:30 P.M.—140 6th St., bum, no loss.
10:56 P.M.—Nicky's Drive-In 990 Upton, teens lighting flatulence, no loss.

Rescue Squad

Friday

10:02 P.M.—1554 Woodrow, Arnold Piesner, 39, beaten by wife.
10:41 P.M.—667 Curtsey, Gloria Gent, 81, ill.
1132 P.M.—1554 Woodrow, Arnold Piesner, 39, beaten by neighbors.
11:52 P.M.—2990 Douglas, Hyman Bremstein, 40, swallowed chess set, to Forrest Lawn mental ward.

Saturday

1:27 A.M.—Corn. Melville and 11th, Ronald LeRoy, 20, beaten by firemen, to Scarsview General Hospital
2:20 A.M.—Paving Park Lover's Lane, Shirley Bartlett, 19, and Harold Netsner, 20, stuck together.
4:11 A.M.—703 1/2 S. Shakespeare, Otis Robinson, 40, snakes and spiders on the ceiling.
6:02 A.M.—667 Curtsey, Gloria Grant, quite ill.
8:49 A.M.—1204 Biltlot, Eric Fetznier, 16, blindness from masturbation.
9:05 A.M.—Sears Store, 2200 Secor, Arnold Piesner, 39, beaten by coworkers.
10:12 A.M.—Licking-Creek Reservoir, Stanislas Slovoki, 25, snagged on fishhook, dead.
11:04 A.M.—1227 Lawnview, Dacron Dales, Tommy Mayes, 7, beans in his ears.
12:02 P.M.—1871 Lasky, Larry Hume, 10, got sick from not washing his hands before lunch.
12:25 P.M.—667 Curtsey, Gloria Goat, 81, really ill.
12:50 P.M.—5511 Telegraph, Jeff Bledsoe, 7, made a face and it stayed that way.
1:48 P.M.—1749 Jermoin Dr., Larry Kroger, 31, mild case of suicide, to Forrest Lawn Hospital.
2:34 P.M.—3440 Taft. Yappy, 3, ate its own vomit.
2:50 P.M.—1660 E. Grant, Burton Torme, 62, hit-and-stayed accident, to Our Lady of Affliction hospital.
3:10 P.M.—1500 block of MacArther Ave., police car buried in mobile home.
3:32 P.M.—1114 Pidgeon St., Earl Edwards, 15, private parts stuck in vacuum-cleaner hose.
4:04 P.M.—Dacron Dog and Kennel Club, 3600 N. Cleveland, 9 people treated for dog bites, 15 dogs treated for people kicks.
4:45 P.M.—667 Curtsey, Gloria Gant, 81, dead.
5-51 P.M.—44020 W. Alexis Rd., Johnny Clutter, 12, tongue stuck to pump handle.
6:19 P.M.1141 Lockdoor, James Kelly, 58, heart attack or wife's goulash, to Calvary General Hospital.
9:50 P.M.—Top of the Building Restaurant, in Trailer Towers, 200 Monroe St., 58 stomachs pumped.

Police Blotter

West Side Cemetery: Joey Hemleck, 18; Ed Plotner, 18; and 3 minor youths, for vandalism, turning over grave markets, attempting to dig up a dead baby and disturbing the peace with loud frightened screaming when apprehended by night watchman.
Corngate Shopping Center, Secore and Monroe: Danny Flegget, 24, and Diane Flegget, 20 for attempted child abuse and baby selling, and Margret Hutchinson, 42, for illegally removing shopping cart from Corngate Food-Clown store.
Buy-And-Pay grocery store, S. Washington Irving and 20th: Patterson Jones, 26, for suspicion of getting caught breaking in.
South Central Ohio R.R. overpass at Buckeyesville Rd.: minor youth for public obscenity with a can of spray paint.
2661 Beaufort St.: Earl Borman, Jr., 28, suspected Nazi war criminal.
I-40 near Monroe St., exit: Willy DiPalma, 18; and Lou Pinnarella, 20, for racing each other in cars; Jerry Goleta, 18, Joe Kersey, 18, and 5 minor youths, for watching them.
Dacron Dog and Kennel Club 3600 N. Cleveland: 2 German Shepherds, 5 Japanese terriers, 1 water spaniel and an otter hound, for fighting.
978 1/2 Taft St.: Dominic Brocolli, 32, for smuggling expensive West Virginia cigarettes into Ohio and trying to sell them in cheap Ohio vending machines.
Cocky-Locky Motel, 413 Upton: Truman Johnston, 26, and Patterson Washington, 21, for impersonating Arab billionaires.
1660 E. Grant: David Diver, 17, for driving like a fool.

Robberies

Ernie's Gulf service station, 750 Avenue of the Ohios, of gas, oil, antifreeze, battery water, air and a map, loss of $11.80.
Irene Sudtz, 6859 Deal Rd. of purse by two men who forced her into an auto, drove her to an unspecified location on the East Side, forced her to wait in auto while they had lunch, then robbed her and returned her to her home, loss of $23 and personal papers.

Burglaries

Buy-and-Pay grocery store, S. Irving and 20th, $140 and 11,000,000 King Korn stamps.
Amaretta Sons Trucking Co., 1250 Dockside, 120 Sony tv's, 40 silver fox fur coats, $1,000 in cash, $40,000 in negotiable securites and 2,000 uncut diamonds taken from an insured truck.
4400 Lake James Rd., home of Ernest J. Truscit, coin collection and other goods taken, house still open.

Larcenies

470 Dremble La., 6-pack of beer stolen from garage by Big-Foot monster.
600 19th St., automobiles of all the basketball game spectators from Benson High School stolen out of Harding High School parking lot.
Trailer Plaza, 3,500-lb. hot dog taken from "World of Weenies" display.

Assaults

Hank's Shell station, Secor and Monroe, Belinda Heinke, 31, assaulted in powder room.
1311 E 9th Pl. Eloise Caulb , 28, beat off rapist.
3296 Brush Ct., Rita Corvest, 27, forced to spend weekend in Las Vegas with male caucasian, 30-35, six feet in height, 160-170 lbs., dark hair, moustache, married, mole on upper left thigh.
1117 Public Housing Cr., Tyrone Wilson, mysterious assailant shot at his wife while he was on the other side of the room looking out the window.

Property Damage

Three Trees Country Club, 7500 Three Trees Rd., human vandalism in $20-a-plate dinner, damage: $20.
W. Trumart and Bycrus, big hole in an empty lot, damage: none.

Other Crimes Reported

600 block of Polk St., sniper or kids on roof with gun or rolls of caps and a hammer.
1540 Crabtree St., missing persons report of Miss Francis Bundle and Mrs. Olive Bundle by Mrs. Bundle's sister Grace Hecky, also missing: Japan.
Anonymous report of dead tree in alley, cracked sidewalk on Spruce St., big dog running wild; low power lines; noisy garbage-men; youngsters downtown and the death of Alf Landon.
1880 Treeleaf, Dacron Dales, missing person report of labor leader Sam Herpsburg, on way to meet organized crime figure, by his wife Lorraine.
Silage Country Jail, escape through hole in wall made with hands by Robinson Brown, 20; Jasper Johnson, 19; Eldridge Jones, 18; and Fred Jackson, 24.

Municipal Court

Abe Binklutz, 450 Datenut, Dacron View Hills, 2,607 counts of petty fraud, trial date postponed forever by his 38 lawyers. Judge Grunwald.
Purdy Spackle, 867 Taft, six counts of grand theft auto, innocent. Judge Dweel.
Bruno Grozniak, No. 558 Singles Village Apartments, two counts possession of marijuana in quantity for sale, three counts possession of cocaine with intention to distribute, nine counts possession of controlled substances, 14 counts of concealing evidence by eating, one count of disorderly conduct and assaulting a wall, trial date postponed to allow time for him to find a lawyer that would take the case. Judge Mumpf.
Maria Teresa Spermatozoa; 211 6th St., impersonating a female, case dismissed upon court's receiving sufficient evidence that she was a female. Judge Grunwald.
Luis Ramonez, 45618th St., operating a vehicle with so many things on the dashboard and hanging from the mirror that he couldn't see out, $20 fine. Judge Hummel.
Elaine Dempsey, 3650 Harding, operating a vehicle in a strange, unheard of manner, $10 fine and a real talking-to. Judge Pipewelt.
Jimmy Bitsner, 244 Lane Ct., Dacron Dells, operating a vehicle under the influence of something the police officer couldn't find, $25 fine, license suspended for one week. Judge Mumpf.
Salley Heather, 1708 Wellsley, speeding, life in prison. Judge Applebower.
Larry Gordon, 2109 Limesand, illegal turn and making faces at a police officer, license suspended for 10 days. Judge Dweel.
Duane Hensettir, 7480-E Coolidge, driving too loud, $30 fine. Judge Grunwald.
Wustes Robinson, 1515 S. Melville, jaywalking, death penalty. Judge Applebower.
Jay Kleepler, 2404 Catalpa Blvd., driving with shoes and socks off, $5 fine, Judge Hummel.
Joey Peterson, 677 Feedlot, operating a vehicle with huge tires and the rear end jacked-up real high $20 fine. Judge Dweel.
Ramon Perez, 1104 S. Longfellow, littering, three consecutive terms of 20 to life. Judge Applebower.

Bad Car Accidents

1900 block of Hoover St.,. auto of David Diver, 17, struck a firehydrant, a tree, a snow shovel, and Enos Murphy, 78, Drive injured slightly, pedestrian broke pipe.
3700 block of P.T.A. Ave., auto of Herb N. Spinks, 38, collided with Eva Louise Jones, 12. Child injured slightly, driver tore shirt and lost expensive gold pen.
1600 block of E. Grant, auto of David Diver, 17, struck Briton Torme, 62. Torme suffered head injuries and broken jaw, driver injured slightly.
1500 block of MacArthur Avenue, auto of Dacron municipal police department struck extra-wide mobile home. Officer George-Benson, 29, injured thumbs, Officer Larren Spokes, 34, broken neck, crushed spine, passenger David Diver, 17, suffered slight bruise.

Noisy Neighbors

Friday

Mr. and Mrs. Andy Maxwell, 5606 Tremansville Rd.

Saturday

Bob Morstonson and 20 or 30 of his friends, 1156 Starling, Apt. 3M.
Trudy Dickenson and her boyfriend, Presidential Trailer Court.
The Felton family, 1171 Whittier.

Annoying Phone Calls

Mrs. Ester Birch at 577-6145: "Is your refrigerator running?"
Miss Amy Munsch at 655-2281: heavy breathing.
Tuft Street Drug Store at 474-3940: "Do you have Prince Albert in a can?"
Sam's Pizzaria at 671-7153: order for 4,000 pizza with everything to go.
Miss Trudy Ellison at 945-4563: caller expressed a desire to eat her lingerie.
Miss Marcie Hellman at 564-5729: ex-boyfriend

Loud Bangs and Thumps

11:05 P.M.— Friday, 3100 block of Dockside.
3:23 A.M.— Saturday, Trailer Towers Building.
6:40 A.M.— Saturday, Plazoria Shopping Center vicinity.

Strange Smells

9:40 A.M.— thru 3:00 P.M.— Saturday, in back of Paul's Steak House, downtown.
4:00 P.M.— Saturday, 1171 Gingko, house of Jack Haven.

Call 555-4070

ACTION FINGER

or write to ACTION FINGER
The DACRON REPUBLICAN-DEMOCRAT
100 Polk Street, Dacron, Ohio 43701

Q. My husband enjoys shooting songbirds from our breakfast room. We would like to attract more of them. What can we do? We are both retired.

Mrs. TRW, Dacron

A. Action Finger's Songbird Expert recommends buying a feeder and stocking it with any commercial seed blend. Every week put out some suet. If your husband will wrap his weapon in a couple of towels, it will cut down on the noise and won't scare away the birds you do attract.

Q. Our son is dying from bone cancer and it has been his dream to talk to Reggie Jackson. Would it be possible to arrange this? We realize it is an enormous imposition but it would bring some joy into the life of a boy who has had none.

RWM, Dacron Glen

A. We spoke with Reggie Jackson's agent and he said that Reggie will telephone your son for $5,000. For $1,500 he will write a letter and for $55 he'll send a get-well card. You may contact Sports Management Inc., Suite 2230, St. Regis Hotel, New York 10012.

Q. I be real mad about giving $500 money to this dude be calling hisself Myron DeCoven for to be locating my Roots and where I came from. All he give me were this card what say, "You come from Africa." I got to be asking how I get more money to take up the place of the money I got cheated away from and I want to know what part of Africa I came from.

RW, South Dacron

A. Action finger has contacted the U. S. Office of Minority Emergency Satisfaction and a check is in the mail. As to where in Africa you came from, Dr. Abuljar Kuwaku, Professor of Blackeology at Dacron Elementary and Junior College, said that you most likely come from Black Africa.

Q. Where can I get some cocaine? I am a chemistry scientist and I need about $35 worth for my doctor degree test. I need it by next Saturday night

W, Dacron Hills

A. Your best bet, according to Dacron Narcotics, Guns and Explosives Division Detective Chester L. Lude Jr., is Willies Shack in South Dacron. Ask for Boss Shark. Remember, however, that cocaine is a controlled substance and therefore possessing it could result in your arrest and imprisonment.

Q. There is a dead tree in my alley. It's been there all day. Also, my sidewalk is beginning to crack. I've only had it 11 years. My sister would like to know why youngsters are allowed downtown. There is a big dog that runs wild in our neighborhood and leaves messes all over and barks too much. Before I forget, could you tell whoever you tell about power lines about my power lines? They seem to be hanging very low. Oh, and remember in last week's letter about garbagemen? They are still just as noisy and sometimes we hear them rattling the cans at midnight! Also, is Alf Landon dead yet?

A. Alf's alive. The dead tree is gone. The dog has been gassed. The sidewalk will be repaired, the power lines just look low, they're fine. You can't do anything about kids downtown. The garbagemen deny that they are being noisy and have never rattled your cans at midnight. The police will check into the matter. In answer to your phone call on Friday-we got your hearing aid replaced, the shower curtain is on order, the bread is safe to eat, cats don't need vitamins, a 45-year-old rug can be expected to wear out, the Supreme Court says blacks have the right to walk in front of any house they want so long as they do not do so on private property, the same goes for Jews and Mexicans, according to the phone company no one is listening in on your calls, cake mixes weigh the same as they did last year, the street cleaner will be sure to go by your home next week, the mayor says "hello" and Rome was not built in a day.

Action Finger answers questions, runs down problems and helps you out. We cannot, however, give you things. You may write us care of the Republican-Democrat, *Dacron. Include your name, address and phone number. We will not accept letters written with anything other than pen, pencil or typewriter.*

Prowler Inflicts Psychic Harm Along Path Of Pain And Anguish

Powder Room Prowler Suspect composite sketch drawn by Dacron Police Department police artists from witnesses' descriptions.

By PETE HAMTRACK
Rep.-Dem. Feature Writer

For almost a year now, the "Powder Room Prowler" has left a trail of mortification, discomfort and, red-faced outrage in the wake of his six shocking attacks upon women in the privacy of their lavatories.

It was one year ago last Valentine's Day when this mysterious, mentally ill person first made his presence known by an attempted assault on socialite photographer Prissy VanHusen: Miss VanHusen was getting ready for a date that night with her then-fiancé Bobby MacAdam. Prissy and Bobby had planned an evening of pre-wedded bliss at the Dacron Heart Association's Annual Heartthrob Charity Ball at the Golfclub Golf Club. Prissy was in an upstairs bathroom of her parents' Dacron Estates home, straightening her hose, when the "Prowler" burst in upon her carrying the instruments of his assaults. Fortunately, Prissy was able to hit her attacker over the head with a hot comb and shove him out the bathroom window.

Miss VanHusen, who has since come to work for the Republican-Democrat, was badly shaken by the near-crime and her life seemed to come to pieces in the aftermath of what narrowly avoided being tragic. "I was so upset," says Miss VanHusen, "that I don't think I even would have called the police except Mom got hysterical when all that broken glass and the 'Prowler,' whoever he is, fell into her prize peony bed which the gardener had just mulched. Then, later that night, my fiancé had a terrible accident when he walked through a sliding glass door. And I guess my whole personality had been changed by what I'd been through and he and I broke up soon after and for awhile things seemed awful."

Two months later, a next victim was not so lucky. She was Bridget Hannihan, 20, a domestic employee in the home of MacAdam Asphalt Co. president Malcolm MacAdam. Mr. MacAdam's son,. Robert, found the girl in an upstairs bathroom where she had apparently fainted from embarrassment. Like Prissy VanHusen only more so, Miss Hannihan's life seemed shattered by the experience, so much so that she was never really able to give the police a very complete account of attack, and the MacAdam family generously aided Bridget in a return to her native Belfast.

Since then, there have been four more "Prowler" assaults: On June 10th, Alice Murdock, 36, here on a shopping trip from Tiffin, was assaulted in the women's lounge of Rosenberg's Department store and left tied to a toilet. And on August 1st, Registered Nurse Ginger Hopkins, 40, was shoved into the ladies lavatory of the Forrest Lawn Memorial Hospital's Emergency Room and attacked with an apparatus that she herself was carrying to a bedridden patient down the hall.

The mild fall day, of Sunday, October 8th, saw perhaps the most vicious of these, crimes when 15-year-old Ellen Blakey, whose name was not released because of her age, was pulled into a comfort facility in Paving Park and assaulted with a parks department garden hose. Miss Blakey was hospitalized for nearly a week with a severe abdominal distension. Then, for four months, the "Prowler" seemed to cease his ravages, only to strike again yesterday.

What has emerged from these attacks? Who is the "Powder Room Prowler"? When will he be caught? Police have few clues. He is a tall young man with a "polite" manner who wears strange high-heeled shoes and has a bag over his head. This much is known. But is it enough? Will it lead police to the "Prowler" and the "Prowler" to jail? For now, no one knows.

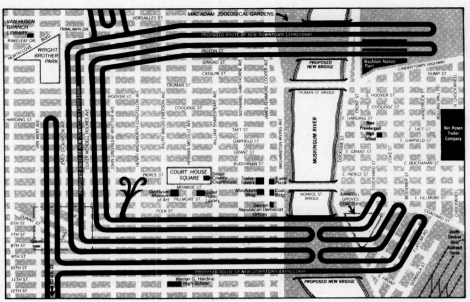

Map Courtesy Gullet Public Library

Map of downtown shows proposed expressway route with special heavy-use loops. Many claim plan will also effect much-needed clearance of southside slums and their residents.

Expressway Would Avoid Snarls

By PETER HAMTRACK
Rep.-Dem. Feature Writer

Highway Commissioner Dan VanHusen says that the new downtown expressway plan, approved by the City Council on Friday, will avoid traffic tie-ups by providing a special series of heavy use back-up loops to relieve traffic pressure during peak usage hours.

Speaking to the press after the Council vote, VanHusen said that although the new plan will cost an additional 480 million dollars and calls for an extra 156 miles of expressway within the downtown area of Dacron, the city will ultimately benefit financially. "More jobs will result from this plan and more jobs means a boost to retail sales

and a revitalized downtown," said VanHusen.

Malcolm MacAdam, Chairman of the Board of MacAdam Asphalt, says that his company alone is planning to hire an additional 4,000 asphalt makers and that the highway construction is expected to create at least 50,000 new jobs in the Dacron area before its projected completion date in 2040.

Landmark Sent To Cleaners

PARIS, Feb. 11 (UPA)— Parisians awoke yesterday morning to find that their beloved landmark, the Eiffel Tower, was absent from the Paris sky. Nearly one million callers notified police and government officials. The famed tower was sent to Germany to be cleaned and painted and will be returned to its site in March.

Hole Being Examined

A large round hole that glows in the dark has been found in a vacant lot at West Truman and Bucyrus near Wright Brother Park. The hole, which is about 20 feet across and six feet deep, emits a greenish-yellow glow similar to that of a radium wristwatch dial. Police say they have no clues yet as to the identity of the vandals who dug this large hole.

30 Million Die in Peking

HONG KONG, Feb. 10 (OPI)—Peking radio has reported that at least 30 million people have died in an industrial accident in the Chinese capital. No details were given.

Missing Link Sought By Sausage Co. Police

The world's largest skinless frank is missing from its display at World of Weenies, the traveling Hot Dog Expo sponsored by the World Weenie Sausage Co. and now on display at Trailer Plaza downtown. The 3,500-lb. red hot was stolen Friday night after thieves broke into a refrigerator trailer where the wiener was stored. Norm Benson, President of World Weenie, says that if it is eaten no harm will come to the diner. "It's fully cooked and ready, and safe to eat."

Police have detailed a special unit to investigate the theft. Citizens are asked to be on the lookout for a hot dog which measures 7 feet in length.

Mass Murderer Given Sentence

OMAHA, Neb., Feb. 10 (UPA)—Daryl Winnducker, who was convicted last month of the lye-throwing murders of his mother, wife, invalid sister and twin three-year-old daughters—crimes which he reportedly committed in order to collect life insurance totaling less than $750—was sentenced yesterday to five consecutive life sentences in prison. Under Nebraska law, he will be eligible for parole tomorrow.

Jews Mailed to Freedom

MUNICH, Germany (OPI)— A family of Soviet Jews arrived in Munich last week by mail. The two adults and three children were sealed inside a carton and sent, undetected by Soviet police, to a Munich address. Later in the month, the family will mail themselves to the U.S., where they will live with relatives. West German sources noted that the family arrived postage-due.

Rep.-Dem. Staff Photo

Dacron Police Department S.W.A.T. (Special Weapons and Tactics) squad apprehended suspected shoplifter at Southslum Shopping Center, Friday. The unnamed suspect had been spotted pocketing a Vu-Liter by Simpkis Jewelry Store manager Sam Shumark.

30,000 Feared Dead in India

NEW DELHI, India (OPI)—It is feared that as many as 30,000 Indians may be dead from starvation. A lack of food is being blamed.

GLOBAL GRAB BAG

The News in Short

NATIONAL NEWS

CIA Drug Use

According to the prestigious Domestic Affairs Quarterly, recent revelations concerning the use of hallucinogenic drugs by the C.I.A. have led to speculation among members of the Carter Administration that certain U.S. intelligence agents may have accidentally dosed themselves with these mind-altering drugs, causing them to hallucinate, among other things, a communist dictatorship in Chile, a winnable war in Vietnam, and air support for the Bay of Pigs invasion.

New Meat Grades

The U. S. Department of Agriculture will soon revamp its system of meat grading, it has been announced. The new rating system will replace the former grades of "U.S.D.A. Prime," "U.S.D.A. Choice" and "U.S.D.A. Good" with three new grades to be called "U.S.D.A. Fabulous," "U.S.D.A. Absolutely Terrific" and "U.S.D.A. Just The Most Wonderful Thing You've Ever Tasted."

Money Seized

Eight billion dollars in counterfeit currency was seized Friday in a New York City hotel. Police were tipped off by a hotel employee who suspected the authenticity of one of the billion-dollar bills.

New JFK Info

The House Assassination Committee has reportedly uncovered evidence that President John F. Kennedy may have been assassinated by a former defector to the Soviet Union who, acting alone from unknown motives, shot the President with a long-range high-power rifle from the window of a building overlooking the route of Kennedy's Dallas motorcade. The evidence, contained in a set of subpoenaed Johnson administration documents titled Report of the President's Commission on the Assassination of President John F. Kennedy, is supposedly drawn from reliable sources.

Fact Finders

Elsewhere in congressional news, all 432 members of the House of Representatives left today on a three-week fact-finding tour of the French Riviera.

UNNATIONAL NEWS

Cambodia

According to information compiled from international agencies, recent political refugees and the monitoring of Vietnamese radio broadcasts, everyone in the country of Cambodia is now dead.

Mass Arrest

Egyptian police have arrested 400 people charged with un-Egyptian activities. The arrests were the culmination of a seven-month investigation by a government un-Egyptian Activities Committee. The 400 are accused of bathing too often, eating with utensils, and working all day. Under a 1964 law, the offenders could face life imprisonment if found guilty.

Drought Aid

The United States will provide six sub-Sahara nations with more than 500 million dollars in foreign aid to help them recover from a devastating three-year drought. The money will reportedly be spent on flood control.

Big Foot Monster Sighted Again– Burglarizes Suburban Garage

By SAM FRESCA
Rep-Dem. Staff Writer

Dacron's Big Foot Monster was spotted again last night in suburban Dacron Glen by a man who said he watched the monster steal a six-pack of beer from a garage. The man, Gordon Lippert of Dacron Glen, was walking his dog when he heard noises coming from the garage at 470 Dremble Lane. "It was about six feet tall with skin like a tweed overcoat,"

Lippert explained. "It had a gorilla head and I think it was wearing sneakers." Police investigated the scene and found a set of the now familiar "tennis racket" footprints. The footprints, which have been found at several other monster-sighting scenes, resemble impressions made by tennis rackets. Mr. Lippert's description matched those given by other witnesses, except that Mr. Lippert said the monster fled on a skateboard when it discovered it was be-

ing observed. "I think it's safe to say there's something out there all right," Police Chief Finch said. "Fortunately, it doesn't seem to be interested in harming people, just stealing beer out of garages and looking in windows. We hope to capture it alive."

Dacron Elementary and Junior College Professor of Animals Stuart Fanbiner said that he and his colleagues believe the monster is a prehistoric gorilla with large flat feet.

S.W.A.T. Team Tracks Sniper

SATURDAY, Feb. 11— Dacron's S.W.A.T. team was called into action this afternoon when shopkeepers in the 600 block of Polk St. reported sniper fire. The special eight-man unit blocked off the street and conducted a rooftop search, but the assailant apparently escaped. "He covered his tracks very well," Sgt. William Gully, second in command of the team, said. "All we found were some kids playing with caps on top of one apartment building."

Witnesses described the gunshots as sounding like rolls of caps being smashed with a hammer, so police speculate that the sniper was using a large caliber rifle. At first report it was believed that six people were shot, however, it turned out that four people had slipped on the ice and two others responded to the shots by falling to the ground. There were no serious injuries.

Police say they have no leads as yet in the incident.

Union Prexy Disappears

Sam Herpsburg, President of International Trash Haulers local 43 was reported missing yesterday by his wife, Lorraine. Mrs. Herpsburg told police that he had left their Dacron Dales home at 8 A.M. Friday morning on his way to a meeting with labor relations consultant Charles Amaretto. According to Amaretto, Mr. Herpsburg never arrived. Police say they have no clues as to his whereabouts.

Ties Identified As Carcinogenic Agents

LANSING, Michigan (OPI)—A group of researchers at Michigan State University have found a link between men's neckties with stripes and cancer. Laboratory animals that had sucked on striped neckties over a two-year period have devel-

oped malignant tumors on their bladders. The group will submit their findings to the Food and Drug Administration early next week. In the meantime, owners of striped neckties are warned against sucking or chewing on the ties.

Negotiations Continue With Air Hijackers

ROME, Italy, Feb. 11 (OPI)—The government of Italy is continuing to negotiate with four armed political hijackers who are holding 240 Air Italia passengers hostage and demanding freedom for everyone in Italian jails. Little is known of this terrorist group, which calls

itself the "Anti-Imperialist Death to Zionism People's Liberation Red Army Black September White Squad," except that its woman leader, who uses the name "Ddb Lzmdc Ouaejk," is reported to have been educated in America. Negotiations are now in their 2,004th day.

Ex-Dacron Man Victim in 'Stash Bag' Murders

SAN FRANCISCO, Feb. 11 (Combined Sources)— One of the victims of the so-called California "Stash Bag" murders is reported to be an ex-Dacron resident, Franklin Furter, 31. The murders, which have been taking place in the Bay area of San Francisco for the past ten years, got their name because the chopped and finely ground bodies of the victims have frequently turned up mixed in with illegal marijuana in one-ounce bags of that drug sold on the street by a mysterious drug dealer known only as "Ed."

Mr. Furter, who graduated in 1964 from Dacron's

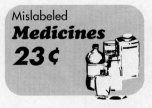

Mr. Furter in a recent photograph.

Kefauver High School, was the owner of an earth shoe repair shop in Sausalito, California. He was reported missing last month by his wife, after he repor-

Cont. Sec. A, Page 29

VanHusen Inc.

Dacron's VanHusen Manufacturing Inc. has presented Mayor Milos Pilegravey with a complimentary limousine manufactured locally for free use during his next four terms in office. Limousine is shown here during mayor's recent test-drive to St. Pete.

Prowler May Be Medico Say Anonymous Docs

By LARRY MICKLE
Rep.-Dem. Staff Writer

SATURDAY, Feb. 11—Police are looking into new suggestions by doctors at Calvary General Hospital that the "Powder Room Prowler's" attacks, which they term "very professional," maybe the work of a professional, a paramedic or perhaps an ambulance driver.

A doctor, who declined to give his name out of fear for his wife and daughter, stated that the acts of assault left no actual damage to the area assaulted and had the medi-cal effect which those acts are intended to have.

Elliot Brisberg, head of Local 11, Medical Semi-Professional Workers, the union that represents paramedics, ambulance drivers, sub-orderlies and unregistered nurses, said there was "no way" anyone in his union was involved. "These are all highly trained people who take oaths of honor and, anyway, none of the girls in the union office have been bothered."

Meanwhile, the special police prowler task force, headed by Assistant Chief Carl Leper, is continuing its investigations.

Eatery Holds Grand Closing

SATURDAY, Feb. 11—McMuggles, the popular fast food restaurant chain, is closing its Dacron facility next Friday. The restaurant will celebrate with a Grand Closing Week promotion which will feature live appearances by Mutts the McMuggles clown. A free soft drink will be offered with each Big Mick and a free order of French fries with each Quarter Kilo hamburger.

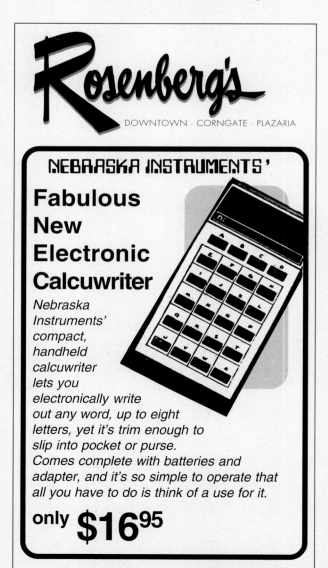

New Ice Age Anticipated

DENMARK, Feb. 10 (OPI)—International meteorologists, gathered for an annual meeting of the U.N. Meteorology Congress in Copenhagen, predict that a continuing accumulation of ice and snow in the earth's polar regions will lead to an expansion of the Antarctic and Arctic ice caps, causing a new ice age within the next 50 years.

Grief-Stricken Jackie Onassis

NEW YORK, Feb. 9 (OPI)—Widowed Jackie Kennedy Onassis, attending the Knee Fund Charity Ball at the Waldorf Hotel doesn't seem upset by the passing of her husband, Aristotle, dead for only two years.

Cap Melting

NORWAY, Feb. 10 (UPA)—Oceanographers from all over the world, here in Oslo for the annual convention of the U.N. Oceanography Congress, believe that a continued warm trend in the earth's atmosphere will cause the Arctic and Antarctic ice caps to melt, flooding most coastal areas within the next several decades.

GOOD NEWS

No news may be good news but the Republican-Democrat thinks there's more to good news than just no news at all. Every day in the Rep.-Dem. we print facts and information that will put a smile and a little joy on your face.

Dacron's violent crime rate is 2% lower than Dayton's.

Today is Boy Scout National Good Sense Day. Scouts will be showing good sense all over America today.

No hurricane has ever struck Dacron.

Rep.-Dem Staff Photo

The 1400 block of South Nathaniel Hawthorne Ave., seen today, is back to normal with the huge piles of garbage that had accumulated now removed.

Garbage Strike Over

Amaretto Hauling, which is under contract to the City Sanitation Department to collect garbage on Dacron's largely black South Side, announced Friday that they had signed contract new contract with International Trash Haulers local 43, ending the two-month South Dacron garbage strike.

Police Crack Cigarette Smuggling Organization

By JERRY BURGER
Rep.-Dem. Staff Writer

SATURDAY, Feb. 11—Police say that they have smashed a major Southeast Ohio cigarette smuggling operation today with the arrest of the smuggling ring's alleged mastermind, Dominic Brocolli, 32, of 978 1/2 Taft St. According to police reports, Brocolli, a close associate of reputed organized crime kingpin Charlie ("The Vending Machine") Amaretto, was buying truck-loads of cigarettes in West Virginia where the state cigarette tax is 15¢ per pack and smuggling them into Ohio which taxes cigarettes at 10¢ per pack. Brocolli was then selling the smuggled cigarette packs at 5¢ to 8¢ above normal Ohio retail prices.

Brocolli had reportedly smuggled more than 3,000 cartons of cigarettes across the Ohio border, but police believe that relatively few of the illegal "butt-legged" smokes had as yet gotten into public circulation.

Rep.-Dem. Staff Photo

The Silage County Board of Estimate has purchased 18 "Mobile Homes of Detention" for use as Silage County mini-jails. According to County Sheriff Joe Welsh, "These movable incarceration facilities will allow us to move our incarcerating capabilities into areas where major emergency incarceration is needed. For example, last year during the rioting in South Dacron which destroyed that pilot low-income housing project. These units would have been very valuable then." The portable jails were manufactured locally by Dacron's VanHusen company.

Authorities Crack Counterfeit Merit Badge Operation In Raid

By LARRY MICKLE
Rep-Dem. Staff Writer

SATURDAY, Feb. 11—Police today raided a home on South Nathaniel Hawthorne Ave. and confiscated a sewing machine and thread and arrested a boy and his mother. The woman, 39-year-old Viola Majors and her son, D.J., 19, were charged with fraud. The two allegedly manufactured and sold fake merit badges to cub, boy, girl and brownie scouts. D.J. Majors had been observed at various grade school playgrounds in South Dacron and was suspected of selling something there. An investigation revealed that youths were buying counterfeit merit badges from him. The badges are given to scout who complete a series of required tasks. The fake badges allowed a youngster to wear a badge without having earned it. They were priced at $5 apiece with the President's Physical Fitness 50-mile-hike badge going for $10.

Commenting on the arrest, Regional Director of the Boy Scouts of Ohio, Gen. Howard Donald Mousse, said, "This is a violation of the basic foundations of Scouting. What's the point of giving badges away if the kids can buy them?" He went on to say that all inner-city Scout troops will be required to undergo badge verification at their next meeting.

Suspects Washington (left) and Johnston (right). Both are claiming diplomatic immunity on the basis of their Black Muslim faith.

Couple Tries Baby Sale

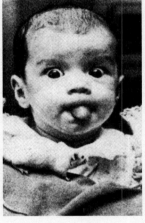

Rep.-Dem Staff Photo

Baby Flegget—offered free with $75 and a set of car stereo speakers.

By JERRY BURGER
Rep.-Dem. Staff Writer

A local couple was arrested yesterday for trying to sell a baby out of the back of their van in West Dacron's Corngate shopping center. Witnesses told police that Danny Flegget, 24, and his wife Diane, 20, had offered to sell their daughter Jill, 1/2, for $500. When there were no takers, the couple reportedly lowered their price to $400, then to $200, then to $50 and then tried to give the baby away for free, even attempting to thrust her into the loaded grocery cart of a passing housewife who made them take her back. By the time police arrived, Danny and Diane were offering $75 and a set of car stereo speakers to anyone who'd take the child. They were charged with attempted child abuse and the passing housewife was charged with illegal removal of a shopping cart from the Corngate Food Clown.

In a statement to police, Mrs. Flegget said that she and her husband had tried to sell the baby because, "Our dog hated her and she threw up if you gave her Pepsi instead of milk in her bottle and we want to go to the West Coast."

Fraud Charged

Cleveland Oilmen Arrested; Not Real Arabs, Police Say

By MICK HOGARTY
Rep-Dem. Staff Writer

SATURDAY, Feb. 11—Two men were arrested early today on charges of impersonating Arab oil billionaires. Police charged that Truman Johnston, 26, and Patterson Washington, 21, represented themselves to members of the Dacron business community as Arab oil billionaires when, in fact, they were actually blacks from Cleveland.

Johnston and Washington, who had been staying in Dacron at the CockyLocky Motel for the past two weeks, claimed that they were from the Middle Eastern sheikdom "Amen" and were here to invest a "quadrillion dollars" of Arab oil money in a new downtown Dacron "Hotel-Motel-Resort-Convention Center-High Income Housing Project-Discotheque Complex" for which they were seeking "local partnerhoods" with shares priced at $5 apiece. Stock in the proposed venture was sold to numerous local businessmen reputedly including VanHusen Vice-President Woolworth VanHusen III, real estate entrepreneur Harvey Sleazebaum, auto dealer Herb Wisenheimer, department store magnate Julius Rosenberg, and Chamber of Commerce president Buddy MacAdam. Close examination by police experts, however, showed the stock certificates to be cleverly altered stainless flatware coupons from a Kellogg's K-Ration breakfast cereal box. The forgery has been traced to a Xerox machine at Bob's Likity-Split Print, a small printing concern in West Dacron and owner Bob Roberts is being held for questioning.

Nobel Peace Prize Revoked

STOCKHOLM Sweden, Feb. 11 (OPI)—The Nobel peace prize was taken away from German biochemist Albrecht Steiner, who won the award for his work with gnats.

After winning the prize, Steiner said he would spend the prize money on sex and drugs. This is the first time the award has been revoked.

Dacron Bar Opposes Recall of Municipal Judge Applebower

By MICK HOGARTY
Rep.-Dem. Staff Writer

FRIDAY, Feb. 10—The Dacron Bar Association issued a statement today defending judge James Applebower, who is presently the target of a recall petition. The petition to Governor Rhodes to have Judge Applebower (who is sometimes referred to as "the Jailing Judge" or "Jailing Jim") removed from the municipal bench was initiated after Applebower sentenced two black youths to life in prison for stealing a stereo and found a young woman guilty of violating a 1787 Northwest Territory ordinance against being a rape victim. According to sponsors of the petition, who include Dacron N.A.A.C.P. President and City Councilman Madison Jones and National Organization of Women People

co-chairpersons Susan Fitzerman and Marylin Armbruster, Judge Applebower has also made a number of other judicial decisions which they say show him to be unfit for his job: They claim that last fall he sentenced 242 Mexican migrant workers, who had taken a wrong turn on their way to pick the Michigan apple crop, to 90 days each in jail for public uncleanliness. He acquitted a confessed wifebeater on the grounds that the deprivation of the wifebeater's wife's services for the three months that she was in the hospital was "punishment enough." He ruled that the East Dacron Ku Klux Klan chapter was a tax-exempt "charitable organization." And he ordered a male hairdresser, arrested for jay-walking, to prove in open court that he was heterosexual. Two hundred thirty-nine of Judge

Applebower's last 236 decisions have been overturned in higher courts, the recall petition sponsors charge (one of his decisions was ruled so erroneous by the Ohio Supreme Court that it had to be reversed three times), and they claim to have the signatures of more than 70,000 Dacron women and blacks on their petition already.

The Dacron Bar Association, in its statement defending Applebower, denies these charges, saying that they are "somewhat exaggerated" and that the petition sponsors have "put the facts in a bad light." The statement of support, delivered by Bar Association and Chamber of Commerce president Buddy MacAdam, goes on to say that the Dacron bar members have "known Jim for a long time," that "he is a regular guy" and has been "a heck of a friend to every one of us."

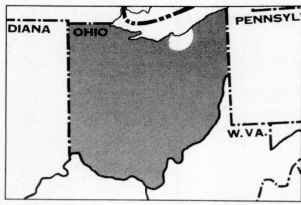

Map courtesy Ohio State Department of Maps

Shaded area is claimed by Indians in court suit. Their lawyers say they don't want Cleveland.

Indians Sue Ohio

COLUMBUS, Feb. 10 (UPA)—Two American Indian leaders, Tom White Feather and William Two Crows, are bringing suit in Federal court to return nearly 95 percent of Ohio to what they call "its rightful native American owners." The area involved in the suit includes almost all of Ohio except Cleveland.

According to the brief filed today in South Central Ohio District Court, the bulk of Ohio's land should be returned to ownership by American Indians because: "American Indians lived in Ohio first, as shown by the state's name, 'Ohio'—an Indian word meaning 'the next state over from Pennsylvania,' therefore Indians must

have used to own it." And, "Nobody can find a canceled check to prove that the Indians ever sold it."

Lawyers for the Indian leaders conceded that no Indian tribe that ever lived in Ohio is still in existence, but they argued that since all American Indians are "brothers in the eyes of the Great Spirit," this is no reason for the state not to be returned to Indian ownership. For instance, although White Feather and Two Crows are both Navajos from Arizona, they have nonetheless proposed themselves as the new Indian owners of Ohio. "Ohio should be returned to Indian ownership, and we're Indians, so we should own it," said Tom White Feather.

Ecologists Tussle With Hunters at Reservoir

SATURDAY Feb. 11— Seven women and six men, part of the Licking Creek Alliance conservation group, scuffled with hunters today at the Lake Muskingum nuclear cooling pond. The group was attempting to prevent the hunters from shooting rabbits and other wildlife that flock to the lake, which is located on South Central Ohio Coal, Gas, Electricity, Telephone & Telegraph Co. grounds outside of Dacron. The water in the lake has an average year-round tem-

perature of 160 degrees Fahrenheit and provides the animals with warmth and fresh, though hot, water. In recent years, hunters have been taking advantage of the situation. "The warmth attracts animals. And when they drink the water, it makes them glow in the dark," Faun Rosenberg, President of the LCA, said. "To hunt animals under these conditions is unfair, besides, hunting at night is illegal."

Spokesmen for S.C.O.C. G.E.T.&T. said the utility

will decide on Monday whether or not to allow hunting at the lake, which is on property leased to them by Silage County. The
Cont. Sec. N, Page 12

Ecology Group Protests Dam Construction Project

SATURDAY, Feb. 11—The Licking Creek Alliance, a group of local environmentalists and ecology conservationists, say they will go to court to seek an injunction to halt construction

Rep.-Dem. File Photo

Environmentalists claim the Licking Creek floodgate will mean the end for the nine-eyed carp.

of a floodgate on Licking Creek. The group claims that the floodgate will endanger the nine-eyed river carp which inhabit Licking Creek. The nine-eye, a large deformed relative of the common carp, appeared in Licking Creek in the early sixties shortly after the Licking Creek atomic power plant was built. It is not known to exist elsewhere. The Licking Creek Alliance fears that the floodgate will wipe out this rare fish. "If we don't stop the floodgate," LCA President Faun Rosenberg said, "we could lose this little fish. It

Cont. Sec. H, Page 23

$3 Bills Nixed

WASHINGTON, D.C., Feb. 10 (UPA)—The U. S. Mint has scrapped plans to issue a three-dollar bill which had been planned for circulation beginning in 1980.

Secretary of the Treasury W. Michael Blumenthal stated today that the new denomination would have been "exceedingly convenient and would have resulted in a considerable reduction in currency printing costs, but extensive research surveys have indicated to us that the public attaches some unfavorable connotations to this particular bill denomination, although we are not sure of the exact source of this 'consumer resistance.'"

The new bill was to have borne the portrait of Theodore Roosevelt, America's 26th president.

A REP.-DEM. INVESTIGATION
Travel Agency Scam?

By TROUT AND BUGBAUM
Rep-Dem. Investigative Reporters

**Bob Trout Carl Bugbaum
Rep-Dem. Investigative Reporting Team**

Last November the Homing Pigeon Tours travel agency of 1221 Monroe Street began offering special trips to Mexico for cancer patients to receive laetrile treatments which are legal there. This seemed like a blatant scheme to cash in on the suffering and tragedy of others and steal the last few dollars from helpless victims of this hopeless disease through the use of medical quackery.

However, after a long talk with Homing Pigeon Tours owner Evelyn Rogg, we have become convinced that laetrile can be a valuable tool in treatment of otherwise incurable cancers and that the use of this drug is an important expression of Americans' constitutional right to self-medication. Besides, the tour packages are very reasonably priced.

Rep.-Dem. File Photo

Members of the Dacron Polar Bear club, who celebrate winter each year with an icy outdoor dip, sponsored their annual Muskingum River Mid-Winter Swim Race yesterday. Contestants swam across the Muskingum River by cutting a hole in the ice, jumping in, getting out and running ten yards, cutting a hole in the ice and jumping in until they got to the other side. Winner was Bob Pollatzy of 1444 N. Scrubwood with 36 holes and a time of 9 hours and 15 minutes, 51 seconds.

Things Stolen

Yesterday the isolated home of Ernest J. Truscit at 4400 Lake James Rd., Dacron Dales, was broken into for the second time in two days. Truscit is a collector of rare and valuable gold coins and is currently on a tour of Europe with his wife. After the first break-in, police officers interviewed in Friday's Republican-Democrat had called the home an "open house for thieves." The second robbery netted the remainder of Truscit's coin collection and an unspecified amount of other goods. The thieves, however, apparently overlooked a wall safe behind the original Audubon drawing in the second-story back den.

Police Arrest Suspected Top Nazi

By LARRY MICKLE
Rep.-Dem. Staff Writer

SATURDAY, Feb. 11— An investigation led by a prominent rabbi in Dacron's Jewish community resulted in the arrest last night of a city dog pound employee accused of being Nazi leader Martin Bormann. An investigation headed by Rabbi Irving Levin, Chairman of the Dacron International Nazi Justice Committee, allegedly uncovered evidence proving that Earl Borman Jr. of Dacron is the infamous Nazi who has not been seen since 1945. Police Chief Finch arrested Borman at his home. Borman was taken to police headquarters for questioning. When asked if he was responsible for the deaths of millions of Jews, Borman answered, "No."

According to a statement given by legal aide attorney Mark Gritten, Borman was born in Lowell, Michigan, in 1949. He moved with his family to Detroit in 1956 and attended Wayne County Junior College in 1967. In 1969 he

OPI File Photo   Rep-Dem. Staff Photo

Is city employee Earl Borman, Nazi murderer Martin Bormann?

enlisted in the United States Marine Corps and served in Viet Nam. After he was honorably discharged, Borman took a job as pet destroyer with the Department of Animal and Pest Control in Dacron. He is married to Bonnita Krimm of Dacron. They have a son, Bobby, who is one year old.

Rabbi Levin and his group claim that Borman was born in Germany in 1900, that he joined the Nazi party in 1925 and rose in the party hierarchy succeeding Rudolf Hess as deputy fuehrer in 1941. After the war, Rabbi Levin alleges, Borman fled to Argentina where he underwent plastic surgery to change his age. Political problems later probably

forced him to settle in Dacron, where he took a job doing the only thing he knew how to do—use a gas chamber.

Rabbi Levin and his group have raised more than $75,000 to send Borman to Israel to stand trial.

VanHusen Inc.

Mayor Milos Pilegravey announced Friday that the City of Dacron will utilize Federal anti-poverty funds to buy trailers for use as low-income housing. The special trailers, shown above, in a South Dacron pilot project last year before the housing riot, will be built by Dacron's own VanHusen company and will be placed on the site of the old Mudroe Lamp Black factory in South Washington.

Chevrolet Dealer Kidnap

SATURDAY Feb. 11— It wasn't a real kidnapping, but a Dacron Chevrolet salesman thought so and broke the General Motors single-day sales record by selling 49 new autos. Herb Wisenheimer, president and owner of Hollerin' Herb Wisenheimer's Psychopath Chevrolet, 2500 W. Buchanan, pulled the profitable stunt on salesman Romeo Boswell. Disguising his voice, Wisenheimer called Boswell and told him that unless he sold four cars an

hour for the 12 hours the dealership is open, his wife and kids would be killed. The wife and children were given money to go out to lunch and to a show so that when Boswell called home, he got no answer. "Romeo went bananas," Wisenheimer said. "When things got slow around lunch time, he bought three cars himself." When the dealership closed at 9 P.M. last night, Wisenheimer informed Boswell of the hoax. "Herb's a real kidder," Boswell said.

New Jackie Escort?

Rep-Dem. Staff Photo

NEW YORK, Feb. 10 (OPI) —Does Jackie Kennedy Onassis have a new mystery admirer? No one seems to know identity of man Jackie was seen with on Madison Ave. today.

Graffitist Nabbed

By LARRY MICKLE
Rep.-Dem. Staff Writer

SATURDAY, Feb. 11—A Tucker Technical High School student has been arrested by police detectives for his role in the defacement of a number of bridges and water towers in the Dacron area. Police nabbed the youth at an overpass stake-out yesterday. The arrest was the result of a new intensive police program to deal with the graffiti epidemic. Walls, vehicles, water towers, structures and streets throughout the Dacron area have been defaced with dirty phrases, words, names, initials and "cultist" drawings and symbols. Effective tomorrow, spray paint, the prime tool of the graffitist, will not be sold to anyone under 21. Anyone caught supplying a minor with spray paint will be subject to arrest and fine and/or arrest and jail sentence. The youth arrested yesterday faces a minimum sentence of two semesters at Silage County Juvenile Work

Scene of the overpass stake-out on East Monroe St. Content of graffiti was not released because accused is a minor.

Farm. Juvenile officers hope to track down the rest of the youthful defacers through handwriting analysis, student informers, and spot inspections at high schools for paint-stained index fingers. Dacron Public School System psychologist Dr. Leonard Townsend says that teens have "a deep-seated desire to express themselves and others by writing all over things with spray paint." All citizens are asked to keep an eye on large blank spaces and inform police of any suspicious index fingers.

A REP.-DEM. INVESTIGATION
Union Election Fraud?

By TROUT AND BUGBAUM
Rep-Dem. Investigative Reporters

**Bob Trout   Carl Bugbaum
Rep-Dem. Investigative
Reporting Team**

Accusations of union racketeering have long been leveled against M. Walter Gizzard, 90, president of local 808 United Coal, Trailer and Asphalt Workers and when, last month, Mr. Gizzard was re-elected to his 36th term by a vote of 19,684 to 2, suspicions of a rigged union election were raised. But an in-depth investigation, plus a long talk with independent labor relations consultant Charles Amaretto, has proven to our satisfaction that the local 808 election was perfectly fair and that President Gizzard is very very popular with all the rank and file members and that those two votes against him were probably clerical errors. And the new local 43 Trash Haulers contract is on the level too.

Does Jackie Have A Headache?

NEW YORK, Feb. 10 (OPI)—Jackie Kennedy Onassis winces during lunch at fashionable LaMange restaurant.

It was Jackie's first appearance in public since last night.

People Poll

People Poll is an independent opinion poll conducted for the Republican-Democrat *by Sidney Epstein Public Opinion Survey and Tax Form Preparation, Inc., Suite 410 Coal Building, Dacron.*

Asked of a cross section of 50 Dacron residents.

HAS YOUR OPINION OF PRESIDENT CARTER GONE UP OR DOWN?
Up: 8%
Down: 62%
Up and Down: 30%

SHOULD OHIO MURDERERS BE GIVEN THE DEATH PENALTY?
Gas Chamber: 56%
Electrocution 42%
Hanging: 2%

ARE YOU GETTING ENOUGH EXERCISE?
Yes: 24%
No: 18%
Sometimes: 58%

HOW GLAD ARE YOU THAT WE ARE OUT OF VIETNAM?
Real: 34%
Pretty: 42%
Not Very: 12%
Don't Know: 12%

SHOULD WOMEN TAKE THEIR HUSBAND'S LAST NAME WHEN THEY GET MARRIED TO HIM?
Yes: 74%
No: 6%
Whatever He Says: 20%

IF DACRON EVER GETS A SUBWAY, WILL YOU BE FOR CUTTING BACK ON SERVICES TO MEET CITY BUDGET DEFICITS?
For: 14%
Against: 76%
Would Drive Children to School Anyway: 10%

CONCORDE: SHOULD WE LET THE SST LAND AT DACRON INTERSTATE AIRPORT?
Yes: 60%
No: 32%
Don't Care Either Way: 8%

SHOULD WE LET THE CONCORDE SST TAKE OFF FROM DACRON INTERSTATE AIRPORT?
Yes: 78%
No: 22%

Dacronian MIA Buried

By SAM FRESCA
Rep-Dem. Staff Writer

The remains of U. S. Army 2d Lieutenant Robert Baxter were laid to rest here yesterday in a burial ceremony attended by his widow, the former Miss Wendy Dempler, and members of the Baxter and Dempler families. Memorial services were conducted by Reverend Andrew Pontlip of the Upton Avenue Lutheran Church and the eulogy was given by Col. Brice Ludlow

(Ret.), commander of Dacron's V.F.W. Post #6.

Lt. Baxter, who in 1964 was captain of the Kefauver High School football team, had been listed as missing in action since June of 1969. But his death was not confirmed until last week when his body and those of two other M.I.A.s were returned to the U. S. According to information received by the Department of Defense, the three had died a month ago in a car wreck outside Stockholm.

Rep.-Dem Staff Photo

Patrick X. O'Garrgle, Archbishop of Ohio, admires sacred trailer to be manufactured locally by the VanHusen company while he visits Dacron's St. Betty's diocese. New mobile home-shrine will be a boon to religious vacationers everywhere. St. Betty is the patron saint of house trailers.

Council OK's Allotment for Handicapped

Friday, Feb. 10—The City Council voted today to allot city funds to establish handicap facilities throughout the metropolitan area. This is the first time the City Council has done anything for crippled Dacronians. The Handicap Access Fund will sponsor the following projects:

– Construct a wheelchair ramp for the Gullet Park sledding hill.

– Purchase one handicap shopping cart for each supermarket.

– Install a wheelchair-height soft drink machine at MacAdam Zoo and MacAdam Field.

– Provide first and second row handicap priority seating at all movie theaters.

Loose Stool Fatal To Zanesville Woman

The death of an elderly woman at a Zanesville Mr. Drippy frozen dairy dessert stand has been blamed on her loose stool. The woman, Mrs. Bradford Finch, 67, was seated on the stool when the rusted base collapsed, hurling her two feet, eight inches to the floor.

She was pronounced dead on arrival at Zanesville General Hospital. Owner of the Mr. Drippy store, Albert Pinari Jr., said that the stool has since been repaired and that the survivors of the dead woman have been given free Frosty Delight chocolate cones.

Come To Our New Suburban Branch Office Grand Opening

Manufacturing Creditors Trust is opening a suburban branch office in the new Plazaria Metro-Shopping-Plex just off I-40 in Dacron Glens. Open a savings account between February 13 and December 1, 1978, and you'll get a lovely gift for deposits of $100 or more.

And we're also giving away free door, floor, wall, and window prizes.

FREE WITH DEPOSITS OF $100 OR MORE

Minimum deposit must remain for 90 days

Bookmark

Manufacturing Creditor Trust Pencil

Matches

Plastic Swizzle Stick

A Dinner Mint

Set of Wooden Toothpicks

"I've Been to the Bank" Button

A Manila Envelope

Personalized Bank Book

Cocktail Napkin

Two Aspirin

A Glass of Water

FREE WITH DEPOSITS OF $1,000 OR MORE

Minimum deposit must remain for 24 months

7-Piece Spatula Set

Kitchen-Magic Asparagus Maker

1,000 Chopsticks

Fold-Away Door Stop

L. L. Bean Two-Legged Camp Stool

Black and Decker Power-Pliers

54-Piece Plastic Ash Tray Set

Set of Three Radio Tables

Plug-In Dimmer– Dims Anything

FREE WITH DEPOSITS OF $10,000 or more

Minimum deposit must remain for 12 years

Electric Salt Shaker

G.E. Digital Hair Dryer

Proctor Electric Bog Home Peat Moss Maker

Milk-Mate Automatic Powdered-Milk Maker

G.E. Electric Wok

Westinghouse Home Electric Meat Pounder

LP Gas Camping-Blanket

AM/FM Clock Iron

G.E. Lite Alarm-Calendar with Snooze-Daze™

Manufacturing Creditors Trust Plazaria Branch Grand Opening February 13th through December 1st

Open 7 days a week,
closed Saturdays and Sundays. 925-9500
Associate member F.D.I.C.
Main office, Secor and Monroe in the Corngate Shopping Center.
(All gifts must be picked up at our Plazaria branch.)

Prisoners In Trailer-Break

Twenty Silage County jail inmates escaped late last night from a county-owned trailer which was being used as a jail annex. It is reported that the prisoners made their escape after one of their number put a large hole in the trailer's outside wall with his fist.

The fugitives were identified as Robinson Brown, 20; Jasper Johnson, 19; Eldridge Jones, 18;

(Cont. Sec. B, Page 14)

Rare Frozen Frog Found

Two local youths discovered an unusual frog frozen in the ice in Licking Creek, last week, near the creek's entrance into the Muskingum River. The small amphibian has been identified by Leonard Frost, professor of biology at Dacron Elementary and Junior College, as an example of Frogus hammerheadae, or hammerhead frog. This frog, says Frost, is related to the hammerhead shark.

Defendant Cleared In Cadillac Theft Case

By JERRY BURGER
Rep.-Dem. Staff Writer

Auto repair shop owner Purdy Spackle was cleared in court, Friday, of charges that he stole six new Cadillacs from the Duke King Cadillac dealership in Dacron Dells. Interviewed after the trial, jury foreman Herbert Wisenheimer, himself a car dealer, cited several compelling pieces of evidence that he said caused the jury to return a verdict of innocent on all charges. Most important, according to Wisenheimer, was the question of the serial number plates attached to the frames of the automobiles. The cars reported stolen were all in serial number series "98601" while the Cadillacs found at Spackle's Dee & Pee Auto Re-Paint & -Pair body shop each had "10986" numbers. Also, the stolen Cadillacs were of various colors while Spackle's Cadillacs had all been painted green.

Hoarding Of Natural Gas Continues Despite Danger

DACRON, Sat., Feb. 11—Despite warnings from South Central Ohio Coal, Gas, Electricity, Telephone & Telegraph Co., a number of Dacron citizens are reportedly continuing to hoard natural gas. Rumors about a possible natural gas shortage for heating and cooking this winter apparently sparked the hoarding spree. S.C.O.C.G.E.T.&T. has denied that there is any substance to the rumors but many customers are shill attempting to hoard gas by filling plastic garbage bags which they inflate by holding over an open stove jet. "They seal the bags shut and store them for future use."

S.C.O.C.G.E.T.&T. warns that the gas is poisonous if inhaled in sufficient quantities to cause harm and is flammable and potentially explosive. "Just a few bags in a basement could poison all the inhabitants in the house and blow the house to Kentucky. So those people who are hoarding natural gas should stop right now," S.C.O.C.G.E.T.&T. experts added. To dispose of the gas, take the bags outside and open them. Many people have brought bags of natural gas to S.C.O.C.G.E.T.&T. offices in order to sell them back, but the company has a policy against making retail gas purchases.

Strike Averted at VanHusen

SATURDAY Feb. 11—A threatened strike against VanHusen Manufacturing by United Coal, Trailer and Asphalt Workers has been averted. A settlement was reached between union leader M. Walter Gizzard and VanHusen Chairman of the Board Woolworth VanHusen II at a meeting at Three Trees Country Club yesterday. The strike, which would have come during the peak recreational vehicle production period, has been postponed until the late summer months, when everyone will be laid off anyway.

State Nets Big Lottery Deficits

COLUMBUS, Feb. 10 (Blurr News Service) —According to state treasurer Anthony Lumber, Ohio has lost more than $28,000,000 in the first six months of its Lucky Buckeye Daily Lottery drawings.

Lumber, in a news conference at the state capitol building, said that he attributed this loss in part to Ohio's practice of using the state's Daily Lottery proceeds to buy Daily Lottery tickets for the state in hopes of increasing the state's revenue if the state gets a ticket with the winning number.

Guest Editorial

Asphalt vs. Concrete—No Contest

Photo courtesy the Keep Fenton B. Sweater in Washington Committee

By THE HONORABLE FENTON B. SWEATER

Southeast Central Ohio's District 19 Congressional Representative

PROGRESSIVE STEPS must be taken to promote safety (and local industry) in the matter of what America's highways are going to get paved with. Progressive steps like my Bill in Congress, for instance, which nears a vote in the House this spring.

AS READERS WILL REMEMBER from previous guest editorials, the Curb Extension/Soft Shoulder and Bridge Abutment Abatement (HR 17533), which I drafted and sponsored, provides for the replacement of brittle, non-resilient concrete paving surfaces with water-resistant, impact-retardant Southeast Central Ohio asphalt road toppings. Not only does this measure promote traffic safety, but it will also benefit Southeast Central Ohio's asphalt producers—an industry generating 6,250 fine jobs in the greater Dacron area.

MY BILL is a five-point proposal designed to be a major step forward for safe streets (and, by extension, safe sidewalks and school bus stops) and will be eligible for 90% federal funding in such local areas as here, thus relieving Greater Dacroners of a severe tax bite when we need it like a hole in the road.

IN BRIEF, MY BILL WILL:

Initiate immediate construction of solid, raised asphalt curbs along all two- and four-lane (federally funded) interstate highways.

Extend all soft shoulders at least 3' (three feet) beyond current inadequate berm specifications.

Subsequently "top" these lethal motoring hazards with a minimum 3 1/2" (three-and-a-half-inch) thick "buffer face" of pure 100% Southeast Central Ohio asphalt.

Begin further safety studies on concrete's non-shock-resistant inflexibility under stress.

Encourage the eventual conversion of existing interstate thoroughfares to heavy-duty, rustproof, top-grade asphalt compositions.

MY PROPOSED MEASURES are considered top priority by many influential safety and asphalt-minded experts in Dacron who share our goal of the re-asphaltation of our nation's 770,000 miles of improved roadbed. But we need the concerned support of all Dacronians young and old to write letters, postcards and telegrams to everybody in Congress all the time until the Bill passes. Thank you.

The Inquiring Picture Taker

By VINCE BLUM

FERRIS   SCRABBLER   ASHLEY   HEMMING   DAVIS   BOBKINS

THE QUESTION
How about all this that's going on in the Middle East?

THE ANSWERS

Larry Ferris, postman: "Can't make head or tail out of it myself."

Gilbert Scrabbler, unemployed rocket scientist: "I guess you'd pretty much have to say it's got me beat."

Bud Ashley, steamfitter: "It's a heck of a thing, that's for sure. One heck of a thing."

Really a heck of a thing. That's what I say. A heck of a heck of a thing."

Mrs. Ted Hemming, housewife: "Oh, gosh, you'd have to ask my husband about that."

Ty Davis, telephone repairman: "You never know. It just goes to show you, you never know. These days, who can tell? You just don't know what's going to happen next, if you know what I mean."

Jim Bobkins, accountant: "You worry and worry about these things and then you step out in front of a car and Boom! Right when you least expect it."

The Rep.-Dem. will pay $2 for each question accepted for this column. Today's award goes to R. Weitzo, 1870 Lawn Dr., Dacron Dales.

Letters to the Editor

Please give name and address with letters. We will withhold both or either on request, maybe.

Dear Republican-Democrat,
I still don't understand why Panama thought it should have that canal. Was it just because it was named after them? After all, Toledo was named after a place in Spain and you don't see a lot of Spanish hanging around asking us to give them that city. Or, at least I haven't heard about it. Also, once they've got the canal, how are they going to get it home?
MRS. FRANK BRESSETTER
1865 Woodley

Dear Republican-Democrat,
You certainly have a wonderful newspaper. I read it every day and love it.
ELINORE HOPPIT
705 Gingko St.

Dear Republican-Democrat,
A lot of people are saying that America has had it because we can send men to the moon but we can't get the potholes in front of the main Post Office on Monroe Street fixed. This isn't true. America is still a great nation.
BILL GREWEL
1102 Paisley

Dear Republican-Democrat,
People ought to remember that Vietnam veterans are real veterans even if it is the War in Vietnam that they're veterans of. My VFW around here won't even let me in because I have a peace tattoo. It's not my fault we lost. I'm still a veteran and should be allowed to shoot pool and buy beer just like I'd been to Korea.
TIM VENNER
109 1/2 E. Polk

Dear Republican-Democrat,
Many people are out of work in Dacron. What I'd like to know is, why don't they all get jobs?
MRS. MARGE BLEEKER
2234 Creekport Rd.

Dear Republican-Democrat,
Many things for sale today are very dangerous but can be purchased by anyone, such as kitchen knives, drain cleaners, and large boxes that a child could suffocate in. Even teenagers may buy these items legally. Let's have more government regulation to make everything safe for everyone.
MRS. EDNA STRUTTON
2784 Shakespeare

Dear Republican-Democrat,
We shouldn't blame people who are bigots. We should feel sorry for them instead. Because when somebody talks like a bigot, they are doing what psychologists call "projecting" and all the bad things that they say about another race are actually bad things that they worry might be secretly true of themselves. For instance, many people who hate blacks are secretly worried that they themselves are actually on welfare and drink a lot of cheap wine and beat their children but don't know it.
CASEY ELLIOT
Dacron Dales

Dear Republican-Democrat,
If people just raised their children right, I'll bet you wouldn't have nearly as much of this "Powder Room Prowler" sort of thing.
MRS. J. JASPERS
Sandusky Blvd.

Dear Republican-Democrat,
I've lived in Dacron all my life and so has my husband. We think it's a lovely town and we're both over 70!
MR. AND MRS.
ARCHIBALD FENDERS
615 E. Truman

Dear Republican-Democrat,
Taxes these days are just awful. They are high as the sky. If you ask me, it's a darn shame.
BUD WILLIAMS
1110 Upton Ave.

Dear Republican-Democrat,
We just got our sewer assessment bill and, boy, was it a lot! Inflation is also terrible.
JOE FASTERELLI
2178 Herman Melville

The Old Grouch Says:

"A 'liberal' - that's a fellow who's not quite pink enough to punch."

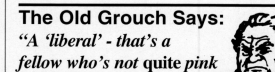

BIRDS OF A FEATHER?

— EDITORIAL —

A Really Sick Person

—is what the "Powder Room Prowler" is, and there's no room in America, or Dacron, for sickness like this which must be stopped! Listen, Mr. Prowler, you read the "Open Letter" to you that begins on page one and turn yourself in, pronto! **You should be ashamed.**

Also Pretty Sick

—are the young ladies and women who have been victims of this so-called "Powder Room Prowler." Sick with embarrassment, that is. We should all feel sorry for them and give them a big hand. They've been great and America needs more girls like these.

Another thing that—

America Needs

—is more house trailers. Or that's what some folks say. Others say America needs more asphalt. And still others say America needs more strip-mined coal (and the gas, electricity, telephones and telegraphs that go with it). But we say that each of these people is wrong. Why? Because America needs more of *all* these things. **So, let's get going America—how about more trailers, asphalt and strip-mined coal for everyone?**

America Doesn't Need

—more of some things, however, and that's for sure. Like meddling government agencies, for example. **So, see here, D.O.T., E.P.A., and F.C.C., we've had too much of you and that's plenty!**

Good Government

—is that government which governs least, said one famous American or another, and he must have been thinking about Dacron's Mayor Milos Pilegravey, who's given us more of that kind of good government than we've ever seen around here for ten years now. Elections are coming up again this fall, Mr. Mayor, and we don't think it's a bit too early for us to throw our 2¢ into the ring with your hat.

Of course, you have several worthy would-be opponents, Mr. Mayor, such as city councilman Charles U. Farley, who has a great deal of very youthful enthusiasm and whose father is a prominent florist, and black city councilman Madison Jones, who is only the third black optometrist in Dacron ever. **Both of these young men would doubtlessly make excellent mayors if either of them knew the first thing about government. But we think it's a—**

Good Idea

—to "not change horses in the middle of a city," and stick with our tried and true-blue present mayor, you.

Speaking of good ideas, how about that new—

Highway

—plan? Those 156 extra (asphalt paved!) miles of freeway should help solve the rush-hour traffic blues once and for all in these parts plus create new jobs aplenty. And how about portable trailer jails, too? There's an idea-on-the-go whose time had come. **Hat's off to whomever thought up either of these! We're with you all the way.**

William F. Ducksward
When Do Those Agencies Quit?

IT SEEMS WASHINGTON'S quenchless bedbugs are yet again engaged in spirited pursuit of a true ne plus ultra, given the ill-omened tenor and Cyclopian bulk of the FCC's most recent exhibition of regulatory Draconia. In an apparent attempt to ablate various commercial radio, television, and newspaper properties from the common control of their extant parent corporations, the Commission will, rather than vitiate the suspected possibility of insidious communicational gallery and deception at the hands of a maleficent, self-serving cabal of media blackguards, instead seminate an entirely antithetical affaire d'contraire wherein newly contentious editors and broadcasters will be forced to out-journalize the truth among one another by, in fact, altering it.

THIS DILATED RIVALRY will generate a monstrous pattern of pizzazz-yielding lies and obfuscatory distortions to lure audiences away from their more veracious program and editorial sources. Honesty and integrity of information will plunge into a turbid declivity of precious rating shares and advertising revenues.

THE ELECTORATE IS COMPELLED by all expedients to resist-tout de suite, and categorically so. Control of America's media, in all of its forms, must remain vested in a small core of efficient and careful conglomerates to ensure that we receive the quality and uniformity of truth hypothecated to us by the Constitution. Maintaining our radio, television, and newspapers under a single, businesslike umbrella just plain makes good syllogistic sense.

William F. Ducksward, America's most celebrated political columnist, is nationally syndicated and well respected throughout the world as our finest author, orator, and oral analyst.

Merl Buchenwald
One Guy's Impact Statement

ALMOST EVERY TIME a guy turns around these days, some self-righteous functionary from the Environmental Protection Agency is poking his big toe into another area of our lives.

Yesterday I was in O'Loughlin's Bar with several members of my Research and Scholastic Society discussing the feasibility of bartering U. S. technology for Chinese oil when I ordered another round from O'Loughlin's kid behind the bar.

"You'll have to hold on a minute," he said. "I need to prepare an environmental impact statement before I can put the drinks on the counter."

"THAT'S RIGHT," one of my associates added seriously, noting the lowered position of my jaw. "All those glasses and napkins and cherry stems and spills will severely alter the appearance of the bar, so it's important we know what to expect."

"YOU GUYS GOT TO BE JOKING," I said. Of course, they were putting me on, but the idea of spending a couple hours predicting what effect a glass of booze would have on a vinyl bar top over the long-term haul doesn't seem too far afield when you consider some of the junk the EPA makes a guy do these days before he can attempt to make a living. And if it's all so damned important, where were they when the Great Manufacturer upstairs permanently loused up the environment with my wife—a noxious waste product if there ever was one. (Or, as they might classify her in the Brooklyn office: a horrendous "goil slick.")

A FRIEND OF MINE in O'Hurley's Bar told me he bought some stock in a mining company that went crashing down to the cellar because the EPA didn't approve of the style of open pit they were digging. "A hole is a hole," he said. "How can you dig a substandard hole?"

"WELL, FIRST YOU GET TWO IRISHMEN," I said, ... one to dig, and one to clear the rocks out of the other's mouth every so often." Although in the case of that joke the Irishmen dug a poor open pit because they were stupid and probably drunk, there are other ways to offend the environment, according to the EPA. Such as digging a pit that will: possibly result in the death of a bunny five million years from now, or possibly offend an incoming visitor from outer space, or possibly even cause people to get cancer by lowering the air level in the area and thereby bending the protective ozone layer. As Eddie over at O'Eddie's Bar says, "Next thing you know, those EPA guys will be want

Cont. Sec. A, Page 32

Merl Buchenwald is America's most funny and popular political humorist, appearing daily in hundreds and hundreds of daily newspapers hilariously enjoyed by untold millions of intelligent, well-informed readers.

Dacron Republican-Democrat

100 Polk St.
One of America's Newspapers
(614) 688-4070
Founded 1851 and 1854 Merged 1958

Published every day by South Central Ohio Coal, Gas, Electricity, Telephone and Telegraph Communications Group, Inc., 100 Polk St., Dacron, Ohio 44307. Elmira Gullet, President; Rutgers Gullet, Editor, Publisher and Vice President

Subscription Rates: Daily Single Copy 15 cents; Sunday 20 cents; Home Delivery Weekly by Carrier Boy 80 cents; By Motor Route 90 cents Remittance must accompany all orders.

Mail Rates	Domestic Mail	Daily and Sun.	Sports Comics Only
	1 month	$5.25	$1.70
	3 months	$10.50	$3.40
	1 year	$42.50	$13.60
	Life	$2,940	$952.00
		Overseas Rates: Much More	

Hunter Standerson with Lester Whitefish
Washington Runaround

Standerson   **Whitefish**

MARSHALL BERNSON, chairman of the National Association of Media Cartels, NAMO, testified last week in hearings before Sen. Beach Byington's Subcommittee on Radio, Television, Newspapers, and Word of Mouth; and the monologue was as pat and predictable as they come. Bernson claimed this country's news media needs to retain its strong, omni-controlling corporate backbone to guarantee a consistency of information, whereas the alternative of free competition would foster a rivalrous tinkering with the actual truth among newly independent and audience-hungry stations and papers.

BYINGTON SEEMED TO LAP UP Brendan's milk and honey with nonchalant credulity, which is interesting, in light of the fact Byington has been utilizing the per sorrel and equipment of the National Security Agency to arrange microwave-transmitted video sex parties with Bernson's two teen-age daughters at Georgetown. It's a running joke at the Czech and Bulgarian embassies that Byington once saw a nude woman in the flesh, and beamed all over himself.

OF COURSE, the Czechs and Bulgarians aren't jibing around simply because they're such ardent humorists—Byington has been funneling U.S. and NATO military secrets to them for years. The telephonic record is intriguing. Byington: "I have some new information for you." Malyv: "Concerning the contingency deployments along the California coast, I trust?" Byington: "Correct. I presume you have the heroin I need?" Malyv: "Yes, it has been taken care of." Byington: "Fine."

AND THE TWO-GALLON paint can full of pure, uncut heroin Byington received was not merely for personal consumption. He and his compadres at NSA are famous in certain quarters for their two- and three-day B-52 drug benders, where Byington and company jet around the world in Air Force bombers and listen to jazz over esoteric SAC frequencies. The narcotics nexus, not surprisingly, often finds its way also into the broadcasting and publishing circles with whom Byington prefers to snuggle so cozily. A personal letter from the Senator to NAMC chairman Bernson reads: "Give the quality drugs I am sending you to your newsmen and talent types. It will keep those high-strung characters low key and easier to handle. Can you get me some teen-age Costa Ricans for my birthday? I am so very bored with your daughters."

AND SO the machine is greased, gear by gear, cog by pinion-with our money, our values, and our future.

Hunter Standerson and Lester Whitefish are carried occasionally by a handful of newspapers due to their extraordinarily unpopular and impractical politics. The Republican-Democrat assumes no liability for the content of their column, offering it solely as a charity gesture to freedom of print.

On This Date 50 Years Ago Today

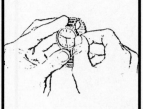

on February 12, 1928:
It was an uneventful day.

How Ohio's Congressmen Voted

HOUSE

	Hubert C. Bucket (R) Dist. 1	Leon Polechute, Jr. (R) Dist. 2	R. Reston Lumpduct (R) Dist. 3	Harold F. Stoopbinder (R) Dist. 4	E. Hummock Feltfart (R) Dist. 5	Benjamin (Buss) Staggers (R) Dist. 6	Elizabeth C. Dipschlick (D) Dist. 7	Charles (Skeeter) Shipsetter (R) Dist. 8	Louis J. Acklewackki (D) Dist. 9	Randolph G. Moot (D) Dist. 10	J.J. (Jack) Nutlap (R) Dist. 11	F. Lawrence Mumblebaum (R) Dist. 12	Paul H. Boatbutter (R) Dist. 13	Arnold R. Gert (D) Dist. 14	Washington Monument Brown (D) Dist. 15	Anthony X. Vespuchio (D) Dist. 16	Ralph T. Footey (R) Dist. 17	Giuseppe V. Lungo (D) Dist. 18	Egon Haverslamp III (R) Dist. 19	G. Gordon Sinkbend (R) Dist. 20	Gerwin B. Mahooey (D) Dist. 21	Fenton W. Sweater (R) Dist. 22	Eustis T. Entwhistle (R) Dist. 23	Totals For	Totals Against
(HR 67834529) Pattermeyer-Hankoff Bill to provide free school lunches to dogs.	N	N	N	N	N	Y	N	N	N	N	N	N	Y	Y	N	N	N	N	N	N	N	A	N	118	310
(HR 46783908) Presidential proposal to create a cabinet-level agency for regulation of lawn care.	N	N	N	N	N	Y	N	Y	N	Y	N	N	N	N	Y	Y	Y	N	N	Y	N	A	N	261	167
(HR 91326935) Himple-Musttoe Bill to make bugs illegal east of the Mississippi.	N	N	N	N	N	Y	N	N	N	N	N	N	Y	Y	N	N	N	N	N	N	N	A	N	196	232
(HR 77629857) Pickerman-Hoot Bill to create a national park on the bottom of Lake Tahoe.	N	N	N	N	N	Y	N	N	N	N	N	N	Y	Y	N	N	N	N	N	N	N	A	N	325	123

SENATE

MCGOVERN-PROXMIRE BILL to take everybody's money away.
Howard M. Metzenbaum (D) no
John H. Glenn, Jr. (D) no
rejected 74 to 25

SPARKMAN-GOLDWATER MILITARY APPROPRIATION BILL to provide $9 billion for development of a mile-wide atomic helicopter.
Howard M. Metzenbaum (D) no
John H. Glenn, Jr. (D) yes
passed 60 to 39

JOHN C. STENNIS BILL to make use of the term "old fart" a Federal offense.
Howard M. Metzenbaum (D) yes
John H. Glenn, Jr. (D) no
rejected 58 to 41

Key:
REPRESENTATIVES:
R = Republicans   D = Democrats   N = Neithers

LEGISLATION
Y = "yes"   A = "absent"   N = "no"   ? = "?"

PROWLER OPEN LETTER

(Continued from Sec. A, Page 1)

I will even beg you. Yes, get off my chair and plead that you turn yourself in to the police and not into a criminal as notorious as Mac the Face or Shame-Dog Coffin.

If you are afraid of the police; you can even surrender to me. I will see you get a fair deal from them and the publishers if you choose to tell your story to both of us.

Just phone me, or write me a letter. Let's talk before you strike again fusing untold embarrassment to the victims, their families and to police.

Prowler, we all go a little off the beam sometimes. I know I have. But that is the time to turn to others for help ... not to a surgical type device that can be dangerous if improperly used by people who have not gone to medical school.

Many people want to help you. To help you with legal costs and with your problems. Understanding, tolerant people in the publishing business as far away as New York have told me so in letters of intent to me.

Prowler, give yourself up to me. Or the police. You're going to be caught sooner or later anyway. If you don't turn yourself in, somebody's father may tear that bag off of your head one day—and maybe your face with it. Please, let's negotiate.

Yours truly,
Donovan Croat
Republican-Democrat
Senior Feature Writer

Smoking, Non-Smoking Dacron Areas Proposed By Commission

DACRON, Fri., Feb. 10— A special commission, set up by young ecology-conscious City Councilman Charles U. Farley to develop a "no smoking area" plan for Dacron, submitted its findings and recommendations to the City Council Friday. The commission studied the smoking habits of hundreds of Dacron citizens during their three-month study. They concluded that most smokers prefer smoking anytime they wanted and anywhere they wanted. Research with non-smokers revealed that non-smoking individuals do not like people to smoke anywhere at anytime. "The only solution," the report explained, "is to begin a long-range reorganization of population according to smoking or non-smoking preference." The commission proposed that steps be taken now to create smoking and non-smoking neighborhoods, districts and suburbs.

Aeronautical Engineer, Bob McKeranski of Dacron Estates, poses with an unarmed prototype of the new CRUISETTE-B missile his small company, McK, Inc., is developing in hopes of a special contract with the international N.A.T.O. organization. The CRUISETTE-B, shown here outfitted for winter targeting, can pull a .5 megaton nuclear payload to nearly anyplace, depending upon the skill of the operator.

Culprit 'Sick, Not Funny' Says School Super

Vandal Rampages Again

Photo by Rep.-Dem. Staff Photographer Vince Blum

Superintendent Cornholt says foot is himself.

By DONOVAN GROAT
Rep.-Dem. Staff Writer

The Dacron Public School system was the victim of its 22nd major act of vandalism in as many weeks, Republican-Democrat reporters were informed Friday in a hastily arranged special news conference called by Superintendent of Schools Dr. Humphrey C. Cornholt. The vandalism, described to be the "work of a seriously troubled rule-breaker or rule-breakers unknown," was discovered in a boy's lavatory of West Dacron's C. Estes Kefauver High School by the school's head custodial engineer Stanislav Dupa immediately following a surprise inspection visit to the school by Superintendent Cornholt himself.

The vandalism, found stopping up a sink as Dupa routinely inspected the washroom for drug use activity, was accompanied by an obscenity on an adjoining wall. Upon closer inspection, Dupa verified that the obscenity was written in the rule-breaker's own vandalism.

The large four-lettered word measuring approximately six by fourteen inches and the attendant vandalism in the washbasin are the most recent of a series of related incidents, according to highly placed Board of Education sources. Dacron high schools have been plagued with similar vandalism since last fall, including willfully defaced plaques, walls, wastebaskets, lockers, water fountains, behind hot radiators, bag lunches, gym shoes, mirrors, school bus gas tanks, teachers' lounge water coolers, cafeteria trays, art supply cabinets, and the new Student Council sponsored Student Suggestion Box at Prendergast High.

In the unprecedented special news conference, Superintendent Cornholt declared that further vandalisms would "not be tolerated, even if it means boarding up all high school lavatories or requiring a buddy system for their continued use."

Dr. Cornholt went on to stress the importance of students' cooperation in identifying the "criminally delinquent" individual or individuals. A number of suspects have already been sent to their respective principal's offices for questioning.

Dr. Cornholt, who was appointed Superintendent of Schools in September 1977, has assured concerned parents, PTA members, and School Board officials that, while vandalisms of such seriousness had never before happened in Dacron's high schools, he was not going to sit idly by while "some sick, twisted youth or youths foul my many unsmudged years as an educator. These vandalisms are becoming a hazard to orderly education, and I think it's time for somebody to put their foot down. That foot is me."

Suspect is Suspected

Twenty-six-year-old Patterson Jones, who broke into the Buy-and-Pay grocery store on the corner of South Washington Irving and 20th St. and stole $140 out of the cash register, is suspected of having committed robbery. Jones entered the grocery store at 1:15 Saturday morning, forced open the cash register with a pry bar and took the money inside it, causing police to suspect him. He is being held on suspicion.

OPI Phone Photo

NEW YORK CITY, Feb. 10 (OPI)—Police today arrested organized crime figure Antonio ("Tony the Vicious Murderer") Callapoloni on a charge of 252 counts of homicide. The arrest was the result of a long-term investigation into Callapoloni's criminal activities which are thought to have included the role of top "hit man" in organized crime's attempt to put an end to long-term investigations of criminal activities.

PAPERBOY OF THE MONTH

Bobby Jameson
1654 Trimlawn Dr.
Dacron

Rep.-Dem. Staff Photo

Bobby, 12 1/2, is a jaunty young fellow with a pert face full of freckles who carries the *Republican-Democrat* along Trimlawn Drive, Pinepanel Lane and Truman St. in West Dacron. He's interested in Little League, skateboarding and rooting for the Dacron Tar Legs, and is shown here posing with *Republican-Democrat* publisher Rutgers Gullet.

Market Analysis

Elliot Gangway Says:

Although the Market had been depressed for several days and was still jittery over the fluctuating prime rate at opening Friday, by mid-morning it seemed to be gathering strength for a noontime rally. Most brokers felt sure that the Market was confident and heading for a major upswing in mood right up until 11:40, when it received an exasperating half-hour phone call from its insurance agent. After that, the Market just fell apart. It was gloomy and vague and told everyone that it felt perfectly useless. Nothing we could do would cheer it up, not even the nice lunch at Delmonico's with some of their really great martinis thrown in. In fact the Market just moped all afternoon, staring out the window and working on a crossword puzzle until quitting time. That evening it watched a little TV after dinner, walked the dog and went to bed early, still not feeling very well. But if it gets a little exercise and catches up on its sleep this weekend, it'll probably be a lot better Monday.

Selected Stocks-Midwex Exchange

	P-E Ratio	Sales (hds.)	Week's High	Low	Last	Net Chg.
A						
ABum	12	1674	19 1/8	16 7/8	19 1/8+	2
ADog	6	106	3 3/8	3 1/4	3 1/8+	1/8
Adork	4	249	21 5/8	20 1/8	20 1/2-	1 1/8
AllBlo	4	823	7 1/4	6 1/2	6 5/8-	1/2
AmBust	...	164	25 1/8	24 3/8	25	...
AmCrap	12	1375	18	17 1/4	17 7/8-	1/4
AmCrud	13	80	16 7/8	16 1/2	16 3/4+	1/4
AmDum	11	6437	45 1/2	43 1/8	43 3/8-	1 7/8
AmFukt	6	327	34 7/8	34 7/8	34 3/8-	1/2
AmSunk	...	2	35	d34 1/2	34 3/8+	3/8
AssHo	10	141	23 3/4	23	23-	1/2
AteBall	12	613	24 3/4	23 1/4	24 3/8-	1/2
ATurkE	8	48	24 1/4	d22 5/8	22 3/4-	1 1/4
B						
Barf	313	318	3 1/8	2 7/8	3 1/8	...
BedWet	12	175	18	16 5/8	16 5/8-	7/8
BetZof	6	364	4 1/4	4	4 1/8-	1/8
BilCo	...	30	10 7/8	10 1/2	10 5/8-	1/8
BloMe	6	296	21 7/8	20 1/4	21 3/8+	7/8
BloOut	4	249	4 1/2	d4 1/4	4 1/4-	1/8
BowWow	12	x1791	31	d30	30 1/2+	1/8
BoZo	16	426	39	38 1/4	38 1/4+	1/2
BugFuk	24	1074	24 1/2	24 3/8	24 3/8-	1/4
BugOff	6	125	29 7/8	29 1/4	29 1/4-	1/2
BumBul	...	2	49	49	49+	1 3/4
BumPoff	8	40	15 5/8	15 3/8	15 3/8	...
BumRap	...	z100	5 5/8	5 5/8	5 5/8-	1/2
BunCo	...	z410	10 1/4	10 1/4	10 1/4-	1/4
BungHo	8	75	25 1/2	24 1/4	25 1/2+	5/8
BurnIt	6	2192	24 1/8	d22 1/4	23-	1
ButFux	7	57	9	8 1/2	8 3/4-	1/4
Buttox	7	x555	29 1/8	27 3/8	28-	5/8
C						
CarSic	7	184	25 1/8	24 3/8	24 5/8-	1/4
Cati	7	172	25 1/8	24 5/8	24 3/4-	1/8
Chump	6	29	35 1/4	d34 3/8	34 3/8-	1/8
ClitWit	...	z6080	24 1/2	d24	24-	1/2
ClumZ	11	213	25 1/4	24 1/2	25+	1/8
ConDum	8	85	9 1/4	8 5/8	9	...
CornHo	6	55	10 7/8	10 1/2	10 1/2-	3/8
CorRupt		15311 u 9	8 5/8	8 5/8	9	...
CoxOut	5	167	20 3/8	19 1/2	19 5/8-	5/8
CoxSuk	...	7	50 1/2	50 1/2	50 1/2-	7/8
CrapE	...	136	15 3/8	15 1/8	15 3/8	...
CrookEd	...	25	19 1/4	19	19 1/4+	1/8
CrumE	8	5280	45 3/8	43 3/4	44 1/4-	1/4
CrumBul	6	420	20 7/8	20 1/2	20 1/2-	1/4
CrumBum	...	27	32 1/2	32 1/4	...	
CumSuk	9	315	10 3/4	10 1/4	10 1/2-	1/4
CuntLap	7	53	5 5/8	5 3/8	5 3/8	...
D						
Damit	15	50	10 1/8	9 7/8	10	...
DamJoos	13	340	31	30	31+	1/2
DedAss	...	658	4 1/8	3 7/8	4-	1/8
DedCox	8	5	28 1/8	28	28 1/8-	1/8
DedDuk	5	x62	23 1/2	22 5/8	22 7/8-	1/8
DefNDum	5	1183	15 1/2	15 1/8	15 1/4-	3/8
DedHed	6	414	13 1/2	12 5/8	12 7/8-	7/8
DiaPer	...	8	17 1/4	16 1/4	16 1/2-	3/8
DidDil	10	94	18 1/8	17 1/2	17 5/8-	1/4
DikLes	9	755	35 3/4	34 7/8	34 7/8-	1/2
DikLip	6	256	27	26 1/2	26 7/8-	1/8
DilDoe	10	1846	14 5/8	13	14 3/8+	3/8
DixOff	3	38	7 3/8	7 1/8	7 1/4-	1/8
DoABM	5	298	27 1/2	24 3/4	25 1/4-	2
DogPoo	7	430	17 3/4	17 5/8	17 5/8	...
DogZas	3	120	19	18 3/8	18 5/8-	3/8
Drudge	5	247	28	26 5/8	27 1/2-	5/8
DukOut	8	3230	15 1/4	d14 1/4	14 1/2-	5/8
DukSuk	4	858	14 3/8	14 1/4	14 3/8-	1/8
DumBo	6	585	17 3/8	16 7/8	16 7/8-	1/2
DumDik	8	173	31 1/2	30 5/8	30 5/8-	1/2
DumFuk	10	4713	13 7/8	11 3/4	12 3/4+	1 1/8
E F						
EatMe	...	52	29 1/4	d27 1/2	27 5/8-	1 7/8
EatOut	14	235	8 1/8	7 3/8	7 5/8-	1/8
EsObe	8	37	8 1/2	8 3/8	8 3/8	...
EZLay	8	x306	17 3/4	17 1/8	17 3/8-	1/8
FagAss	10	2146	50 1/4	49 3/8	49 5/8-	3/8
FagIt	34	61	11 1/4	10 3/4	10 7/8-	1/8
FatBut	8	490	38 7/8	38	38 3/4+	3/8
FedDup	...	18	51	50 1/4	50 1/2-	1/2
FellUn	138	311	4 3/8	4 1/8	4 1/8-	1/4
FistFuk	8	1087	15	14	14 3/8-	1/8
FlimZ	11	x214	17 3/8	d16 3/4	16 3/4-	1/8
FooFam	...	z30	51	51	51	...
Fudge	...	z510	30 1/2	29 3/4	30	...
FukAll	...	z350	28 1/4	28	28	...
FukDup	8	x767	14 7/8	d13 3/4	14-	3/8
FukIt	8	637	23 1/2	22 1/2	22 1/2-	3/8
FumBul	13	420	14 3/8	13 1/2	13 7/8-	1/4
G						
GetBent	6	143	22 7/8	21 3/8	21 1/2-	1 1/8
GetClap	8	1101	32	31	31 7/8+	1/2
GivHead	6	1553	18 1/4	d17	17-	1 1/2
GonZo	8	x373	10 7/8	10	10 1/4-	3/8
GoofO	4	2798	4 1/2	4 1/8	4 3/8	...
GotCha	5	169	28 1/8	27 5/8	28	...
GotDTs	...	112	9	8 5/8	8 5/8-	3/8
GoToLA	7	1558	28 7/8	27 5/8	27 7/8-	7/8
GotVD	...	316	1 7/8	1 5/8	1 5/8-	1/4
Grump	7	13	6 7/8	6 5/8	6 3/4-	3/8
Grunt	6	225	39 5/8	38 3/4	38 7/8-	3/8
GumDup	...	149	23 1/2	22 3/4	23+	1/4
GutLes	7	94	26 3/4	25 3/4	26 3/8-	1/8
GypU	11	526	20 7/8	20 1/4	20 1/2-	1/8
H I						
HafAss	...	149	4 1/2	4	4 1/8-	1/8
HafWit	...	45	7 3/4	7	7 1/4-	3/8
Herpes	...	395	5 5/8	4 7/8	5 1/8-	1/8
HoBo	13	1331	9 1/8	8	8 3/4+	1/4
HopeLes	...	1	10 3/4	10 3/4	10 3/4	...
HopHed	...	134	23	22 3/4	22 3/4	...
HunGup	6	567	17	16	16 3/4+	1/2
IckE	...	13	66 1/4	64 3/4	66+	3/4
ImaBum	3	3643	13 3/8	12 1/2	12 1/2-	3/4
ImaFag	11	520	34 1/2	33	33 3/4-	3/4
InDebt	7	35	29 3/8	29 1/8	29 1/8-	1/4
InDutch	8	510	22 1/4	21 1/2	22+	3/8
InJail	...	z250	47	46	47+	1
InShit	...	z3100	106 1/4	104	106 1/4+	3/4
IsJunk	...	z1560	107	105	105 1/2	...
J K L						
JakOff	8	421	13 1/8	12 3/4	12 3/4-	1/4
JakTof	5	283	10 3/8	10	10	...
JerkMe	...	20	12 1/2	12 3/8	12 3/8	...
JoyRag	4	1694	16 3/8	15 3/8	16+	1/2
KiZoff	...	20	12 1/2	12 3/8	12 3/8+	...
Klod	...	x33	22 1/2	21 1/2	21 3/4+	1/2
Klutz	12	564	8 5/8	8	8 1/8-	3/8
LamPre	5	229	21 1/2	20 3/8	21 1/8-	1/4
LesBux	7	237	12	10 3/8	11 7/8+	7/8
LesBo	6	404	4 1/2	d4	4 1/8-	3/8
LikDik	10	2828	20	19 1/2	20+	1/4
LikSpit	...	z220	47	47	47-	1
LoBall	6	177	11 3/8	10 7/8	11-	1/4
LoCo	5	256	11	10	10 3/8-	3/8
M						
MacAd	9	91	18 7/8	18 1/2	18 1/2-	3/8
MBezL	...		25	24 3/4	24 3/4-	1/4
MeFlit	...	83	16 1/4	15 1/2	15 7/8-	5/8
MePuke	15	1061	34 3/4	33 1/2	33 3/8-	1/2
MesDup	12	1096	24	23 3/8	23 3/8-	1/4
MIA	7	1370	44 1/4	43	43 1/4-	1
MoFuk	7	194	20 3/8	18 1/2	19 3/4-	1/8
MoFux	...	173	3	2 5/8	2 3/4-	1/8
MTBank	5	226	16 5/8	15 1/8	15 1/4-	7/8
MuchBO	...	3	35	35	35	...
Mucus	7	127	8 3/4	82 1/4	8 1/4-	3/8
MudDux	6	1155	17 5/8	17 1/8	17 1/8-	5/8
MudPak	...	4	39	38 1/4	38 1/4-	7/8
N						
NasT	...	y390	49 1/2	48	48 3/8+	1/2
NatSwat	...	y4060	u57 3/4	55	56+	2 1/4
NigErz	...	x135	82 3/4	80	80+	1 1/8
NitPik	...	y7320	85 1/4	82 5/8	82 5/8+	2 5/8
NoBux	...	x213	84 1/2	81 5/8	82 1/8+	1 3/8
NoDice	...	x22	26 1/4	25 1/2	25 1/2-	1/8
NoDoo	...	3	73 3/4	73 1/4	73 1/4-	1/8
NoHope	...	z10	12 3/8	12 3/8	12 3/8-	1/2
NoLoss	5	816	50 3/8	48 7/8	49-	1 3/8
NoLuck	...	3	56 3/8	53 1/2	53 1/2-	2 7/8
NoNuts	...	2	54	54	54-	3 7/8
NotZee	8	402	30 1/2	d30 1/8	30 3/8	...
NoUse	...	484	25	24 5/8	24 3/4-	1/4
NoWay	6	611	24 7/8	241.2	24 3/8+	1/2
NutLes	26	172	14 7/8	14	14 3/8-	3/8
NutsO	...	218	3 1/2	3 1/8	3 3/8	...
O P Q						
OfukU	5	363	24 1/4	23 5/8	24 1/8+	1/2
OHeck	48	505	4 3/4	4 1/4	4 3/4+	1/4
OhOh	...	30	18 1/2	18 3/8	18 1/2+	1/8
OnDope	7	682	11 3/4	11 3/8	11 1/2-	1/8
OnLam	...	14	33 1/2	33	33-	1 1/2
PasGas	12	283	26 1/4	25 3/4	26-	1/4
PeaU	8	208	20 3/4	20 1/8	20 1/4-	1/2
Pester	...	1	88	88	88+	4 1/2
Player	4	124	6 1/4	5 3/4	6-	1/8
Pudge	9	2075	25 3/4	24 7/8	24 7/8-	7/8
PudNoz	...	z100	23 3/8	23 3/8	23 3/8-	1/8
Putz	...	z100	26 1/2	26 1/2	26 1/2-	7/8
Quack	...	z100	28 3/4	28 3/4	28 3/4+	3/4
QuimSuk	...	165	49 3/4	d48 5/8	48 7/8-	3/4
R						
RatZas	4	861	14 7/8	14 3/8	14 5/8-	3/8
RCox	11	2322	15 1/8	d14 1/4	14 1/4-	7/8
RFukt	...	61	6	5 7/8	6+	1/8
RipPoff	...	17	10 5/8	10 3/8	10 3/8	...
RiteTof	...	z100	78 5/8	78 5/8	78 5/8+	1/8
RobErz	...	z110	83 3/4	831.2	83 3/4+	1/4
RotGut	...	z1600	94 3/8	94	94+	3/8
RPrix	...	z320	115	114	114+	1
RumDum	...	40	23 3/4	23 1/8	23 1/2+	1/4
Rump	9	37	25 1/2	25	25-	3/4
RUNutz	7	172	24 1/8	23 5/8	23 3/4-	3/8
RunOut	...	2	86	d86	86-	1
S						
SCOCGE	14	673	17	16 1/8	16 3/8-	1/2
SellMe	...	202	38 1/8	36 3/4	36 7/8-	1 5/8
Shelt	4	43	12	11 3/4	12+	1/8
ShuDup	8	58	22	d21 3/8	21 3/8-	1/8
Simp	8	967	35 3/8	33 7/8	34-	1 1/8
Slantl	6	177	13 1/4	12 3/4	12 7/8-	1/8
Sludge	...	21	16 5/8	d15 5/8	16+	1/8
Slump	...	34	18	17 3/8	17 3/8	...
Smirk	...	90	2	1 3/4	1 7/8-	1/8
SnotRag	7	77	40 1/4	38 7/8	38 7/8-	1 1/4
SnoUse	9	14	14 1/8	13 7/8	13 7/8-	1/4
SoAnSo	8	148	27 1/4	26 3/8	26 5/8-	1/2
SoDum	16	701	21	19 7/8	20 1/8-	1 1/8
SoSorE	6	617	40 1/8	38 7/8	38 7/8-	1 1/4
SpamCan	8	69	21 1/4	20 5/8	20 7/8-	1/4
StifDik	8	2957	39 3/8	d36 7/8	37 1/2-	2
StinkE	13	952	u10	9 1/4	10+	7/8
StuPid	6	9518	29 7/8	d27 1/4	27 1/2-	1 5/8
SueMe	...	6	53 1/2	53	53-	1/2
SukAss	...	54	51 1/4	d49 1/4	49 3/4-	1 1/4
SukDix	...	52	59 1/4	d58 1/4	59+	1/2
SukOff	...	75	54 1/4	d53	53 1/8-	1 1/8
SumCox	...	1	76 1/4	76 1/4	76 1/4+	1/2
SureDum	7	1	76 1/4	76 1/4-	1/2	
SyfDik	10	99	16 1/2	16	16 3/8+	1/4
T						
TaxLos	9	653	9	8 3/8	8 3/8-	1/4
TeeDof	5	x274	31 7/8	30 3/8	30 1/2-	3/8
TGIF	6	2675	21 7/8	19 7/8	20-	3/4
ThroUp	6	546	20 1/2	19 7/8	19 7/8-	1/8
TitLes	6	x113	20 1/4	19 1/8	19 1/8-	3/4
TooDum	5	1399	23	22 3/4	22 7/8+	1/8
ToyLet	...	19	75	74	74 1/2-	1/2
Tripe	...	z450	50 3/4	49 1/2	49 1/2-	1/2
Trudge	...	11	53	52 1/4	52 5/8	...
TufLuck	8	696	24 3/4	24 1/8	24 3/8+	1/8
TurkE	...	21	64 1/4	62 1/4	63-	1/4
Twat	5	1053	23 1/2	22 1/4	22 1/2-	1
Twirp	6	966	38 7/8	d35 1/8	35 1/4-	3 3/8
U V						
UnBrite	...	3	62 1/2	62 1/2	62 1/2-	1
UnDeez	7	544	28	d27 3/8	27 7/8	...
UnDone	...	30	58 1/4	57 3/4	57 7/8-	1/2
UnFukt	...	7	57 3/4	56 3/4	57 3/4+	1/2
UnGood	4	1760	16	15 3/8	15 1/2+	1/8
UnWasht	8	632	25 7/8	25 1/8	25 1/2-	1/2
UpChuck	...	z340	107 1/2	107	107 1/2	...
URAFag	...	18	27 1/8	16 1/2	26 1/2-	1
URGypt	10	540	32	30	30 3/4+	7/8
UseLess	8	624	33 3/8	d32 1/8	32 1/4-	1
USmel	...	1	42 3/4	d42 3/4	45 3/4-	3 3/8
UTrou	10	331	16 1/4	15 1/8	15 3/8-	7/8
VanHus	8	1525	28	27 3/8	27 3/8-	3/8
VomMit	...	175	26 7/8	26 5/8	26 3/4	...
W X Y Z						
WacKof	6	512	48	d46 3/8	46 3/8-	7/8
WeeWee	4	1301	13	12 1/2	12 1/2-	1/4
WitLes	...	103	3/8	3/8	3/8	...
WhakO	...	113	24 3/8	23 1/4	23 1/4-	7/8
WhaZat	...	193	11 1/4	11 1/8	11 1/8+	1/8
WhaZit	7	x380	32 1/2	31 1/4	31 5/8+	1/4
WorthO	6	92	13 1/8	12 3/8	12 1/2-	1/2
XPence	12	74	53 7/8	51	51-	2 3/4
XWife	7	753	21 5/8	20 1/2	20 3/4-	1/8
YBuyIt	...	z5500	85 1/4	84 1/4	84 1/4-	1 3/4
YMee	...	z100	89	89	89-	1
ZipUp	...	z270	120	119 1/2	119 1/2-	1/2
ZitPop	8	117	8 3/4	81.2	8 5/8	...

S. Central Is 'Fighting Media Monopoly'

By BRIAN TORST
Special to the Republican-Democrat

WASHINGTON, D.C., Feb. 10-Federal Communications Commission Chairman Richard E. Wily, in a speech before Congress today, called Dacron's South Central Ohio Coal, Gas, Electricity, Telephone & Telegraph Communications Group a "fighting media monopoly." FCC Chairman Wily cited S.C.O.C.G.E.T.& T. as a prime example of a large corporation with near total regional dominance that is resisting by every possible means all FCC attempts to increase competitive freedom in the communications marketplace. S.C.O.C.G.E.T. & T. owns controlling interest in Dacron's WOIO AM and FM radio stations, WOIO-TV, three not-yet-operational pay and cable TV franchises, and this newspaper. Richard E. Wiley noted that his agency has brought 2,348 lawsuits against S.C.O.C.G.E.T.&T. and went on to say that he expected court rulings in favor of the FCC in all of them by spring.

MacAdam Has Role Lowering Cancer Rates

By BRIAN TORST
Special to the Republican-Democrat

WASHINGTON, D.C., Feb. 10-Environmental Protection Agency spokesperson Miriam Breer told reporters today that the closing of MacAdam Corporation's Dacron asphalt plant could have an important role in reducing the cancer rate in the Ohio River valley and elsewhere. She pointed out that carcinogenic effluvia from the MacAdam plant here has been linked to incidences of the disease as far south as Natchez, Miss. Ms. Breer said she expected the agency to order MacAdam Asphalt shut sometime within the next month. The plant employs some 6,250 people, about 10 percent of the Dacron work force.

Local Firm to Produce Oil

By CLARENCE STIMVEK
Rep.-Dan. Science Editor

A new Dacron firm has found a way to beat the high cost of Arab oil-they're making their own. Dacron New Energy Associates have begun the manufacture of high-grade low sulphur crude oil. In nature, oil is created by tremendous pressure being exerted upon dead and decomposed organic material such as leaves and dinosaur corpses. Dacron New Energy is following that same procedure in hopes of finding a new source of inexpensive energy. "We've got a hundred tons of organic matter buried in the ground and we've put about 300 tons of rock and solid debris on top of it plus trucks drive over it every day on their way to a quarry," Phelps Trent, president of DNEA said. "We'll open the pit in about 30 years and hopefully we'll have some oil." The project will not be profitable, says Trent, until they can expand about 200 percent and open 30 to 100 new pits. At the moment, the crude oil will cost approximately $9,000 per barrel. "The price will come down as we increase production," Trent says.

EARNING REPORTS

AMALGAMATED INDUSTRIES
Earned Plenty

GENERAL MANUFACTURING CO.
Earned a Bunch

AMERICAN FABRICATING
Really Earned a Lot of Money

EASTERN CONSOLIDATED
Is Rolling In It

The Armchair Investor
Asphalt, Trailers Are Portfolio Virtuosos

By MORTON KROFF

If you're looking for something safe (and profitable!) to put your life savings into, VanHusen Manufacturing common stock is definitely the answer: 1978 is going to be a banner year for VanHusen. They have a full range of terrific new products in the hopper-a mobile tree house, a grassmobile, three new water trailers to haul behind your boat, and a complete line of work and school vehicles to complement their recreational vehicle lineup. The nation's top investors are pouring every cent they can get hold of into VanHusen stock, and financial analysts all over the world are saying that that's the right thing for them to be doing.

Another company that offers terrific investment opportunities is MacAdam Asphalt. Basically this is because their product is just one of those sure things-no matter what state the economy is in, no matter what happens in world politics, people are still going to need pavement. Besides, these days, kids are making everything out of asphalt. So watch for a huge boom in asphalt bonds.

Now, if blue chip securities are your bag, there's a once-in-a-lifetime opportunity this week to get in on a new issue of South Central Ohio Coal, Gas, Electricity, Telephone & Telegraph convertibles. S.C.O.C.G.E.T.& T. is a conglomerate with excellent diversification. They're involved in coal, gas, electricity, telephone and telegraph operations and their communications group owns one of the top newspapers around. This is certainly a company that the smart money is headed toward.

MacAdam Photo Gallery

South Central Ohio Coal Gas, Electricity, Telephone & Telegraph Company, in cooperation with MacAdam, Inc., has finished a pilot project to reclaim strip-mined land in north-east Silage County. State and Federal conservation funds were utilized to pave more than 950 acres with asphalt.

VanHusen Inc. to Aid in Trailer Safety

By BRIAN TORST
Rep.-Dem. Washington New York, Boston, Cleveland and Foreign Correspondent

Washington, D.C., Feb. 10-Secretary of Transportation Brock Adams announced today that the Department of Transportation is ordering Dacron's VanHusen Mfg. Co. to recall every house trailer it has ever built. The D.O.T. cited potential safety hazards involving wheels, tires, brakes, frames, lights, wiring, stoves, heaters, sinks, refrigerators, air conditioners, springs, axles, floors, ceilings and walls. VanHusen Inc. has been manufacturing house trailers since 1931.

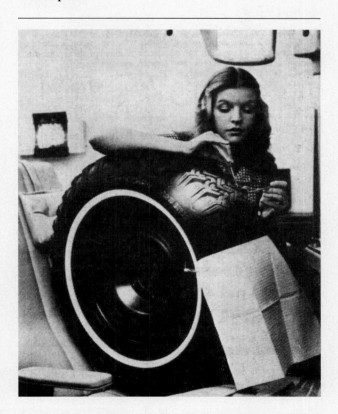

DentaTred, a national chain of automotive tire dental offices, will open four DentaTred drive-in auto dentistry locations in Dacron within the next few months according to William Havitts, DentaTred vice-president in charge of the Southern North-East Mid-West region. "Tire treads need a dentist just like your teeth do because tire treads can be crooked, need cleaning, have cavities or have to be re-capped just like your teeth," says the DentaTred V.P.

Dacron Business People in the News

MORTON KNIGHT, 30, has been promoted to Brand Manager at MacAdam Asphalt, supervising sales and marketing of "AsphaBrite,"

Rep.-Dem Staff Photo

Morton Knight—Promoted.

MacAdam's new lemon-freshed asphalt care product. Knight stated it will add a deeper, richer luster to fading pavement. The company's "Glossier Streets Are Safer Streets" slogan is already well-known in the Dacron area.

BOB McKERANSKI, president of McK., Inc., announced the signing of a long-term and exclusive "needs" contract with South Central Ohio Coal, Gas, Electricity, Telephone &

Telegraph Co., wherein the latter will supply McK. with certain raw materials essential to the construction of its new CRUISETTE-B nuclear land missile. "It is indeed fortunate that we have the pleasure of purchasing these rare and delicate materials right here in our own backyard," commented McKeranski—long-time believer in spending dollars right here in the Dacron area.

BOB TROUT and **CARL BUGBAUM**, top Republican-Democrat investigative reporters, received the local 808 United Coal, Trailer and Asphalt Workers' "Trophy for Excellence in Investigative Reporting" at a special awards dinner Thursday night. The trophy was accompanied by a "Check of Appreciation" for $50,000. This is the first time that the "Excellence in Investigative Reporting Trophy" has ever been awarded by local 808, which just created the award last week.

ROSENBERG'S DEPT. STORE has hired a woman Negro.

Photo Courtesy Rosenberg's Department Store

Woman negro—Hired.

VAN HUSEN MFG., INC. has transferred associate VP HUGH VAN to its Formica Procurement Division, in an effort to strengthen the company's overall style appeal. Citing a general consumer trend toward the more luxurious, natural style of living environment, Van noted that, "We in the trailer sector must take immediate advantage of fast-breaking design breakthroughs in the veneer industry." "I am confident the new knotty

pines, parquets, and Brazilian rosewoods will give our interiors the earthy, uncomplicated feel your modern trailer owner demands," he said afterward.

HERB WEISENHIMER'S Hollering Herb's Psychopath Chevrolet has been designated

Courtesy Dacron Elementary and Junior College Department of Art Education

Seurat's "Saturday Afternoon on the Grand Jatte"—To be destroyed.

a South Central Ohio Automobile Dealers' Assn. Foundation Fellowship Dealership for its sales excellence over the past year. As a permanent Fellow, Weisenhimer has received a grant to develop various experimental campaigns and promotions for

Foundation members. Mr. Weisenhimer has already mapped out the first initial television spots in which he will threaten to destroy a very realistic copy of Seurat's "Saturday Afternoon on the Grand Jatte" with an Ouzi submachine gun until, as he puts it, "local eggheads buy every unit on the lot."

Money Talk

By ABE BINKLUTZ

I am retired with a fixed income of $450 a month, and am interested in tripling it if possible. Can you give me some advice?
BRUCE EAZLEY, COLUMBUS

I'd be inclined to steer you toward a new mutual fund approach to commodities, which takes advantage of the 300% gains we often see in the futures arena, while adding the added protection of a mutual fund insurance feature, wherein the fund, acting as underwriter, actually guarantee your 300% profit in case of an unforeseen loss.

For a more exhaustive discussion of how you may take

advantage of today's lucrative mutual funds, send $5.95 now for my booklet: Mutual Fund Bonanza, in care of this newspaper.

I am going to sell my window air-conditioned soon because I won't be needing one anymore. It's an old model, but I still think I'll get enough money for it to make it worth my while to invest. Do you have any hints?
SPUD BROWN, TOLEDO

There is a tempting argument for your getting into the new Series F high-yield municipal chain bonds, not only because they are tax exempt, but also because of the unique and profitable system by which the bonds are transferred. There is space for five

signatures on the face of the note—you simply cross out the first name and sign your own at the bottom. You then mail a $5.00 transfer fee to the person whose signature is on top. To sell the bond, you mail copies to five new persons, who will send you within a relatively short period of time up to 27,000 times your original investment.

A more thorough, step-by-step explanation of how to invest in Series F municipal chain bonds is contained in my pamphlet: Series F Municipal Chain Bond Goldstrike, available to you by remitting $7.95, in care of this newspaper, today.

Is there a plan where I can make money without

investing anything?
B. ADZE, DAYTON

This is the most popular plan of all, and consequently available in numbers and varieties too numerous to mention here. Under the general heading of Life and Casualty Insurance, most companies specializing in this area return handsome dividends, on demand, in cash, to the investor, provided only that he or she sign the proper requisition in advance of the demand for money, or at least telephone.

To completely familiarize yourself with the modern Life and Casualty Insurance picture, mail $6.95 immediately for my brochure: Life and Casualty Insurance Jackpot, in care of this newspaper.

Metal Fasteners Held Their Own In U.S. And Abroad

U.S.	*		100
Eur.			50

*War in Cambodia
[1]Courtesy, U.S. Bureau Labor Statistics
[2]Seasonally adjusted, post-1974 years

1975[2]   **1976**   **1977**

South Central Ohio Coal Gas Electricity Telephone & Telegraph Presents:

11 Tips to Help You Save on Gas and Electric Heating Bills

- Air your house out frequently during cold snaps. Don't let old, stale, over-warmed air accumulate in your furnace.

- Turn heat up at night to avoid "peak heating" hours.

- Save money by reusing old furnace filters. Leave them in an extra year this winter.

- Thermostats function most efficiently at 75° Fahrenheit.

- Use your electric stove to heat the kitchen.

- Keep windows open. It helps your furnace "breathe."

- Pay your gas and electric bills months in advance to improve household budgeting.

- Encourage kids to play outdoors. Running back and forth, in and out of the house all the time, will help them keep warm.

- Put felt or rubber weather stripping, about an inch wide, around all your indoor plants.

- Use your air conditioner during winter months when there's less demand for home cooling.

- Put six inches of S.C.O.C.G.E.T.&T. "Asphalt Wool™" insulation on your basement floor. Much of your home's heat escapes through basement floors.

This advertisement is provided as a private service by

South Central Ohio Coal Gas Electricity Telephone & Telegraph, Inc.

Coal Building
Dacron, Ohio 43701

This announcement appears as a matter of great good fortune to the canny investor.

$6,750,000
South Central Ohio Coal, Gas, Electricity, Telephone & Telegraph

Convertible, Sedan, Coupe, and Sensible Station Wagon Bonds

Due Any Minute

The undersigned think these notes are grand. Get in touch with us right away.

Ruff & Tumble Incorporated

Matthew, Mark, Luke & John, Inc.

Fife & Drum Co.

Katz & Jammerkidz, Inc.

Pudding & Tane Incorporated

Over, Andover & Dover Incorporated

Redd, Inc.

February 13, 1978

This announcement appears as a matter of record only, but it's a great deal and you'd be a fool not to get in on it.

NEW ISSUE

$4,000,000
33 1/3% Yield
Asphalt Bonds

Maturing in 1990   **Payable in Asphalt**

The undersigned arranged the private placement of these securities and urge you to buy a bunch of them.

Merrill Lynch, Inc.   Pierce Fenner, Inc.
Lynch Smith, Inc.   Merrill Pierce, Inc.
Merrill Lynch, Pierce, Fenner & Smith
Incorporated

This advertisement is an offer to sell and a solicitation of offers to buy any and all of these securities. You bet.

NEW ISSUE   February 13, 1978

350,000

VanHusen Manufacturing Company, Incorporated

Uncommonly Swell Stock

Price $12.00 Per Share But, For You, Only $9.98
Copies of the prospectus may be obtained by picking one up off the sidewalk after we drop them from planes all over the city.

E. F. Mutton & Company, Inc.   Rodger Will Co.   Roland & Martin, Inc.
Grabbit & Runn Incorporated   Winkin, Blinkin & Nod Incorporated
Sturm & Drang Incorporated

 **Rosenberg's**

DOWNTOWN · CORNGATE · PLAZARIA

Fabulous combination Valentine's Day and Lincoln's and Washington's birthday sale

MEN'S CLOTHING

Men's One-Piece Pantless Suits

50%off

Famous and Pretty Well-Known Brand Winter Suits

$39.99

Now in cuffless, beltless, and vestless styles, these finely tailored suits are woven from a special blend of wool and plastic and are available in brown, green, green brown, brown, or green. Regular sizes, Sub-Regular sizes, Post-Regular sizes and Fat. Hurry in for best selection.

LUGGAGE

Colorful Japanese Paper Luggage

Save on our

100%

Luggage Sale

Every Piece of Rosenberg's Luggage Is 100% On Sale.

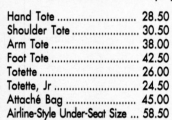

Paper—that traditional, magical material of the Orient—is now available in beautiful imported luggage. You'll love these paper-thin, paper-weight pieces of matched-look baggage— they're light as a sheet of stationery yet strong as a grocery sack. And no one knows paper like the Japanese!

Hand Tote	28.50	In-Seat Size	62.00
Shoulder Tote	30.50	Two-Seater	82.50
Arm Tote	38.00	Two-Suiter	61.50
Foot Tote	42.50	One-Suiter	57.00
Totette	26.00	No-Suiter	42.00
Totette, Jr	24.50	Over Nite	32.00
Attaché Bag	45.00	Over Nite & Part of	
Airline-Style Under-Seat Size	58.50	the Next Day	44.50

SWEET SHOPPE

For that Special Valentine

Candy-Shaped Heart-Flavored Chocolates

ALSO
• Butterwelsh Candies
• Fish Mints
• Brut™-Filled Bonbons
• Crimean Taffy
ALL only
$3.99 per lb.

only
$2.99 a box
Flavored with genuine baby beef hearts.

YOUTH BEAUTQUE

French Three-Legged Jeans

$18.99

Super selection of stripes, plaids, patterns, paisleys, polka dots, batiks, tartans, argyles, brocades, moires, and African prints. All 100% polyester genuine denim double-knit. S, M, L, XL, XXLL, XXXLLL.

With any $5 purchase **FREE** Parallel parking anywhere downtown 9PM—9AM

Powder Room Prowler – A Psychological Profile

By LARRY MICKLE
Rep.-Dem. Staff Writer

The well-known Dacron psychologist, Dr. Barry Steinkopf, has developed a psychological profile of the "Powder Room Prowler" for Dacron police to aide in their search for the criminal who has made most area women frightened to go to the bathroom alone. Using all available data including eyewitness reports of such things as mannerisms, clothing, voice, odors, etc. and running this all through a computer, Dr. Steinkopf, who heads the Social Arts & Sciences Department of Dacron Elementary and Junior College, has created a chillingly accurate description of the criminal's mental make-up. If you know of anyone who matches this description, call the police immediately.

The Powder Room Prowler as he is envisioned by Dr. Steinkopf.

"This man is between the ages of 21 and 40," says Dr. Steinkopf. "He is of medium build. He is white, with both parents living. His father tends to dominate the household. His mother's love for him is deep, but she often scolded him when he did things that were wrong. As a teen-ager, he. was obsessed with girls. He often created fantasies in which girls were featured unclothed and in provocative situations, As an adult, he suffers from some sexual insecurity. When he deals with women in real situations, he tends to worry about his appearance, breath, cleanliness, manners, clothing, etc. He chooses only to associate with and contact women who are attractive and personable. He likes compliments and enjoys doing things that bring him satisfaction. He does not like punishment or ridicule. He is particularly fearful of being publicly humiliated by women. He is nervous about embarrassing himself in public. He insists on keeping the bathroom door closed when he uses it. He is very sensitive about having people watch him defecate."

Miss Cerebral Palsy Found Safe As Kidnap Suspect Nabs Self

By JERRY BURGER
Rep.-Dem. Staff Writer

A day of worry ended last night when police returned Cathy Ann Polaski, Miss Cerebral Palsy of Ohio, to her Columbus home. Miss Polaski, 16, had been abducted earlier in the day at a Cerebral Palsy Pancake Festival fund-raiser at the First Reform Presbyterian Church of Dacron Dells. Miss Polaski reportedly wheeled herself outside for some fresh air when she was approached by Rufus Leaking, Dacron's 1977 Mr. Retarded Trainability, who was attending the Cerebral Palsy Pancake Festival as part of a new Ohio Disease and Affliction Cooperation Program. According to police, Leaking, 32, took Miss Polaski to Wright Brother Park where he removed her dress and undergarments. As Miss Polaski struggled with the boy, she struck him on the nose and he began to bleed. He panicked and drove to a nearby McDonald's restaurant and attempted to surrender to the manager. Police arrived moments later. Dr. Donald Pelvin, Director of Childhood Diseases at Forrest Lawn Memorial Hospital and the founder of the cripple exchange program, apologized to Miss Polaski and her family. Miss Polaski's father, Jonosh was not appeased, however, and has threatened legal action. "I'd like to rip his underpants off and use a twig on him and see what an apology does," he said.

Dr. Pelvin explained that Leaking is not licensed to drive and stole the vehicle he used in the abduction. "Rufus has always been very gentle and well-behaved. We are shocked that he did this. But we are also gratified that he has responded to trainability therapy so well that he was able to drive a car," he said.

Despite the abduction, the Pancake Festival managed to raise a record-breaking $410.80 for cerebral palsy research.

Photo by Rep.-Dem. Staff Photographer Prissy VanHusen

Newspaper Publisher Launches Drive Against Child Porn

By PATTY PLANT
Rep.-Dem. Feature Writer

SATURDAY, Feb. 11— Rutgers Gullet, publisher of the Dacron Republican-Democrat, announced today that he was launching a major drive against child pornography in Dacron.

So far there has been no child pornography in Dacron, Mr. Gullet told this reporter during an interview right in his office where he had called this reporter into, but, he continued, we will all have to become very vigilant to keep it out. As a first step in his announced drive, Mr. Gullet will leave Tuesday for a brief tour of Los Angeles, San Francisco, and the 42nd St. district of New York in order to better identify the problem before beginning local activity here in Dacron.

They "Figure" They're Equal

N.O.W.P. Holds Contest

SATURDAY, Feb. 11— The Dacron chapter of the National Organization of Women People held a bathing suit competition yesterday at the Dacron Antelope Lodge. Fifteen beautiful women modeled bikini bathing suits for the 450 men who paid $3 for the pleasure. The event raised over $1,200, which will be used to further causes of women's rights in Dacron. The organizer of the competition and Co-Chairperson of the Dacron N.O.W.P., Ms. Suzi Fitzerman, told the au- dience at the conclusion of the competition that "Dacron is living in the 20th century so far as the way women are treated."

Not many men can Equal this: **Wanda Petosky models a little something from Rosenberg's St. Pete Shop.**

Photo by Rep.-Dem. Staff Photographer Vince Blum

She's Guilty In Child Abuse Case

By LYN ELLBOWN
Rep.-Dem. Staff Writer

FRIDAY, Feb. 10—Family court judge Albert Dunne ruled "guilty as charged" today in the much-publicized child abuse case involving Mrs. Emily Lambretta of 6635 Cabana La. in North Dacron. The Dacron district attorney's office had charged that Mrs. Lambretta, 31, had been repeatedly beaten, starved and locked in a closet for periods of up to two days by her 13-year-old daughter, Tammy. Tammy was remanded to the custody of Silage County Juvenile House. She is believed to be the first Ohio child to be convicted of abuse. Her younger sisters, Heather, 8, and Melanie, 5 1/2, were cleared of accomplice charges in family court proceedings earlier today.

Mrs. Lambretta, the former Emily Praeger, is a lifelong resident of Dacron and divorced. Her estranged husband, Vincent Lambretta, manager of a local men's clothing store, testified that he had no knowledge of the ongoing abuse although he did notice that his ex-wife had seemed to be "not looking very well lately." Mrs. Lambretta, who was not available for comment, is reportedly in fair condition in Calvary General Hospital.

City Champ

Rep.-Dem. Staff Photo

Miss Lemmer, 11

Clinton Grade School 6th-grader Margret Lemmer, 11, of 1201 Gatewick Dr., won the Dacron Public Schools Annual Counting Bee Friday. Perry School 5th grader, Elaine Kahn, 10, of 1009 Wedgewood, came in second after tripping up on 7,964. The contest was held in the Kefauver High School auditorium.

High Court KOs Welfare Abortion

By SAM FRESCA
Rep.-Dem. Staff Writer

FRIDAY, Feb. 10—The Ohio Supreme Court ruled today that the state's welfare agency does not have to provide Medicaid funds for a local Dacron woman's abortion. The woman, Mrs. Jefferson Jones, 28, of 766 South Shakespeare, had sought the abortion even though she is not presently pregnant. Her legal aid lawyer, Mark Finiman, argued that Mrs. Jones has been pregnant six times in the past ten years and since there was every likelihood that she would get pregnant again, Medicaid should be able to give her funds for a "layaway" abortion. This would cut down on red tape and future bookkeeping expense, lawyer Finiman argued. Mrs. Jones, who is separated from her husband, would then owe the state welfare agency one abortion which she would deliver whenever necessary, though, in the meantime, Finiman admitted, she intends to use the Medicaid funds to buy a television.

By providing entertainment to the Jones household, Finiman went on to say, this plan might also result in lower future abortion expenditures. The high court did not agree.

Malpractice Suit Brought

SATURDAY, Feb. 11—A Dacron man has filed a 16.6 million dollar malpractice suit in Silage County superior court against an area dentist, Dr. Leon Macky. The man, Nate Goldner, 36, claims in his suit that the dentist, Dr. Macky, left a mirror in his mouth following oral surgery. The mirror, according to the suit, caused Goldner excessive pain and mental anguish and estranged him from the affections of his wife. "This young man suffered from the mistakes of a very wealthy, and possibly incompetent, dentist who caused grievous injury to this fine young man," Goldner's attorney Meyer Saperstein said after a Friday afternoon preliminary hearing. Dr. Macky declined to comment.

Disabled Gal Has 'All The News That's Fit To Phone'

By PATTY PLANT
Rep.-Dem. Feature Writer

Attractively handicapped Dacronian Ursula Wattersky wanted a business of her own but needed a financial enterprise that didn't include leaving home much.

"I talk on the phone a lot," says Ms. Wattersky, 31, "and I guess that's when I got the idea for *The Corngate Bell*—I was talking on the phone all the time and I said to myself, Talking on the phone can really be a lot of work, so why shouldn't I get paid for it?'" That was the beginning of Ursula's unique weekly telephone shoppers' newspaper, *The Corngate Bell*, which comes to everybody on the West Side free once a week when Ursula calls them up to tell them everything about recent cub scout activities, church socials, zoning board meeting schedules, and much more, plus, of course, many complete details on valuable bargains and special sales at Food Clown and other fine shopping places unless you get your number unlisted.

"It's the only telephone newspaper in the world," says Ursula, "that I know of, anyway. It's usually 20 minutes long or so. We don't have any photos," she laughs, "but I'll tell people what stuff looks like. Naturally I have to call almost around the clock to make sure everybody gets 'delivered to,' so sometimes people get a little fussy around 1 or 2 A.M., but most folks just love it. Especially the shut-ins and Mrs. Ablemann, who doesn't see very well. I'm hiring two extra girls next week so we'll be
Cont. Sec. B, Page 30

Following Up On The News

• Reffly Roos, the "Puppy Killer" who angered Dacron pet owners in late 1968 when he mutilated a neighbor's litter of six puppies, has been arrested in San Jose, California, and charged with decapitating 11 elderly residents of a nursing home where he was employed. Roos had spent three months in an Ohio mental institution but won release in 1969 after a book of his poems was published.

• The three half-frozen boys who were found in a boxcar here last winter have been found half-frozen in a boxcar in Toledo.

• Little Becky Brighte, the 10-year-old Dacron girl with extremely rare cancer of the tip of the tongue, has been successfully cured. Doctors at Our Lady of Affliction Hospital performed the delicate operation last Wednesday. Little Becky managed a brave smile about her operation, saying, "I hes I han't hick my hung hout hat my hittle ruther hany more."

• The story about Gerald Ford retiring to Dacron turned out to be just a rumor.

• No one has contributed to the Autos for the Poor Drive and the program has been dropped.

• Dacron Area State Senator Abe Mudroe's legislation to make asphalt the state gemstone of Ohio has passed 104-12 and now goes to the state house of representatives.

• The congressional proposal to build a national forest here died in committee.

City To Buy New Trailers

FRIDAY, Feb. 10—The Dacron Department of Highways will purchase 42 new 60-foot house trailers to be used as storage facilities for the city's 1978-79 winter road salt supply, Highway Department Chief Dan VanHusen announced today.

Citizen Foils Telephone Pest

Miss Anna Gibbile of 1827 Jermain Dr., who called police last week to report continuing threats and abuse from an anonymous phone-caller calling her at 262-6449, has had her phone number removed from listing and changed to 261-6338.

CORRECTION

Arnold Piesner of 1554 Woodrow, Dacron, did not commit a violent act of homosexual assault on his next-door neighbor's seven-year-old son as was erroneously reported in Friday's *Republican-Democrat*. The assaulter was a Mr. Andrew Neebler and the incident took place in San Jose, California. We regret any inconvenience this error may have caused Mr. Piesner with his family, in his neighborhood or at his place of work.

Suicide Attempt Spoiled

Saturday, Feb. 11—A local high school guidance counselor attempted to take his life yesterday afternoon by leaping from the second story window of his parents' home at 1749 Jermain Drive, Dacron. The man, Lawrence Kroger, 31, finished lunch with his parents and excused himself to go upstairs. "He said he was going to kill himself, but I didn't think I heard him right," Mrs. Fredrick Kroger said. "Next thing I knew, there were policemen on my lawn." Dacron's Police Negotiating Team made verbal contact with Kroger, who was hanging from the gutter threatening to let go if anyone tried to rescue him. Lt. Sgt. Gerald Omstead spoke to Kroger from a bedroom window and convinced him that suicide was only the beginning of something even worse than life.

After nearly an hour in which several ministers, a friend, a radio disc jockey, family members and the Negotiating Team tried to get Kroger to come down, Lt. Sgt. Omstead brought the distraught Kroger in. "I talked

Photo courtesy Mr. and Mrs. Fredrick Kroger

Mr. Kroger as he appeared at a recent high school reunion.

him down from the eaves," Lt. Sgt. Omstead said.

"I told him that if his life was so lousy, his death would probably be lousy too, so why make a fool of himself for nothing. It did the trick." After being rescued, Kroger was taken to Forest Lawn Hospital to have his stomach pumped, because his mother discovered an empty bottle of Midol in Mr. Kroger's bedroom. "We are grateful to the Police Negotiating Team for saving Larry," Mr. Fredrick Kroger said. "But we're puzzled. Larry's never committed suicide before, I don't know why he'd want to do it now." Kroger was the first suicide case for the Police Negotiating Team.

A Perfect Record

Dacron's Police Negotiating Team

The Dacron Police Negotiating Team was created in June, 1976, to deal with hostage situations, suicide attempts, kidnapping and sieges. Three officers, Lt. Sgt. Gerald S. Omstead, Lt. Daniel Crosse Jr., and Sgt. Donald W. Beever make up the highly touted team. The three officers underwent a six-month training program at Dacron Elementary and Junior College and attended a two-day F.B.I. Contemporary Crimes Workshop in Chicago last winter. Until the Kroger suicide attempt, the Negotiating Team has not seen action but were ready for it nonetheless. So far, there have been no civilian fatalities in cases where the Police Negotiating Team has been called into action.

Deer Wreck

A fast-moving deer belonging to the Ohio Fish and Game Department collided with an auto in Woodtrim State Park last night. The automobile was unharmed. Damage to the deer is estimated at $250.

Answers to
YOU'RE WRONG!
(Quiz on Page 16, Sec. B)

1. Belgium during the late 1870s.
2. They aren't.
3. In a car.
4. He buzzes his scales very rapidly. If the female accepts this courtship gesture she explodes, scattering eggs over two-foot area of fen.
5. Lunch thumbs.
6. Top right dresser drawer under the cuff link box.
7. 2 lbs. scallops, 2 cups dry white wine, 1/4 cup butter, 4 finely chopped shallots, 24 finely sliced mushroom caps, 2 tablespoons minced parsley, 2 tablespoons flour, 2 to 4 tablespoons whipping cream.

N.O.W.P. Wins Battle At VanHusen Mfg.

SATURDAY, Feb. 11—Women's Liberation has won "a battle but not the war" at VanHusen Manufacturing according to VanHusen Employee Relations Engineer, Bruce Blecht. The giant local trailer manufacturer has agreed to allow women employees to leave work and receive full pay on Friday to have their hair done. National Organization of Women People's Dacron Co-Chairperson, Suzi Fitzerman, organized a successful "cramp-in" during which VanHusen's 59 women employees complained of stomach cramps and locked themselves in a powder room and refused to come out until their demands were met. Woolworth VanHusen II, chairman of the board of VanHusen Mfg., okayed the new rule.

"If men had to spend two hours in the beauty parlor every week," Ms. Fitzerman said, "then the whole world would get off early on Friday." Mr. VanHusen arid Ms. Fitzerman agreed on one point, however—no employer wants unkempt, unattractive women workers on the job.

Dacron Pair Elected To Nat'l Geographic Society

Mr. and Mrs. Herbert Wilkie of 2390 Versailles, Dacron, have been elected members of the National Geographic Society. Mr. Wilkie entered his name for consideration several weeks ago and last Thursday received his first copy of the Society's magazine. "The check for $8.50 came back cashed and the magazine arrived so Dorothy and I are definitely members of the Society and we are honored," Mr. Wilkie told the Republican-Democrat in a telephone interview. Mr. Wilkie is also a member of the Freemasons.

Kitchen fires begin at home!
© 1954 American Accident Association

Dacron News-Makers In The News

As part of his special second-class scout project, Dacron Second Class S c o u t JEFFERSON STILLWELL, 12, designed and set up a three-mile "Citizenship Trail" through his neighborhood. By barricading driveways, streets, and alleys with large rocks, Stillwell will divert local traffic along a special path marked by strategically felled shrubs and trees. Each segment of the trail is devoted to a different kind of "good citizenship." In the "Look Both Ways Before Crossing" portion, small tree-bark and rope children will pop up in the middle of the trail before there is time to stop. Further on, in the trail's "Don't Litter" section, the community-conscious young man has whittled 800 cubic yards of realistic-looking debris, and placed it everywhere to make the point. At trail's end, Stillwell's backyard, the talented Scout and his patrol will act out a symbolic stage play starring beavers that have the good citizenship not to sniff glue.

M R S . A V E R Y GLEASEN has rearranged her patio for the second time in as many weeks (despite the cold snap!). A firm believer in an interesting and up-to-date patio, Mrs. Gleasen moved the lounge chair to the extreme left corner, where she says it will be close to the backyard, as well as still on the patio. In other changes, the wrought iron coffee table was permanently anchored to flagstones by Mr. Gleasen to prevent an unfortunate tip-over, such as occurred last summer with snacks at a patio gathering.

MR. AND M R S . HERBERT WILKIE, recent ind u c t e e s into the National Geographic Society, are busy Dacronians indeed, combining their N.G.S. activities with active memberships in numerous other national groups, too. Charter members of the Book Club, a literary organization with headquarters in Peterson, Virginia, the Wilkies also participate in a variety of programs administered by The Record Club, the Music Cassette Society, The Universal Alliance of Federated Magazine Clearing Houses, and the Automobile Club of Dacron. "It takes up quite a bit of our time, but we're an active couple," notes Mr. Wilkie. As new National Geographic Society members, the active couple expect to experience their maiden viewing of the Upper Nile next month, in addition to a brief look at the last remaining wide-gauge railroads of the Caribbean. A hefty itinerary, when you consider the already hectic schedule of other viewing and listening the activity oriented couple maintain.

Dacron philatelist, ART LANGDON, has acquired an uncancelled block of 13-cent U.S. commemoratives from a well-known stamp sales firm. The colorful issue, bearing a red, white, and blue engraving of the United States flag on a white background, is very popular. Langdon is reported to have purchased the four-stamp block for 52 cents.

S K I P Y E A T S has just ret u r n e d from a vacation to Cincinnati, where he stayed with the Skott family on W. 155th St. The Skotts have a lovely two-story white colonial home, with plenty of room for guests since the children are older and have moved out. In fact, Yeats had the house to himself, because Mr. and Mrs. Skott were in Youngstown visiting the Taylor family. The Skotts and the Taylors are old friends and so is Yeats. In fact, Yeats was married to Kirsten Taylor, who introduced him to the Skotts. Although Skip and Kirsten are now divorced, all remain friends.

25 Years Ago In The *Dacron Republican...*

"Members of the Local 808 Coal, Trailer, and Asphalt Workers Union whose leadership is riddled with Communists and Communist fellow travelers, continue their three-week-old strike today, bringing economic hardship and financial misery to everyone in the Dacron area. But now Ohio Senator Robert Taft has had the courage to publicly request that Governor James A. Rhodes call out the state militia to halt union violence, and public opinion is seen to be in favor of this move."—Feb. 12, 1953

25 Years Ago In The *Dacron Democrat...*

"Management at South Central Ohio coal mines, MacAdam Asphalt and Van-Husen Trailer Truck Company, whose owners are members of huge nationwide monopolistic cartels, continue their three-week-old lockout today bringing economic hardship and financial misery to everyone in the Dacron area. And now Ohio Senator Robert Taft has had the nerve to publicly request that Governor James A. Rhodes call out the state militia to crush legitimate union protests, but public opinion is seen to be opposed to this move."—Feb. 12, 1953

Government Charges Vet In Dacron Medicare Fraud Here

By LARRY MICKLE
Rep.-Dem. Staff Writer

Dr. Elton Tuttle, a prominent local veterinarian, was arraigned in Federal circuit court Friday on charges of defrauding the Federal government out of more than $15,000,000 in Medicare funds over a six-year period. Dr. Tuttle pleaded innocent. According to Tuttle's attorney, Morris Slumberg, a senior partner in the Cleveland law firm of Grabgold, Slumberg and Slimstein, Tuttle is the victim of a simple misunderstanding.

Slumberg claims that Dr. Tuttle had made no attempt to conceal the identities of his patients, filling out all Medicare forms with their proper names, such as "Yappy" or "Fluff," that he had simply been under the mistaken impression that Medicare covered dogs and that he had only treated old dogs anyway. "Many of these dogs were 13, 14 years old," said lawyer Slumberg. "An old dog like that deserves Medicare. It's part of the family. It may mean a lot more to the kids, for instance, than grandma."

? ? ? ? ?
? ?
Did Ya Know?

By LES PRATTLE

It would take over one billion major league home runs to reach the moon.

Clams don't have eyes.

Medical scholars report that people who stutter are less likely to lisp, but people who lisp are more likely to stammer.

In Alaska less than 1% of the population stutters.

Hogs have been trained to answer the telephone and mow lawns.

Babies need constant care.

The tuba is the musical instrument closest to the human voice.

TODAY'S PAPERBOY

Jimmy Hopkins
645 Ridemower La.
Dacron Dales

Rep.-Dem. Staff Photo

Jimmy, almost 12, is a sleek, slim, coltish chap with a headful of touseled locks and a glint of mischief in his eye. He delivers the *Republican-Democrat*'s *Suburban Edition* in his Dacron Dales neighborhood and collects baseball cards, a rare 1948 Joe DiMaggio example of which is about to be presented to him by the fatherly figure of *Republican-Democrat* publisher Rutgers Gullet.

Cute Coed Misses Her Hemisphere

While it's the middle of winter here in Ohio, Australia, on the other side of the equator, has hot sunny weather this time of the year. Pretty Meg Smither, 19, from Sydney, Australia, is now a co-ed at Ohio State University but, as Meg says, "Where I come from, it's summer." Meg is majoring in elementary education.

Finch Calls For Licensing Feet

FEBRUARY 10— Dacron's first woman City Councilman, City Councilperson Olive Finch, today called for a measure which would require all citizens to wear small license plates on their shoes. The plates would be issued to all Dacron residents and eventually to all Ohio residents, and hopefully to everyone in the U.S. Ms. Finch claims that shoe plates would help police trace lost and stolen shoes and track down foot criminals. "Most women who get attacked get attacked by people on foot," Ms. Finch said. "When she's lying on the ground, it's very easy for her to see the back of a shoe and take note of its license number." Ms. Finch also pointed out that shoe plates would generate revenue for new sidewalks, steps and floors. "It will also serve as an official acknowledgment of the importance of the foot in solving our energy problem," Ms. Finch added. The Council voted to sleep on Ms. Finch's proposal.

Oldest Girl Scout Honored

Mrs. Elinor Harmon, of 854 Catalpa St., was honored at a special awards luncheon Friday as Dacron's oldest girl scout. The luncheon, which was held in the Tea Pot Room of the Hotel Warren Harding, was sponsored by the Dacron area chapter of the Girl Scouts of America, who presented Mrs. Harmon with a special plaque. Mrs. Harmon, a Scout First Class in the North Irving Avenue Congregationalist Church Troop 44, is 27.

Prowler Cans Toilet Use

By LYN ELLBOWN
Staff Writer

Public restroom use by Dacron women has fallen off alarmingly, according to Ellis Sinclair, who owns the Dacron area franchise for GoPay-Em, a Cincinnati-based pay toilet company. "Apparently they are 'holding it' until they get home, " said Sinclair, who estimates that the year-long series of ladies' lounge attacks by an unidentified assailant has cost him as much as $800 in uncollected dimes. Sinclair also pointed out that the continued assaults pose a grave threat to the livelihoods of the more than four local women who are employed as ladies' room attendants in three Dacron restaurants and the hotel downtown.

LOCAL HIGH SCHOOL NEWS

Youthful news writers from area high schools bring you the area high school youth news every week in the *Republican-Democrat*.

Ezra Taft High School   Bobcats

By Suzi Lister

Meow, Meow, Hiss!
Meow, Meow, Hiss!
Hit 'Em Like That!
Hit 'Em Like This!
YEA BOBCATS!!!

Everybody at Ezra Taft Benson is rooting their heads off for the Bobcat basketball team! Especially after they won a basketball game last week against Benedict Arnold and just about won another one the day before yesterday night in the Warren Harding High School gym down on the south side, even if that game was marred by some pretty unhost-like activities by a small but vocal minority of Harding students who stole all our cars. Everybody is also rooting their heads off for the Bobcat wrestling team with "Buggsy" Frunch (127 lbs.) and "Spider" Humple (103 lbs.) both getting out of the hospital sometime this week.

Elsewhere in school, fun was had by all at the Senior Ground Hog Night dance where Patty Epsomer won first prize for best ground hog costume. And debate is still being argued about whether the class play will get to be *Hair* or not. Faculty theatrical advisor Mrs. Girkins is for it. But our principal, Mr. Mannsburden,

says he won't let student actors stand up in their underpants. The 1978 Student Straw Primary for the Mayor's election was lost by City Councilman Chuck Parley who sort of looks like the Governor of California, Jerry Brown, if Jerry Brown were fatter. 36% of students polled said he was "too young to run the city." 34% of other students said he was "too old to go to a KISS concert." Present Mayor Pilegravey, whose daughter Leda goes to Benedict Arnold and everybody says she's real sweet, re-won, and City Councilman Madison A. Jones got a vote from a certain member of the basketball team.

C Estes Kefauver High School   Kangaroos

By Janie Praeger

Everything's coming up Kangaroos at Kefauver! Our basketball team is practically in first place, not counting Warren Harding and Tucker Tech, and everybody is "jumping for joy." Even all the sophomores that have to spend the rest of the year in detention study hall because of a lack of racial understanding during sophomore lunch period last week. But let's not have any prejudice against sophomores. It's not fair to blame all sophomore

students for the actions of some rowdy class members. In fact, five sophomores were out sick that day. Besides, Brian

O'Malley, Pat McPhee and Joey Brunelli probably just slipped and fell onto the sharp edge of cafeteria trays in their backs the way the public defense lawyer says they did and we shouldn't let one unfortunate small incident lead to hatred between friends and neighbors such as Cleon Jones and the Murphy brothers that ran him over in the parking lot who live right next door. After all, certain minorities have suffered years of oppression, such as having to repeat 9th grade three times, for instance, and we should view their struggles and aspirations with understanding even if Cleon did set fire to their house.

The JV basketball team is doing great, too, and is expected to do even better as soon as the police quit using our gym for temporary detainment so that they can practice more.

Benedict Arnold Day School   Turncoats

By Tish Sweater

Well, *lately*, life at Ben Arnold has just been positively wonderful. There've been *scads* of fabulous parties all week long and the whole Corvette-Set has been in an absolute tizzy.

PUFFY MAC ADAM gave *beaucoup de fete* Sunday last while parents were in St. Pete and governess was *avec* Dad's chauffeur (if you get my French). *Couldn't* have *been* more fun except for poor GABBY VANHUSEN who was *n'est'ce pas de* invited due to GAB's big sis PRISSY giving PUFF'S brother BOBBY the here's-your-hat. Well, that's life in the Big Suburb. "Dumb her" says B.A. D-School cafeteria society. For a man of 27 that

BOBBY is *mmmmmmm*. ... He dropped in on PUFFY'S party, borrowed somebody's pumps, put a bag over his head and was *soooooo* amusing. Let us at him, Puff!

Then all Tuesday night, while Le Folks were at *Man of La Mancha* opening night in Cleveland, GABBY had open house herself and *tout le high school* was there. Except PUFF, of course, who just *wouldn't* come. PUFF is so *loyal*.

Then, Wednesday, when the *mere et pere* of simply everyone plays canasta at Three Trees Country Club, cute little LEDA PILEGRAVEY (her dad practically runs this town) "borrowed" the keys to the PILEGRAVEY summer cottage on Punt Lake. LEDA goes with a college man and he brought along just *pounds* of... Well, I'll say no more, but *some people* drove through a store window on the way home and *boy* did *they* get a talking-to from the Dacron Estates policemen.

And, of course, Friday night was divine. That was when we had the Hunt Club Cotillion. Boring, yes, but that BIFFY MUDROE (her Dad's the county-famous City Councilman) put *enas je ne sais pas* what in the punch and the overdressed Rosenbergs (who only got into the Hunt Club by the skin of their money anyway) went *quelle flip-out*, took off all their clothes and tried to sell Israeli Defense Bonds to the furniture. Their much-divorced and artistic (if you know what I mean) daughter FAUN had to be called away from her modern dance potluck to drive them home. Well, tsk-tsk and ciao-ciao till next.

Warren Harding High School   Hyenas

By Pearlette Jefferson

This Hyena Pride Week so that all us Harding Students are evidencing our Hyena Pride. Right on. And this

drug Education Week too and all us Harding Students are told not to be taking no dumb drugs. There been hardly no rapes lately in the halls either and the basketball team be first all over town. There a whole mess of new courses to take at Harding High School here. We got Black Home Economics, Afro-American Industrial Arts, Minority Math, and History of the Great Ancient Civilizations of Africa where we goes outside and sits in the practice field and braids our hair with mud, way they did back in the Great Ancient Civilizations of Africa. I got to take my sister to the store.

Boss Prendergast High School   Lampreys

By Buddy "Brain-Bash" Bashniak

Breaker. . . Breaker. . . How about that Boss Prendergast High? . . . Come on . . . Come on ... So far this semester has been strictly Boogie-City on the old East Side. True, the hoop-shooters ain't so hot, but we've been winning all the fights after the games. Especially after the Harding game Friday before last. Man, we got daylight savings time now, because what I mean is that it's going to be a long time before it gets "dark" again in this neighborhood. Only trouble is City Council went and passed a law that we can't have any more home games until 1980, What a bummer. But, anyway, "Bush" Bushshinski and "Tom-Tom" Wackkadecki are starting the world's first Polish Ku Klux Klan chapter. Only the Bush and Tom-Tom are both good Catholics so they aren't going to burn any crosses—they're going to burn cars instead. Let's see, what else is new... Well, "Ape" Cannelli got thrown out of Mr. Bohack's shop class for reading National

Rep.-Dem. Staff Photo

Students at North Dacron's Ezra Taft Benson High hold annual Girl's Choir Dog Wash next Tuesday at 1100 Soft Pine Highway (corner of Soft Pine and North Secor). Money raised will go to send Benson Girl's Choir on a Spring Vacation Goodwill Tour of six Michigan cities.

Lampoon while he was supposed to be cleaning a lathe. So Ape hung around the back of Bohack's house for about a week and finally got this Polaroid of Bohack's giant pig of a wife getting into the bathtub and sent it to True Facts and the Toon printed it! Can you dig it! Then there's a KISS con-cert coming up next week and Jimmy Chezsky is working on a giant shrapnel bomb to set off in the audience. I'll bet those dudes in KISS will really flip for that one. Then Buzzy Malone has been working on his van some more and as soon as he gets his tires upholstered he's going to figure out a way to turn the whole insides of it into a giant bong. That's about everything I can think of so . . . *Here's laying all the good numbers on ya . . . Keep the beaver down and your handle on top, Boss High'll catch ya on the big flip-flop ... We down and gone to school!*

St. Vitus Parochial High School — Penguins

By Missy McHannihan

A big "Hi" from a big "High"— that's us, all the boys and girls at St. Vitus and we've got news to spare . . . Monday was our annual sex education class for all consenting senior girls over 18. Sister Theresa gave the lecture, which was tided "Don't." Tuesday, Father Coach Gilhooey announced the new Penguin B-ball center, Seamus Muldoon, who'll replace both the Murphy brothers that we lost to Kefauver High when their dad joined the Free Masons and that Kefauver lost to Juvenile Hall where they unfortunately will only play second string. Seamus is 5'11" and was the tallest person in Cork before his family moved here. Wednesday, heavyweight wrestler Serge Grumbulski broke his own foot when he accidentally put his famous toe-hold on himself during a practice match with sophomore Jumbo Slapelli. But the Penguin arm-benders are still expected to beat any school without a Pope. Thursday, Mike O'Pork was awarded an academic scholarship to Notre Dame for winning the Midwest Parochial Schools Essay Contest with his entry, "The Role of the Blessed Virgin in the American Revolutionary War and Pro Football." Congratulations, Pork-Head!

Friday we got off because it was Assistant Saints Day. And the same goes for next week when it's Ash Monday, Palm Tuesday, Feast of the Deaccession, St. Lanolin Eve, and Bad Friday.

Notes and Tidbits: Sophomore Maria Scalliano has decided to become a nun and will start taking nun courses as soon as her baby is adopted. New St. Vitus Dress Code will allow St. V. girls to wear patent leather shoes as long as they have dark underwear on (but no black). And Archbishop of Ohio Patrick X. O'Garrgle was here last week and said that anybody who went to the KISS concert had to say 11,000 Hail Marys before they could take communion again.

Tucker Tech Vocational High School — Wingnuts

By Joe Humski

Everything at Tucker Technical High is going real good. All the sports teams are going real good. We have won a lot of wrestling. And also pounded Kefauver's basketball team. Tucker Tech now has girls that go to it. This is something that began this semester. They study beauty shop operating. Some of these girls are cute but most of them are dogs. Most of the white guys still date their sister's friends that go to St. Vitus. Willy DiPalma dropped a Rat engine in his Vega down in auto shop and stomped Louie Pinnarella's old Mustang out on 1-40 last night about 2 in the morning.

Silage County Rural Consolidated High School — Farmers

By Bob Snope

Luke Dubber's prize heifer up and died on him last week and that sure was a shame. Winter wheat looks good. Hog prices have been way up. Lou Ann Packle says she will get married this spring to that fellow from up to Mt. Vernon. Folks that have met him say he is real nice. He's got a factory job and they plan to live in a trailer up there but will visit down here, regular. Supposed to be a early thaw this year. Least, that's what they say.

AREA HIGH SCHOOL SPORTS EVENTS

thru Feb. 18th (Won-Lost record in parentheses)

BASKETBALL

AT HOME		Just Visiting
Wed., Feb. 15		
Silage Rural Consolidated (6-6)	vs	Middletown John Foster Dulles (15-0)
St. Vitus (7-5)	vs	Akron Dewey (13-0)
Fri., Feb. 17		
Benedict Arnold (0-12)	vs	Warren Harding (12-0)
Tucker Technical (10-2)	vs	Ezra Taft Benson (3-9)
C. Estes Kefauver (9-3)	vs	Boss Prendergast (8-4)
St. Vitus (7-5)	vs	Silage Rural Consolidated (6-6)

WRESTLING

Tues. Feb. 14		
St. Vitus (8-1)	vs	Warren Harding (6-3)
Thurs., Feb. 16		
C. Estes Kefauver (5-4)	vs	Boss Prendergast (7-2)
Tucker Technical (6-3)	vs	Silage Rural Consolidated (0-8)

OTHER SPORTS

Mon., Feb. 13
Squash: Benedict Arnold vs Groate Preparatory

Tues., Feb. 14
Paddle Ball: Benedict Arnold vs St. Sissy Boy's School

Wed., Feb. 15
Water Polo: Palmolive Day School vs Benedict Arnold

Thurs. Feb. 16
Contract Bridge: Miss Melton's Finishing School vs Benedict Arnold

Sat., Feb. 17
Puff Billiards: Benedict Arnold vs Gullet Military

Dacron Public Schools Luncheon Menu

Monday, Feb. 13 through Friday, Feb. 17

MONDAY
Choice of
Cheese Chow Mein
or
Individual Franks & Beans
Pickled Beets, Creamed Corn Niblets
Bun
Chocolate Dairy Drink
Butterscotch Pudding du Jour

TUESDAY
Choice of
Bologna Sandwich
or
Macaroni & Cheese
Sauerkraut, Chili Squares
Sweet Pickle
Slice White Bread, Pat Margarine
Neapolitan Ice Dessert Brick

WEDNESDAY
Choice of
Sloppy Joes
or
Knockwurst a la King
Pickled Egg, Stuffed Pepper
Grapefruit-Ade
Soft Roll Lime or Fish Jello

THURSDAY
Choice of
Olive Loaf
or
Spaghetti & Meatball
Cauliflower au Gratin, Succotash
Slice Date-Nut Bread & Cottage Cheese
V-8 Juice or Hot Prune Cobbler

FRIDAY
Choice of
Assorted Cold Luncheon Meats
or
Fish Sticks au Jus
Food Chowder & Oysterettes
Deviled Broccoli, Cream of Washroom Soup
Cranberry-Ade
Graham Cracker w/ Topping

ASTROLOGICAL FORECAST
by Sybyll Beeks
For Sunday Feb. 12, 1978

IF FEB. 12 IS YOUR BIRTHDAY, you are creative, frank, a perfectionist and prone to nit-pick and nag until everyone around you is crazy. You often laugh at things no one else thinks are funny and even though you try to hide it, people know you are insecure. Leo and Capricorn persons are most likely to accept your many shortcomings. June is the best time of year for you, as most people go away on vacation during that month.

Aries (March 21-April 19): You asked for action—now you get it. A family member outlines plans and desires and teaches you a lesson you'll never, ever forget. Also, your gas bill will fall due.

Taurus (April 20-May 20): Keep a close watch on loved ones—they're in the mood for a conflict. Co-workers could be plotting. Keep out of shadows. Cover face when entering darkened rooms. A Sagittarius at Rosenberg's (Basement) and the Leo mailman will figure in your future.

Libra (Sept. 23-Oct. 22): If you are the Libra who was out with a certain Gemini on Friday night and went to a certain dark restaurant and was observed by a certain Cancer who happens to know the Leo you are married to, you can expect a problem in the very near future.

Scorpio (Oct. 23-Nov. 21): You will be embarrassed by something that will happen when you least expect it. Although you will not be seriously injured, you will spend a few hours in Calvary General Hospital with a nurse.

Sagittarius (Nov. 22-Dec. 21): Whatever happened yesterday will happen again today only it won't come as such a surprise.

Capricorn (Dec. 22-Jan. 19): Doesn't your spouse look strange today? There is something about him or her that just doesn't seem right. New hair style? New glasses?

Aquarius (Jan 20-Feb 18): Nothing can harm you as you enter a "lunar protection" phase. Good time to see how fast the station wagon will go.

Gemini (May 21-June 20): Something you threw away years ago will come back to haunt you. Stay away from the Dacron Medical Clinic and a dentist with a goatee. Listen to your heart, feed your stomach and refold your linens.

Cancer (June 21-July 20): Keep your nose off other people's grindstones—Mrs. T.'s especially. Bud G., something very important will get lost in the mail. Mary N., a fortune will slip through your fingers, but you won't find out about it for many years.

Leo (July 23-Aug. 22): It would be a good idea to steer clear of Wright Brother Park, Trailer Tower and Oliver Wendell Holmes Ave. It is wise to postpone picnics, potluck suppers and out-of-town shopping trips until Venus gets out of the way of your moon.

Virgo (Aug. 23-Sept. 22): Dig deep into a neighbor's past. If you know someone at the bank, he or she could help you obtain credit information. Ask lots of questions. Children can be helpful.

Pisces (Feb. 19-March 20): Today is a good day to meet someone new and start a close personal relationship. Seek this new person on a street corner, at your place of business or at the bar at the Cocky-Locky Motel's Chanticler Room.

Rep.-Dem. Staff Photo

Participants in this week's iturgical Debate Corner, left to right: Reverend Elliot Dotter, North Melville Avenue Presbyterian Church; Reverend Andrew Pontlip, Upton Avenue Lutheran Church; Reverend George Sheele, Christ Church of God; Reverend Travis Demaree, Christ Methodist Church; Reverend Daniel Condense, St. Andrew on the Mall Episcopal Church and Reverend W. W. Anode, James K. Polk Church of Christ Christian Church.

Church Debate Corner

Each week, clergymen from a number of Dacron faiths are invited by Jason Halstrom, Republican-Democrat Church editor, to debate an important religious question. This week, our pastors were presented with the question:
Do people benefit from going to church?

REV. ELLIOT DOTTER, NORTH MELVILLE AVE. PRESBYTERIAN—Well, yes, I would have to say that I, as well as other Presbyterians, believe that going to church is a benefit. We think we should all go to church.

REV. ANDREW PONTLIP, UPTON AVE. LUTHERAN—Yes, as Rev. Dotter said, going to church is beneficial for us. He is right when he says we should all go to church, and I agree. The Presbyterian and Lutheran churches are very much in agreement on this point, all should go to church, and I agree.

REV. GREGORY SHEELE, CHRIST CHURCH OF GOD—Although many people do not attend church, I agree with Rev. Dotter and Rev. Pontlip that we should go to church. Yes.

REV. TRAVIS DEMAREE, CHRIST METHODIST—Oh, yes, I am very much in agreement with my colleagues, Rev. Dotter, Rev. Pontlip, and, of course, Rev. Sheele. We certainly should all go to church. That is a firm tenet of the Methodist faith.

REV. DANIEL CONDENSE, ST. ANDREW ON THE MALL EPISCOPAL—Rev. Dotter, Rev. Pontlip, Rev. Sheele, and Rev. Demaree reflect the Episcopalian view that we should all go to church, because there is a definite benefit that we receive by going to church.

REV. W.W. ANODE, JAMES K. POLK CHURCH OF CHRIST CHRISTIAN—Going to church is good for everyone, just as Rev. Dotter, Rev. Pontlip, Rev. Sheele, Rev. Demaree, and Rev. Condense have said so nicely. Yes, I believe that church is a benefit to us all, and that we all should attend.

Next week: "Is God important?"

Group To Have Religious Rally

Followers of the Korean Rev. Sun Nyung Moon, who call themselves "Moonies" after their leader's last name, are holding a public rally at the Buchanan St. Theatre on Thursday, Feb. 16, starting at 5:30 in the morning. According to Dacron Moonie member Naomi Eggenschwiler, the event will be "beautiful." There will be a free movie.

Church Notes

REV. DAVID BEKEL, rabbi of the New Beth Ouzi Temple of Dacron View Hills Jewish church reports that recent vandalism to the front of his temple has been temporarily covered over; however, he states that sandblasting and an entire new coat of plaster will be necessary to fully efface the large black symbols painted by the wrongdoers. Rev. Bekel suspects a causal relationship may exist with a new bookstore in East Dacron, which he says sells literature and other materials bearing similar insignia from which the perpetrators may have drawn their inspiration. An unexplained explosion at the bookstore has hampered efforts to check out the connection.

RIGHT REV. DOMINIC O'McGREGLIORELLA of Our Lady of the Exit-Wound West-Side Catholic parish announces that mass in perpetuity for the souls of 2,500 pagan babies have been purchased by his parochial school students with funds raised from their annual door-to-door X-acto knife sale.

MOST REV. MIKE GENK of St. Betty's East-Side Catholic parish informs us that his parochial school pupils have bought masses for 156 more pagan babies than Our Lady of the Exit-Wound has, with money earned at the school's recent "Las Vegas in Gethsemane" Nite. Competition between the two parishes has been spirited, with a grand total of 5,156 pagan babies being the real winners. Each of the heathen infants, many dead for nearly 2,000 years, will hopefully get into heaven soon, as a result of all the masses being perpetually said.

REV. SAMMY "BLACKSHOES" JOHNSTON of South-side Jesus Luxury Mission announces the premiere of a slide and lecture program prepared by Dr. Ecru Muhammed Aswan during his recent visit to the Soviet Union as part of a multi-denominational delegation of the United Algerian Religious Council's World Friendship Task Force. Dr. Aswan's presentation includes details of a $25 million Soviet grant-in-aid to finance American Negro visits to Russia, North Korea, and East Germany so the different cultures may share their common aspirations and foster a warm friendship. The program is entitled "We Share Your Dream," and will be given continuously from 8 P.M.

REV. GREGORY SHEELE of Christ Church of God advises his church will be closed Wednesday, Feb. 15, for minor repairs to the phonograph needle of the steeple's clarion bells which suffered damage while playing some 2,000 choruses of "White Christmas" over the Xmas holidays.

THE OLD COUNTRY PARSON'S CHRISTIAN PULPIT WITH —

Rev. Endochrine O. Spicketts

Today, when most of us look about we often find more questions than answers. In a world so complicated by machines and speed and competitive pressure, the ordinary man discovers that more than ever before he must turn to a higher, less worldly, source of comfort if the confusion and alienation of modern daily life is to be relieved. Some have tried all manner of escape such as drugs, books, and suicide; while still others have simply "dropped out" into self-imposed isolation, abdicating their role in the Father's Plan.

Please take a moment and listen to what the Bible says: Chronicles 28:19— "All this, said David, the Lord made me understand in writing by His hand upon me, even all the works of this pattern." The Lord's own Word soothes our singed and battered and splayed souls, while other wickedly candy-coated secular diversions merely abominate our lives, turning a beautiful world into an ugly, living hell; rife with the stink and horror of moral putrefaction and hopeless tomorrows. Witness the words of Matthew, 19:1—"And it came to pass, that when Jesus had finished these sayings, He departed from Galilee, and came to the coasts of Judea beyond Jordan." Clearly, the concurrent wisdom and solace therefrom to be had dramatically exceeds the grandest of earthly "pleasures."

For as Isaiah says in 30:4—"For His princes were at Zo-an and His ambassadors came to Ha-nes."

You know, a woman came to me a short time ago who had indeed suffered immensely, having been frightfully disfigured in a car accident; occasioning her despair. 2 Samuel 21:18— "Then she spake, saying, they shall surely ask counsel at Abel: and so they ended the matter," I quoted to her. Another individual with whom I am acquainted couldn't find a job. I opened my Bible to Psalms 70:3—"Let them be turned back for a reward of their shame that say, Aha, aha." Virtually everywhere I turn in the Holy Bible, I find the answers I need to help me through this life. Answers that don't come in pills, motel rooms, on 6th Street, in back seats of cars or dice games. Turn to the Bible with me, won't you?

"So, I got a girdle according to the word of the Lord, says Jeremiah 13:2, and put it on my loins."

Today's Guffaw

Plenty of fellows are married to wanton women—first they're "wanton" this, then they're "wanton" that...

Submitted by
**Borden G. Klinger
Pith-Dipper, MacAdam Asphalt**

The Republican-Democrat will pay 50¢ for each humorous item accepted. Mail to: Today's Guffaw, The Republican Building, 100 Polk St. Dacron, Ohio 43701

Church Directory

Obituaries

AUKSCHTENZ—Knule B. Avid fisherman and outdoorsman Knule Bauhaus Aukschtenz, 31. of 222 W. Villa de Manzana, died of an illness described as radiation poisoning according to officials. He was active in many outdoor organizations, including the Licking Creek Alliance, in which he had been leading a campaign to clean up Dacron's ponds and lakes which he claimed were "threatened." Services will be held on board the naval destroyer *U.S.S. Erie*, from which the special lead and zinc funeral cannister will be lowered two miles into the ocean off the coast of American Samoa. Officials could not pinpoint the source of Aukschtenz's exposure to the massive concentration of strontium 90 found in his body, commenting only that "he could have picked it up most anywhere." He is survived by a wife and two children, now residing in Europe.

BENTWICK— Oscar L, Jr., 56, died Saturday at Scarsview Hospital of complications following foot surgery. He is survived by his beloved wife, Dorri, faithful sons, Harrison W. and Gerald S. and devoted dog, Hotcakes. Services Monday at Scapula's Funeral Home. Family requests cash in lieu of flowers.

BUNKERS—Helen, 60, died Friday in her car at the corner of Truman and White Pine of cancer. She is survived by her husband, Daniel, and sons Red and Darrel. Mrs. Blinkers will be buried at home.

DOE—Mary. Unviable and unnamed fetus, Mary Doe, 0, no address, died before birth in the recently waxed aisle of Rosenberg's Dept. Store on the afternoon of Feb. 10. Miss Doe might have weighed approximately seven pounds and four ounces at full term, with dark hair like her mother's, and eyes resembling those of her father. According to Mr. and Mrs. Doe, she would have been a strikingly beautiful girl.

METZ—Lorraine. Dacron citizen Lorraine Gay Metz, 18, died of a heart attack suffered during a young men's pre-nuptial smoker at the Royal 600 Motor Court on Feb.16. Born on April 1,1961, Miss Metz was officially enrolled at Victor Wertz Elementary School as a student, where she attended classes under a variety of instructors in successive grade levels one through eight. Following graduation, she went on to become a fully registered pupil at Benedict Arnold High School, receiving further Special Education in general arts as well as general sciences.

During this period, she also found time to live with her family at 1802 E. Onyx, with whom she shared a great many hours of t.v. and meals. Although

Miss Metz was a solitary girl, she touched the lives of many, as evidenced by the fine turnout of 2,482 students from Benedict Arnold who were in attendance at the funeral following permission to leave classes to attend. The crowd was so large that many mourners were backed up all the way to the Kreemy Freeze dairy treat outlet several blocks away. As one of the young men remarked who had been present at the motor court where Miss Metz passed away, "She had a soft, deep, warm spot for the entire gang, and then, bang!, she was gone."

PESCADOR—Ralph M. Longtime Dacronian Ralph Mann Pescador, 74, of 118 W. Coco Circle, died in his home after a long and painful illness. Pescador first became aware of his affliction in late 1976 when routine blood tests revealed a serious bone marrow deficiency, further borne out by urine and tissue samples taken at a private clinic in Cleveland. Although he had suffered occasional listlessness and analgesia, the full effect of the disease did not become overtly manifest until June or July of 1977, when Pescador was con-

fined to his bedroom, barely able to take care of himself. His condition progressively degenerated. Various family members found it necessary to move into the Pescador home to administer around-the-clock medication, manage the household, and arrange the dying Pescador's financial affairs in legal order. The last weeks were particularly stressful for everyone. Pescador was intermittently conscious, often incoherent, and tempers flared. The end came in the evening. Pescador's survivors, his wife, Olivia, and his daughters, Margarette, Hazelique, and Yvonne, were shopping.

REILLY—Omarr, 58, died Saturday morning in his home at 312 Gingko St. of middle age. He is survived by his dear wife, Marjorie, dedicated son, Lawrence, and unusual daughter, Berna-dette. Mr. Reilly will be shipped to the University of Ohio Medical Dept. on Tuesday following a brief private ceremony.

Deaths Elsewhere

AUKSCHTENZ—Grettl K., one-time Dacronian resident Grettl Krug Aukschtenz, 33, died in a European hospital recently of an overdose of radiation. She had apparently been exposed to an active nuclear contaminant sometime ago, having possibly come in contact with it "most anywhere," according to officials. A widow, she is survived by two children.

CRIBBETS— Verna, 66, was frozen moments after death by doctors at the Or-

ange County Hospital in California where she has lived since retiring. Miss Cribbets was a former head librarian with the Dacron library system. Her body will remain frozen until medicine finds a cure for gunshot wounds. She is survived by her sister, Mithune Patterson, of Dacron.

HELQUIVE—Ambrose V. Former Dacronian Ambrose Victor Helquive, 68, Cleveland, Ohio's largest manufacturer of lightweight cutlery, died in his home. He is credited with inventing the first plastic silverware sold in the United States, which he marketed under the name of "Knives," "Forks," and "Spoons." Helquive, reportedly a billionaire, is survived by his wife, Elaine, and a son, Shelley, who state that most of the deceased's estate will be used to finance a world cook-out, given in his honor at a site either in the Hunan district of Northern China, or Colorado, depending upon the weather. Brazil will bring the cups. Services are to be held for Helquive at the Muerto del Vide Mortuarial Shrine in Dacron, where he will be interred in the family basket. The viewing picnic will be Tuesday at 8:00 P.M.; eulogy at 10:00.

Clinic Ordered Closed

By MICK HOGARTY
Rep.-Dem. Staff Writer

SATURDAY, Feb. 11—A local methadone maintenance clinic is under court order to close its doors today in the wake of an investigation which showed that none of the clinic's patients had ever been addicted to heroin.

The clinic, run by Dr. Mitchell Larmgrove and known as the 7-11 Medical Center, has been operating for four years at South Longfellow and 12th Streets, m a statement issued through his lawyer, Dr. Larmgrove categorically denied accusations that he misused state and Federal anti-drug funds. "The methadone maintenance program has great validity," said Dr. Larmgrove. "Many of these patients are heavy drinkers, almost everyone of them smokes cigarettes, some even smoke marijuana.

There is no doubt in my mind as a doctor that virtually all of my clinic's patients would be addicted to heroin if it were would be addicted to heroin if it were more easily available in the Dacron area."

Investigation of the 7-11 Cont., Sec. B, Page 19

Mystery, Disease Strikes

By LARRY MICKLE
Rep.-Dem. Staff Writer

At least seven men have sought medical treatment for an undisclosed illness at Our Lady of Affliction Hospital. The men are all members of the Dacron Hot Bags, Light Manufacturing Bowling League team, causing their ailment to be dubbed "Bowling Leaguer's Disease" by some. One woman who does not bowl with the men but is described as a fan was treated at Scarsview Hospital at the same time the men sought treatment. Doctors at both hospitals refused to reveal any information about the disease except that it does not appear to pose a public health threat at this time. The woman, who describes herself as a professional modern dance specialist, is from Toledo, which leads some to believe that she may have brought the disease from there and passed it to the bowlers.

Report:
Giant Mice On I-40

Saturday, Feb. 11—State police yesterday investigated a report of giant mice harassing cars on Interstate 40 near here. A caller reported the pack of dog-size mice running near the highway and said that several of the giant mice growled at her as she stepped out of a.comfort facility at an I-40 rest stop. Police searched a 20-mile stretch of roadway but found no sign of the mice. "There is some possibility that these dog-size mice may be dog-size dogs," State Police Lieutenant Howard Holwanger speculated.

THIS YEAR'S TOP PAPERBOY

Tommy Shane
1011 1/2 E. Taft
Dacron

Rep.-Dem. Staff Photo

Tommy, going on 13, has deep mysterious blue eyes and the entrancing look of a young fawn. There's a hoydenish grace to all the engaging movements of his young limbs as he carries his heavy bag of newspapers along the gray avenues of Dacron's East Side. Tommy's hard-working fatherless family has been greatly aided this past year by thoughtful assistance from *Republican-Democrat* publisher Rutgers Gullet, a frequent visitor to their modest abode.

Man Tries to Rape Her But She Beats Him Off

Eloise N, Caulb, 1311 E. 9th PL, East Dacron, was sexually accosted in the driveway of her home yesterday by an unknown assailant, police authorities disclose. Miss Caulb, a divorced cocktail waitress, told detectives she resisted the attacker for several minutes, but he quickly overpowered her and she became helpless. However, as he struggled with her, the aggressor, whom she described as exceedingly strong and ruddy, became entangled in her garments and lost his concentration. "At that moment, I hit him over the head with my purse, then I kicked him in the stomach, clawed his eyes with my nails, cracked him in the face with

Cont. Sec. J, Page 12

City Council Notes

Council Session of Friday, February 10, 1978 Mayor Milos Pilegravey Presiding

Motion by Councilman Buzz Mudroe to have city purchase site of the old Mudroe Lampblack factory, 1040 South Washington, for use as low-income housing site.
For: MacAdam, Mudroe, O'Garrgie, Snope, Hunch, Shellmonzak, Grosso, Welsh, Finch
Against: Parley, Jones
Motion Carried 9-2

Motion by Mayor Pilegravey to use Federal anti-poverty funds to buy VanHusen trailers to be used as low-income housing on site of the old Mudroe Lampblack factory.
For: MacAdam, Mudroe, O'Garrgie, Snope, Hunch, Shellmonzak, Grosso, Welsh, Finch.
Against: Parley, Jones.
Motion Carried 9-2

Motion by Councilman Madison Avenue Jones to ban home athletic games at Boss Pendergast High School when Prendergast High is playing against Warren G. Harding High, until 1980.
For: MacAdam, Mudroe, Hunch, Finch, Parley, Jones
Against: O'Garrgie, Snope, Shellmonzak, Welsh, Grosso
Motion Carried 6-5

Motion by Councilman Buddy MacAdam to approve new downtown expressway plan.
For: MacAdam, Mudroe, O'Garrgie, Snope, Hunch, Shellmonzak, Grosso, Welsh, Finch.
Against: Farley, Jones
Motion Carried 9-2

Motion by Councilperson Olive Finch to require all Dacron residents to wear small license plates on their feet.
Mayor Pilegravey invoked his tie-making powers. Motion Tabled.

Special Commission set up to investigate problem and have lunch.

Motion by Councilman Charles U. Parley to create no-smoking areas within Dacron city limits.

COUNCIL MEMBERS

Buddy MacAdam (R)—present
Buzz Mudroe (R)—present
Francis J. O'Garrgie (D)—present
Tom. T. Snope (R)—present
Preston Hunch (R)—present
Gus Shellmonzak (D)—present
Victor Grosso (D)—present
Leon Welsh (R)—present
Olive Finch (R)—present
Charles U. Parley (I)—present
Madison Avenue Jones (D)—present

For: Finch, Parley.
Against: MacAdam, Mudroe, O'Garrgie, Snope, Hunch, Shellmonzak, Grosso, Welsh, Jones.
Motion Defeated 9-2

Motion by Councilman Preston Hunch to allot city funds to establish handicap facilities throughout the city.
For: MacAdam, Mudroe, Hunch, Shellmonzak, Grosso, Welsh, Finch, Farley, Jones
Against: O'Garrgie, Snope
Motion Carried 9-2

Motion by Councilman Charles U. Parley to ban the Concorde SST from landing at Dacron Interstate Airport.
For: Hunch, Finch, Parley, Jones
Against: MacAdam, Mudroe, O'Garrgie, Snope, Shellmonzak, Grosso, Welsh
Motion Defeated 7-4

Motion by Councilman Buddy MacAdam to postpone annual crackdown on 96th Street "amber light district" until Lola Palooza finishes her engagement at the Buckeye Burlesque Theatre.
For: MacAdam, Mudroe, OGarrgle, Snope, Hunch, Shellmonzak, Grosso, Welsh, Parley, Jones
Against: Finch
Motion Carried 10-1

Motion by Councilman Gus Shellmonzak to seek 1988 Winter Olympics site at Dacron.
For: Shellmonzak, Grosso, Parley, Jones
Against: MacAdam, Mudroe, O'Garrgie, Snope, Hunch, Welsh, Finch
Motion Defeated 7-4

Motion by Mayor Pilegravey to eliminate school bussing in Dacron public schools and institute "school trailering."
For: MacAdam, Mudroe, O'Garrgie, Snope, Hunch, Shellmonzak, Grosso, Welsh, Finch, Parley.
Against: Jones.
Motion Carried 10-1

FARM NEWS

By FRED GRACKERN
Special Rep.-Dem. Farm
Correspondent

THE McCORMICK-HALSTON IMPLEMENT CO. will be demonstrating its new Designer Series hay balers this coming week at the Peggy Jo Potts farm on Route 8. The company says they're a lot like ordinary hay baling machines except that they come equipped with a selection of baling frames that mold the hay into a dozen different shapes. Among the available bale styles are "sphere," "pyramid/' "kidney," "teardrop," "rhomboid," and "Crazy Bale" — a mixed-up, every-which-way formation that comes out different each time. The farmer can choose a single shape, or combine several into an attractive grouping. McCormick-Halston says its Designer Series balers restore some of the lost glamour to farming.

TURNS OUT THAT IT IS NOT A RABIES EPIDEMIC which has resulted in the deaths of hundreds of Silage County livestock and has scared area farmers. It is a virus which looks and acts like rabies. Mock Rabies is the common name for the virus which causes rabies-like foaming at the mouth, erratic behavior and death. It is highly contagious. "We do not have a rabies problem," Silage County Agriculture

Dept. Director Hermann Belmont said. "There is no reason for farmers to destroy livestock they think have rabies, as they will die anyway."

ACCORDING TO A BULLETIN from Washington, D.C., the Dept. of Agriculture has launched a special farming satellite, called "Almanac I." The unique craft is expected to assume a solar orbit by 1983, from .where it will transmit crop timetables, weights, measurements, historic facts, weather predictions, and various other helpful communications to intelligent farmers that may exist on other planets. "We all know how useful an almanac can be in running a good farm here on earth, so there's no reason to imagine that other folks in outer space might not also appreciate the information, and thus want to be friends rather than destroy our crops," said the Dept. of Agriculture.

LUKE DUBBER'S prize heifer, Dolly, apparently choked herself to death on some cud she caught in her throat Tuesday last, says their veterinarian. The playful cow had become fond of running sideways into culverts and machinery, and it seems like this time Dolly went a little overboard and knocked the cud she had been chewing down the wrong pipe. It was a mystery that we're all glad to have cleared up.

Fatal Ravioli Kills 27 Persons

CINCINNATI, Feb. 11 (Pan-Ohio Press Service)— Faulty equipment at the United National Household Products Company has resulted in the deaths of 27 persons throughout Ohio. The Cincinnati plant processes food and packages a toilet bowl cleaner called "Wow." At one point in the plant, the pipes that carry the toilet bowl cleaner from a mixing area to the packing area pass directly over the Mighty-Good Brand Canned

Ravioli as it moves along an exposed "hot" conveyor. A leak in one of the pipes sprayed deadly poisonous toilet bowl cleaner onto the ravioli which was packed and shipped to stores. Before the leak was detected, UNHP estimates over 700,000 cans of the killer ravioli had been shipped. A full-scale operation is underway to retrieve and destroy them. All consumers are asked to check their shelves for the toxic food.

Black Slant On The News

By TYLER JEFFRIES
Special Rep.-Dem. Black
Correspondent

Johnston   Washington

TRUMAN JOHNSTON and PATTERSON WASHINGTON of Cleveland, Ohio, are both black men and it is heartening to all minority members to find this out. Many people had previously thought that these prominent investment men were Arab billionaires.

WILLIE SHARK, 5870 S. William Shakespeare Ave., is a Black businessman on the go. He lives like a millionaire, and makes earning all that money seem real easy.

SHELDON HADLEY, Director of Ebony Studies at Warren Harding High School, is a prime mover behind the introduction of several new Black-oriented

Shark   Hadley

classes at Harding High. Such courses as Black Home Economics teach future adult Blacks how to get the most out of wine, where to buy

okra, and the practicalities of hand-me-down pork. Minority Math accents relevant arithmetical concepts which include odds and numbers, while Hadley's Afro-American Industrial Arts course emphasizes such skilled trades as locksmithing, glass cutting, bolt cutting, and security systems. Blacks are pleased.

MYRAN DeCOVEN is Dacron's resident Black genealogical expert who can trace your "roots" authentically and expertly. Says DeCoven, "Every Black person that was sent from Africa to America had a bill of lading attached to him. Once you get the shipper's registration number, you can cross-reference it to port of embarkation

DeCoven   Robinson

emigration files and come up with a copy of a passport, birth certificate, fingerprints, and military and criminal records. Then it's a simple matter of running the information through the Afropol computer up in Cleveland which will print out a complete ancestral jacket on any Negro born or residing in Africa after 2800 B.C. It's really a very routine sort of investigation."

ODELL ROBINSON'S Cadillac Funeral Palace is a prominent Black business in town, where Negro funerals

are a specialty. The "Soul Food in Paradise" funeral has been an especially nice success for Cadillac. The Robinson family has been in Dacron for 20 years, all of them as Negroes.

MADISON AVENUE JONES, Dacron City Councilman, will soon be voting on many issues, that are of concern to Dacron Blacks, because as an elected city official he is in a position to do so, since he is in a position of power and importance.

LINDORA DJABOUNDI, 3803 S. Nathaniel Hawthorne Ave., announces that she has been hired as a full-time member of the Rosenberg's Dept. Store retail merchandising point-of-purchase staff. After completing a special employers' W-4 form, Mrs. Djaboundi participated in an intense store orientation clinic, and later began to map out plans for her first assignment in the children's sneaker bin area. The hired

Jones   Djaboundi

Mrs. Djaboundi intends to participate in several state, federal, and F.I.C.A. withholding programs, and in addition, will be incorporated into a company-provided work schedule.

BE A
Republican-Democrat
NEWSBOY

You'll Make Money
and Have Lots of Fun, Too

WANTED:
Young fellows between the ages of 11 and 13 to deliver the daily Dacron Republican-Democrat door to door. Must be well-groomed and should have a pert upturned nose.

Apply in Person to: Rutgers Gullet, Publisher,

DACRON Republican-Democrat

Republican Building, 100 Polk Street Downtown

Dacron Republican-Democrat

Living Life

formerly the Women's Pages

• Cooking • Cleaning
• Taking Care of the Kids

SUNDAY, FEBRUARY 12, 1978

SECTION C

Midwinter Fashion Preview

Top Haute House Garments Shown

By CARMELITA DURANGO
Rep.-Dem. Fashion Editor

DACRON'S MIDWINTER house apparel season got off to a smart start Friday with Housecoat '78, a fashion showing of the newest in around-the-house garments and accessories. The world's top housecoat, slipper, and hairnet designers were represented in the stunning show hosted by Rosenberg's Department Store. "The house has been neglected as a fashion area," Troy La Fey, Rosenberg's fashion buyer, said. But certainly not for long, judging from the fresh, vibrant

Photo Courtesy Rosenberg's Department Store

This Oscar of Manila combines warm nylon with cuddly soft orlon to create this stunning housecoat that features two cozy pockets. Pompom slippers are by American Rubber Soles Shoe Co. Just one of the many smashing housecoats featured at Housecoat 78 and on sale at Rosenberg's.

designs, and huge colorful plastic hair-rollers that made Housecoat '78 the smash of the fashion year so far. (Even better than Apron Expo!) Seoul 'n' Shore captured overall popularity honors with its sassy "After 8 a.m." collection, dominated by those bold, luminous anchor and ship's-wheel "Neo-Nautique" pocket motifs that are currently all the vogue.

Is Your Child A Dip ?

By Dr. BARBARA DERRING

DIPPINESS, which most frequently strikes male children between the ages of 6 and 12, can have lasting effects on physical and emotional health. There's considerable debate among

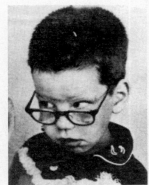

Rep.-Dem. Staff Photo

Dippiness can have lasting effects on a child's physical and emotional health.

physicians as to its cause—though most agree that it seems to be transmitted through the mother—and there's an even greater debate as to its proper treatment. Can dippiness be cured? So far, we don't really know. If caught early, it can apparently be controlled and it often disappears by itself in early adulthood, though it may reappear during middle age. But much about the "dip" is still a mystery to us.

WHAT CAN YOU DO if you suspect that your child is one?

First, take the following quiz. Some of the most common symptoms of developing dippiness are given below. Score one for every "yes" answer.

Does your son . . .

1. look funny?
2. have an unusual odor?
3. eat paste or "nose dirt"?
4. frequently sniff his fingertips?
5. read?
6. have invisible friends?
7. eat bugs?
8. fear the basement?
9. swing a baseball bat with his "foot in the bucket"?
10. wear glasses?
11. wear glasses with an elastic band around the back to hold them on?
12. play "house"?
13. wet the bed?
14. wet the bed during the day?
15. wet the rug?

16. willingly wear:
    a. snow pants?
    b. rubbers?
    c. blue jeans with red-flannel lining?
    d. undershirts?
    e. long underwear?
    f. hats with fold-down ear flaps?
    g. clips to attach mittens to his coat?
    h. mittens?
    i. shorts?
    j. red hen shoes?
17. refuse to fight smaller boys?
18. get into your lingerie drawer?
19. enjoy kissing his aunts?

Cont. Sec. C. Page 18

Up In Your Attic!

Those Superb Collectibles Findable In Your Home

By CARMELA SAVIN

DEAR CARMELA,
I have friends who collect things and they seem to enjoy themselves. How can I get started?
Dorothy P.
Erie, Pa.

Collecting things is lots of fun and easy to do. Simply get something, then get another one and another and so on until you have a whole bunch of them. Other than that, all you'll need is my book, "Collecting Things," which can be yours for $9.99 through this newspaper. Sorry, no C.O.D.'s.

DEAR CARMELA,
My husband was cleaning out the garage last fall and he came across a whole carton of jelly glasses. Many of them date back to the early '60's. Are they worth anything?
The Drumonds
Chicago, Ill.

Yes! At a California auction recently, a complete set of Flintstones/Welch's Grape Jelly glasses sold for $32, If your glasses are in good condition, it may be worth your while to go out and clean the garage again. For more information, send $7.95 to me c/o this newspaper and I will send you my color brochure, "Jelly Glass Collecting for Profit."

DEAR CARMELA,
My nephew bought a farm and when we were visiting him, my husband found this great big huge giant black round thing that stands shoulder high and has ridges that are real big all around the edge. What

Cont. Sec. C. Page 2

DEAR DOROTHY

Friends Indeed?

DEAR DOROTHY: At a luncheon at a friend's house I discovered that there was no toilet tissue in the bathroom and as I needed some I had no choice but to use a hand towel. I put the hand towel into my purse fully intending to take it home, wash it and return it the next day. However, a while later my friend asked to see my new handbag. Needless to say she found the towel and accused me of stealing. What should I do now?

EMBARRASSED
PORTLAND, OREGON

DEAR EMBARRASSED: Anyone who entertains and doesn't have the sense to check her toilet tissue supply isn't considerate enough to have friends. If she's really your friend, I'd hate to meet your enemies!

DEAR DOROTHY: I had a few friends over for lunch the other day and as we were visiting I noticed one of the gals was acting very peculiar. I suspected something right away and asked to see her purse. She was very reluctant to give me her purse and with good reason—she stole one of my towels! I'm shocked at her and don't quite know what to do.

ANGRY
PORTLAND, OREGON

DEAR ANGRY: Anyone who steals from her friends is no friend at all! Drop her like a hot brick!

DEAR DOROTHY: I am very generous about loaning things, but I'm really miffed. I loaned a neighbor my expensive good guest hand towels for a luncheon party. When she returned them the next day, one of them was stained and smelled of urine. What could be wrong with her?

REVOLTED
PORTLAND, OREGON

DEAR REVOLTED: I think your friend needs a hygiene lesson. And you need friends like her the way a cat needs swim fins.

DEAR DOROTHY: I'm the son of a family that's very prominent locally and I've committed six pretty serious sexual assaults around town in the past year. I know I need help and I intend to surrender to the police, but is there some way that I can turn myself in without causing bad publicity for my folks?

NAME WITHHELD
BY REQUEST
DACRON, OHIO

DEAR WITHHELD: It certainly does sound like you need help. However, I'm afraid there is really no way that you could turn yourself in without attracting attention.
Maybe you should reconsider. Are you sure that you wouldn't be hurting your family more than you would be helping yourself?

Continued from Page C-1
is it and how much is it worth?

Donna Wirtz
Indianapolis, Ind.

It sounds like a tractor tire and it may be very valuable if properly restored. You can get my valuable pamphlet, "Restoring Tractor Tires for Fun and Money," by sending $4.98 to me c/o this newspaper.

DEAR CARMELA,
I collect soda and beer can pop-tops. Are they worth anything?

Lorry Y.
Detroit, Mich.

Some are quite rare. I have a list of these available for only $3.49. c/o this newspaper.

DEAR CARMELA,
We collect early Tensor lamps. Is there an organization we can join? Also, what is a 1968 GE Walnut-look Student Series Swivel Head Lamp going for?

Wally and Irm,
Pittsburgh, Pa.

You may Join "Carmela's Tensor Lamp Club" for $14 (for two) for one year. You will receive information about lamps, and you'll attend meetings and seminars. Send your check or money order to me c/o this newspaper. As for the GE Swivel Head, it is a very rare lamp that will sell for $40 to $45 depending on condition.

DEAR CARMELA,
I have enclosed my aunt's collection of perfume bottles. She died and left them to me. They are from China and they are real old and made out of ivory. I'd rather have money, so how much are they worth?

Gilbert Reynolds Sr.
St. Louis, Mo.

They are practically worthless. First, they are very old and yellowed. They are not Ivory but plastic or wood. They are not from China. They are not valuable at all. I have sent you a check for $25 for all 75 of them. I'll see if I can unload them and recover the $25 I sent to you.

Happy Collecting!

Engagements

Miss Eileen Roth

Roth and Wobblestone

Eileen Roth and Larry W. Wobblestone both of Dacron, have announced that they are engaged to be engaged. A June 1979 engagement will be followed by marriage in 1980.

Miss Dolores Stangferd

Reilly and Stangferd

Evert Reffly and Dolores Stangferd were engaged Friday night at the wedding of Miss Stangferd's sister in Denver. The couple does not plan to marry.

Miss Karen Woodie Jenks

Jenks and Peterson

Karen Woodie Jenks and Northrup Peterson Jr. of Dacron and Detroit, Michigan, will wed this June at the First Church of Christ Biologist in Dacron. The engagement is the first for Mr. Peterson, the fifth for Ms. Jenks.

Miss Rose Wonko

Wonko and Kozak

King Janos Tene Wonko and Queen Mary Mother Kozak signed engagement papers for Rose Wonko and Stavo Kozak. A marriage will be planned when the couple reaches maturity.

Miss Marcie Hooverman

Hooverman and Jantinez

Marcie Hooverman and Diego Jaminez announced their engagement at a birthday party for their son, Roaldo, at the Pimwick Restaurant in Zanesville. An October wedding is planned.

Wedding Announcements

Simpkis   LeMauve   Smith   Bendix   Fartle   33241-9866-214

Gradomowski   Eggschwiele   Binder   Tomes   Schwartz   Washington

SIMPKIS — LeMAUVE

Evelynn Bird Simpkis and Francois LeMauve were married in a private ceremony last week at the bride's home in Dacron Hills. Evelynn is the daughter of Francis and Mary Simpkis, owners of the Simpkis jewelry store chain. Francois is the son of Beatrice Le Mauve. The marriage was the seventh for Francois, the first for Evelynn. Francois is a dance instructor. Evelynn is a senior bookkeeper for the Simpkis main store downtown. The couple will honeymoon in Paris, France.

GRADOMOWSKI — EGGSCHWIELE

Rennee Lisa Gradomowski exchanged wedding vows with Dr. Aaron Eggschwiele Saturday in ceremonies at the nondenominational Jet-Propulsion Chapel of the University of Toledo. Rennee is the daughter of Mr. and Mrs. Jansch T. Gradomowski of Elk Lane, Dacron Dales. Dr. Eggschwiele's parents were gassed by the Nazis. The couple will honeymoon at the Smithsonian Institute in Washington.

SMITH — BENDIX

Sharon Smith and Earl Bendix, both of Dacron, were wed at midnight Thursday at the International Amphitheater in Chicago during a performance by the rock and roll ensemble KISS. The ceremony was performed by a minister in the Church of the Holy Robot Head. The couple will honeymoon in their van in the parking lot of the Amphitheater. Earl runs a poster store in Dacron Dales.

BINDER — TOMES

Diana Beth Binder and Thom Tomes Jr. were married in an emergency ceremony at Mercy General Hospital. Diana is the daughter of Dr. and Mrs. Hermann Binder. Thom is the son of Mr. and Mrs. Lester Tomes Sr. of Truman St. The couple will complete high school at C. Estes Kefauver before going on their honeymoon. Thom has one more year and Diana, who has been visiting an out-of-town aunt for the last eight-and-a-half months, has two years before she graduates.

FARTLE — 33241-9866-214

The United States Post Office was the setting for the wedding of Edith Beatrice Fartle and 33241-9866-214. Edith is the daughter of Homer P. and Blythe S. Fartle of Farm Rd. 33241-9866-214 is the son of Bertha Gray and Jimmy Bob Gray. Edith is a lab technician at Feces Analysis Associates in Dacron. 33241-9866-214 is employed in the laundry room of the Ohio State Reformatory in Mansfield. The couple plan a Niagara Falls honeymoon in 12 to 20 years.

SCHWARTZ — WASHINGTON

The South-Side Afro Baptist Church was the setting for the wedding of George Washington Washington and Glinda Schwartz. Glinda is the daughter of Myron and Naomi Schwartz of Dacron Dells. George is the son of Ida Mae Washington and Mr. Joe Van Snooker or Mr. Clevester Jones.

A reception was held at the Rocket 88 Lounge in South Dacron. Glinda's parents were unable to make it to the wedding due to a sudden illness. The couple will honeymoon in Gary, Indiana. George is unemployed. Glinda owns real estate in Chicago and a hotel in Hawaii, due to the kindness of her late grandfather.

 **the thinking cap**
By LEON BURDWIC

Score one point for each correct answer. The last question counts for five points. 0-2, Dumbbell; 3-6, H.S. Grad; 7-8, Scholar; 9-10, Nobel Prize Winner.

1. Blood flows.
A. UPSIDE DOWN   C. AROUND
B. IN AND OUT   D. FAST

2. Who or what was the Washington Memorial named after?
A. WASHINGTON SENATORS   C. GEORGE WASHINGTON
B. WASHINGTON APPLES   D. WASHINGTON D.C.

3. Medicare is a health plan for
A. OLD PEOPLE   C. OLD SOLDIERS
B. THE SICK   D. PEOPLE WHO WON'T WORK FOR A LIVING

4. Which country is not a neighbor to Germany?
A. BELGIUM   C. EAST GERMANY
B. FRANCE   D. LATIN AMERICA

5. Match the famous Dacronian with his accomplishment:
a. Will Finnery
b. Hansen Bilbous
c. Alice Brent Ed
d. Fred Wright
e. Homo Ohiopithacus

1. Invented a chemical goose wormer.
2. Sold a gas water heater to Warren Harding's sister.
3. Founded Aunt Ed's Pie Co.
4. The third Wright Brother.
5. First man in Dacron.

(Answers in Sec. B, Page 19)

Society Shows It Has a Heart at Heart Association's Annual Heartthrob Ball

Valentine's Day Fete Is Held at Three Trees Country Club

Everybody who's anybody in Dacron seemed to grace the banquet room at Three Trees Country Club Friday night for the 14th Annual Dacron Heart Association's Charity Dinner and Dinner Dance. Guests included such luminaries as Woolworth VanHusen II of VanHusen Manufacturing fame, who is this year's Heartthrob Ball chairman, and lovely wife Alma, Chairmanette. Young Woolworth III was on hand too with his wife, Snooky (he's VanHusen Vice-President in charge of helping his dad, she's nee Knickerson from Atlanta with a father prominent in banks there). Woolworth's adorable little sister Prissy was also on hand, but in a professional capacity, snapping stunning

pics for the local paper, which is this.

Of course the MacAdamses, those wonderful asphalt folk, were there in force — father Malcolm and gracious wife Flora in a dress by Cleveland's most exclusive department store. Son Bobby came stag. And Malcolm's younger brother Buddy brought third wife Doreen. Buddy's the politician in the family—a prominent city councilman, president of the Chamber of Commerce and "Dacron's Goodwill Ambassador to the World" in general.

The ever-wonderful Mrs. Elruira Gullet, still kicking up her feet at age 84, came on the arm of her son, Rutgers, the important publisher. Mrs. Gullet doesn't let

being a golden-ager stop her a smidgen — she's got her hands on the reins at South Central Ohio Coal Gas Electricity Telephone and Telegraph, the company her husband did so much to buy.

Also present were nursing home magnate Merv Hackleweeze; Mayor Milos Pilegravey and wife of the mayor, Betty; Police Chief Bruster "Bud" Finch; labor leader Walter Gizzard and his business associate Mr. Charles Ammaretta; popular local judge James Applebower; Superintendent of Schools Cornholt; and department store proprietors Mr. and Mrs. Julius Rosenberg plus more luminaries too luminous to mention.

Photos by Rep.-Dem. Staff Photographer
Prissy VanHusen

Labor relations consultant Charles Ammaretta has his friends discuss business problems for him with police Chief "Bud" Finch. Some folks just can't quit talking shop!

Trailer wizard Woolworth VanHusen II extends an enthusiastic hand toward young Bob MacAdam, heir to asphalt fortune.

South Central Ohio Coal Gas Electricity Telephone and Telegraph Board Chairman Mrs. Elmira Gullet confers for a moment with son, Rutgers. He's Vice-President of S.C.O.C.G.E.T.&T.'s Communications Group.

Shocked Dr. Humphery Cornholt, Superintendent of Schools, looks on as an ex-student of his, City Councilman Charles U. Farley, discovers that the high-school-wide vandalism problem may be spreading to country clubs.

Elaine (lovely daughter of leading Dacron nursing home owner Merv Hackleweeze) and Elaine's beautiful new young stepmother, Charollette, let *Republican-Democrat* investigative reporters Bob Trout and Carl Bughaum know how wonderful they thought this newspaper's story about Hackleweeze nursing homes, written by Bob and Carl, was.

Judge Applebower checks under his table for illegal aliens or North Vietnamese. "A judge is never off duty," he says.

Popular and youthful Dinner Theatre in the Dell director Forrest Swisher mistakenly thought it was a costume party but enjoyed himself anyway.

Tall, gracious young Bobby MacAdam, paving scion arrives at the Heartthrob gala. Bobby's a real fashion plate, always up on the latest in Continental men's wear-unusual shoes and paper accessories have been his trademark this past year.

Mr. Julius Rosenberg and Mrs. Ethel Rosenberg sit down at a reserved table for special kosher food. It was delicious! They own a department store.

LADIES WEEKLY TELEVISION REVIEW

By PATTY PLANT
Rep.-Dem. Feature Writer

DARK IS THE NIGHT— Angie found out that Drake is really her older brother who moved away when their parents were divorced and she drove off in her car and had a breakdown at the gas station. Beth sold cocaine to a cop but didn't get arrested because she let him wear her clothes because he was a transvestite who liked to wear women's clothing. The Bartlett twins decided to get sewed back together as Siamese twins because they were lonely. Sugar Ross married herself in the mental institution. (Ch. 2, 10:00 AM)

SEARCH FOR A HOSPITAL—Maggie opened her shop and had a miscarriage. Sven drugged Ramona but decided not to go to Brad's funeral. Leslie tried to kill herself because Dr. Beaumont told her she had to wear a neck brace to Clive's party. Claudia's nose fell off and she wants Bill to sue Dr. Dover. (Ch. 2, 11:30 AM)

GENERAL DISTRESS— Dr. Pitt was arrested for molesting Sally while she was in traction for the broken back she got when she jumped out of Dan's car. Norrie Benson lost her baby at the rodeo. Darren refuses to go outside since he had his colon removed. Ruth says she still loves him but wants to find an outside sex partner because sex with him is so spooky. Steve recovered from his drug addiction and got shot by a prostitute. (Ch. 4, 11:30 AM)

ALL MY PROBLEMS— Donna Sue and Dick decided not to get married because Dick is dying of cancer and Donna Sue is opening a tennis club which would take most of her time. Donna Sue told Dick that she might marry Lance Walworth if he can come up with $25,000 seed money for the club. Barry Newmeyer has amnesia which he got after Buck Derringer hit him with a pipe. Barry can't remember where he dropped his children off and Mrs. Newmeyer is threatening to sue if they are not found. Barry is arranging to have Mrs. Newmeyer die in a house fire. (Ch. 13, 11:30 AM)

LIFE LUMBERS ON— Eugene lost his leg when a terrorist bomb went off in a locker at his high school and he is depressed. Jackie Blake spent the night with Chet while Chet's wife was out of town at her parents' funeral. Pete the handyman took movies and threatened Chet with them. Chet gave him $10,000. Pete bought a new car with the money and accidentally ran over Jackie Blake. Chet wants his money back. (Ch. 13, 11:45 AM)

Name the 100 Thousand Eels at MacAdam Municipal Zoo

The "Petting Zoo" at MacAdam Zoological Gardens is holding a contest open to all Dacron-area grade school students, grades 1 through 8, to name the Zoo's new baby eels. First prize will be an aquarium tank full of live baby eels for the winner's school classroom. Second, third, fourth and fifth prizes will be additional eel tanks. Leading the contest so far is Bobby Allis Jr., grade 4, of McKinley school, who has submitted more than 1,200 eel names including Billy, Sue, Tim, Ed, Tom, Karen, Molly, Kathy, Jack, Larry, Alice, Fay, Carol, Diane, Joe, Earl, Alex, Marcia, Leonard, Martin and Hank.

Words of Wisdom
We are alone in a fearful world where no one cares about us at all and we're going to die.
—Seneca

Contact Bridge

By Wilhelm Konrad and Monk Meyer

Both are vulnerable. As South you hold:

♠Q10972 ♦QJ105 ♣KQ83

The bidding has proceeded:

West North East South
1♥ Pass Pass 1♠
Pass 3 NT Pass ?

East weighs in at 230 lbs. and has an excellent jab and a good left hook. West is small but wiry. Your partner likes to hit high but has a glass jaw and tissue-paper nose. You are good all around but excel in your quick moves. What action do you take?

Make a quick movement to the right, then fake to the left and go straight into his gut from the right. As he drops his cards, seize Spades. With your left foot, overturn the table. Your partner hammerlocks West and redoubles. You give West a punch in the face and spin to kick East, who should be coming to. When both East and West have been dropped, lead with Clubs and protect your left side as action continues. If your moves are anticipated and you lose your element of surprise, go for the pencils.

Learn to find that winning attack with William Konrad's "Drawing and Keeping First Blood." For your copy, send your check or money order for $5.95 to Contact Bridge c/o this newspaper.

SURPRISE HER! COME HOME IN A TUXEDO TONIGHT!

Won't she be surprised when you come home in a tuxedo from Delux Tux. Try our Sombre Roma at the Elegant Guy.
Rental available for one night, one week, one month, or longer if your plans call for it. Don't wait for someone to get married—come home in a sharp-looking Tux tonight!

"A Tux from DeLux Is De-Tux"
DeLux Tux

Checking Up On Your Babysitter

By DONNA WZCZSCK

THE RECENT STORY about a local baby-sitter who was using her customers' homes to smoke marijuana in focused attention on a new area of concern for parents. Of course, every teen-ager who babysits is not a thief or a drug addict, but so long as you trust your home and your possessions to someone, you should be watchful of any nonsense or improper use of your home. Here are a few simple things you can do to "check-up" on your baby-sitter.

1. A hair strung across each drawer in the dresser will tell you at a glance if your baby-sitter is a "drawer snoop."
2. Mark your liquor bottles discreetly. If she's playing cocktail waitress with her friends, you'll know.
3. If your children are old enough, have them do a little innocent "spying."
4. One evening, announce that you will be back very late. Wait an hour, park your car around the block and sneak back to your house. A peek in the window will be very revealing.
5. Leave 25 single dollar bills in a careless pile somewhere obvious. When you come home, count the money.

But, be careful! Once you've cleared your baby-sitter, don't just go to sleep—adolescents often undergo rapid personality changes.

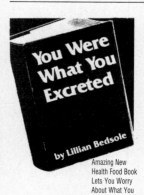
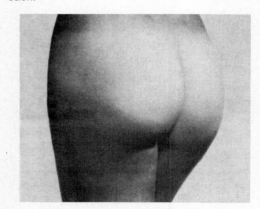

The Eyes Are On The Men At Show
Finkle's Features Fashions

By CARMELITA DIJRANGO
Rep.-Dem. Fashion Editor

THE MEN'S DEPARTMENT at Finkle's Corngate department store hosted a showing of menswear designer Yve St. Bass's summer collection, Friday. Warm, earthy, masculine colors and practical, longwearing fabrics were the main themes while styles had a new bold, take-charge look with slightly padded shoulders and tailored waists. This is Bass's fifth collection of sum-

Cont. Sec. C, Page 16

Photos by Rep.-Dem.
Staff Photographer Prissy VanHusen

Fashionable swimwear, an oft neglected area of men's wardrobes... while his conservative but stylishly tailored suits are ideal for daily business wear.

Practical sportswear by Bass combines casual elegance with freedom of movement ... Bass After Midnight formal wear is handsomely distinctive yet classical in its design.

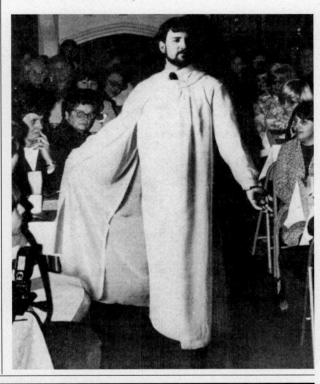

Working Woman's Cookbook:

CHINESE FOOD

By LIZ CARLTON

Chinese food is perfect for the working woman. She doesn't want to spend hours in the kitchen, yet she wants her family to have an interesting and wholesome meal. Chinese food is very easy to serve and it's delicious and nutritious.

CHINESE FOOD

CALL:
Your favorite Chinese food carry-out restaurant

ORDER:
egg rolls
egg foo young
chicken chow mein
pork subgum
fried rice
almond cookies

SERVE WITH:
large spoons

BEVERAGE:
milk and/or tea

NEXT WEEK:
Pizza With Everything Except Anchovies

WHAT AILS YOU?

By Dr. DENNIS DUMONT, M.D.

The Sniffles — *Secret Crippler*

Knowledgeable medical doctors often call sniffles "the secret crippler," and it's true. A small case of the sniffles, if neglected, can lead to a larger case of the sniffles, which can become a bad cold accompanied by a nagging cough and hoarseness that may indicate strep throat, which could develop into scarlet fever resulting in rheumatic fever which, if left untreated, can cause crippling damage to the heart muscles.

READERS' INQUIRIES

DEAR DR. DUMONT,

Our son Larry put a pecan up his nose and my husband and I can't get it out. We are worried it might travel up and poke his brain. What can we do?

Larry's Mother

Dear Mother,
There is plenty of this going around. Don't worry about the nut, it won't move up to the brain. Have Larry plug his clear nostril, close his mouth, and blow as hard as he can. This should free the nut.

DEAR DR. DUMONT,
How can I prevent another heart attack? The one I had last year was real inconvenient.
Hermann Bauer

Dear Hermann,
Eat right, get lots of sleep, and avoid sudden shocks and starts.

DEAR DR. DUMONT,
Every time our phone rings, I have a bowel movement. Is this normal? What can I do?
Pooped

Dear Pooped,
I can't say that your condition is exactly normal, but, then again, maybe it is. I suggest that you disconnect your phone during those hours when a trip to the rest room is most inconvenient (late night, bathing, eating, etc.).

TO "SCARED TO DEATH" — What happened to you is perfectly normal. It hurts at first, then the pain goes away. Your photographs indicate that you are very normal and very attractive in that particular region. You will be fine. I will look forward to more photos as development progresses in that region progresses.

Send Reader Inquiries to Dr. Dumont c/o this newspaper.

THE FAMILY DENTIST

A Public Service of the American Family Dental Association.
® 1978 A.F.D.A.

My teeth seem to be fine, but they are slightly yellow colored.
— Mrs. L.R.
Indianapolis, Ind.
Better consult your family dentist.

Sometimes when I buy gum, I get a little piece of the foil wrapper in my mouth by accident and if the foil touches a filling and wow!, does it ever hurt!
— G.T.
Lansing, Midi.
Frequent visits to the family dentist can often prevent or cure a condition such as this.

How do I select the right toothbrush?
—Mrs. Y.W.
Eriei Pa.
Sounds like a job for your family dentist! Make an appointment right away.

My husband says I occasionally grind my teeth in my sleep. Is this normal?
—Mrs. M.N.
Matoon, 111.
A difficult question. Your family dentist will have the best answer.

Don't forget: Fight decay tooth and nail with monthly dental checkups for the whole family.

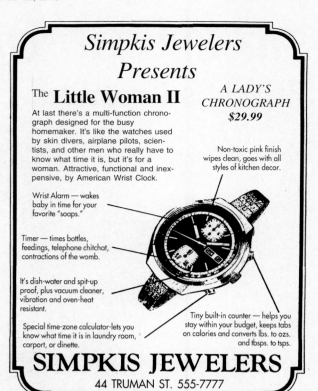

Recipe Nook

*Mud Pies
—Kids Love 'em!

By RACHEL WARNER

Prepare:
Any type of Baked Pie Shell
Combine in a double broiler:
1/2 cup mud
2 tablespoons mud
4 to 5 mud lumps
Cook and stir these ingredients over – not in – hot water, until thick.
Add:
1 pinch of mud
3 teaspoons of muddy water
Cool the mixture.

Preheat oven to 400° F.
Whip:
1/4 lb. of mud
until stiff, but not dry.
Fold in:
1 pt. mud
Mix this lightly into a previously prepared mud. Fill pie shell. Brown pie in oven for about 10 minutes. Serves everyone in the neighborhood.

First Aid: Choking

Kick choking person from behind.

Last year, 100 times as many people died from choking on food in restaurants than died from being hit in the face with live game fish. Do you know what to do if someone begins to choke on food in restaurants? Quick action could save their life.

Social Notes

By NIGEL DUMPSTER
Rep.-Dem Society Editor

'Twas a week awash with glamour in Dacron! Our town being the scene of not one but another glorious social fete. First was the Hunt Club Cotillion which, this year, was held on a weekday night. That's because weekday nights are considered so chic nowadays and also because of a tiny tiffette between MALC MAC ADAM, who's president of the Hunt Club, which was originally going to have its dance on Friday night, and WOOLY VAN HUSEN II, who's Chairman of the Heart Association's Heartthrob Ball, which was also going to have its dance on Friday night and did. You see, neither fabulous celebration could be held on Saturday night as MRS. MAC A had promised to visit her lovely mother in Youngstown then, so a compromise was had to be had, but MALC and WOOLY hardly came to blows at all in the Maple Room of the Downtowner Club, contrary to some reports. And also contrary to some reports, there's just not a single bit of bad blood between THE VANHUSENS and THE MAC ADAMSES over PRISSY V's breakup with BOBBY M, after she was attacked by a mysterious "Powder Room Prowler." "That's a lot of fluff," says Prissy's mom, ALMA. "We wouldn't do a *thing* to ruin their family's reputation."

Speaking of young BOBBY MAC ADAM, he was causing comment aplenty at aforementioned Cotillion with more of his amusing fashion firsts this time it was open-toed men's strapless pumps by CALVIN KLEIN and an YVES ST. LAURENT brown paper bag hat. But, if you ask me, people are just envious of the ever-amusing BOBBY's avant-garde taste and charming abilities to entertain. Remember how we missed him while he was in the hospital with those headaches during last August's Summer Wonderland Dance at the Country Club country club? And wasn't he the life of the picnic at the MacAdam Asphalt company get-together in Paving Park last fall? Who couldn't help but love the wonderful BOBBY.

Anyway, the Hunt Club Cotillion was an absolute smash success even counting the fact that certain very naughty teen-agers "pepped-up" the punch, causing the poor (of course, not *really* poor) ROSENBERGS to feel not at all themselves and be asked to leave.

Then Friday it was the Three Trees country club's turn to host the Heart Association Ball, and so much fun was had that practically everybody stayed way past eleven. Be sure to see the lavish photo spread of this mirthmaking occasion elsewhere in today's paper!

As if that weren't enough, so much else has been going on besides! Lovely Indianapolis socialite and ex-Dacroman TWINKY CROUP DIELEMEYER came back to town yesterday and was interviewed on WONK's noon-time "People Talk" show. Her husband's the largest paving contractor in Indiana. TWINKY said she loves the excitement of big city life but sometimes wishes she'd settled here in her own home town. "You know," she told interviewer HAZE HAWSLY, "sometimes I think it would have been perfectly grand to have just married some fellow like Larry Kroger—he was a boy I knew in high school and I understand he's still in high school. I mean teaching, of course and settled down to a fabulous little life with oodles of kids and dogs right here." TWINKY is absolutely adorable. Don't you think so? And hasn't lost the common touch one bit.

And last Wednesday night PINKY ALBRIGHT FARLEY and her city councilman husband had a party for several of their friends who are attractive couples. WOOLWORTH and SNOOKY VAN HUSEN III were there and so were SUZI (nee Fitzerman) and HOWARD LIPBAUM, and a number of other nice-looking young marrieds. The kids were at grandma's so the party just went on and on and *on*.

And last on my list, but not least, was the Tuesday night opening of "Man of La Mancha" in Cleveland which drew VAN HUSENS, GULLETS, MAC ADAMSES, THE PILEGRAVEYS, REPRESENTATIVE SWEATER and HIS WIFE, plus YOURS TRULY and the very talented Dinner Theatre in the Dell director FORREST SWISHER all the way to Cleveland to see DON KNOTTS as Don Quixote, while local stage star BERTON GROMMEL played Sancho Panza, and LESS TRAMLIN and TAD FELTER played his mule. *Devine! Devine! Devine!*

Housewife Humor

By SHIRLEY PETZER
Author of *The Rug Is Always Yellower Under the Dog*

REMEMBER THAT TV commercial where Josephine the lady plumber helps her friend who's visiting from St. Louis clean that old New York apartment house sink with kitchen cleanser, and the friend says she'd better take some of that cleanser back home with her because "We've got some pretty old sinks in St. Louis, too"? Well, I always get a kick out of that because I live in St. Louis and we do have some pretty old sinks, although ours is practically new.

YOU KNOW WHAT tickles me? The kids will spend all day Saturday picking up newspapers for the school paper drive, but just try to get them to pick up the clothes in their room! My husband's the same way. He gets hotter than heck if I borrow any of his tools and leave them in the kitchen junk drawer or under the sink instead of putting them back on the pegboard over his workbench in the basement, but then he'll turn around and leave his clothes all over the bedroom. Aren't husbands something? And kitchen junk drawers now that I've mentioned it, I have to laugh when I think what a mess ours is. Isn't yours?

MY LITTLE NEPHEW Bobby, my sister Edith's youngest boy (he's 1 1/2), said the funniest thing the other day. He always says "Wawa" when he wants water. And the other day he said, "Can I have a glass of wawa?" So my sister said, "Don't say 'wawa,' say 'water.'" And Bobby said to her "But I can't say 'water,' I can only say 'wawa!'" Isn't that the funniest thing you ever heard?

Cleanin' Wif Miz Lottie

CLEANING THEM WINDOWS

Ya'll noticin' when winter make them windows real dirty an' you be wanting to make thems clean again but it be too cold outside to be doing that, what you do now be take you some real hot water an' put your ammonia in that an' some of that nonfreezing radiator car things? That water don't freeze on your windows nohow. It look so clean and so fine you be feeling like spring inside even if it be still winter. And yo' man, he be fussing about you like a bear be fussing about his honey on account of them windows.

Today's Pattern

A Handy Nose Mitten

By MARABELLE THUMBLES

The first thing to get cold and the last to get warm is your nose. This handy nose mitten will keep your nose as warm as toast in temperatures as low as 15 degrees. It's easy to make and fun to wear.

Materials
5" x 7" square of blue fur cloth
8" elastic
blue thread

Instructions
Draw panels A and B and Bottom Gusset on the back of the fur cloth. Use pinking shears to cut. Allow 1/4" for seams. Cut Breathing Holes in Bottom Gusset. Cut Grommet Hole M in PanelA. Cut Grommet Hole N in Panel B. Insert Grommets M and N. Sew Panels A and B to Panel B along Seam L. Sew Bottom Gusset to Panels A and B along Seam J and K. Turn right side out and attach elastic (being sure to measure head of the family member who will be wearing the nose warmer) through Grommets M and N.

How the completed nose warmer will look finished.

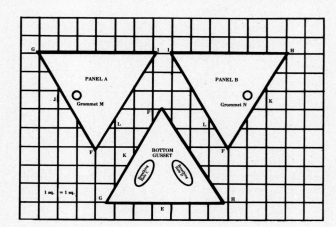

Le Home Decor

Give Your Home a Vacation Look

By Rachel Warner

WHAT'S MORE EXCITING than that moment on a vacation when you open the door to your new motel room? There it is clean, comfortable, and beautifully decorated.

Haven't you often wished your own home looked half as good? Well, it's not really so difficult (or as expensive as you might imagine) to get that smart "motel" decorator look and give your den or bedroom a fun "I'm-on-vacation-right-in-my-own-house" feeling.

FLOOR COVERINGS are one important key to the "motel look." Fecal-colored industrial grade wall-to-wall carpeting is available locally from three different

Cont. Sec. C, Page 20

Drawer Bibles make tasteful and inexpensive accent pieces.

The "motel-look" can give your den or bedroom a fun "I'm-on-vacation-in-my-own-house" feeling.

Rosemoot Paper Products, 234 Polk, carries a complete line of toilet seat hands in many decorator colors and prices to suit any budget. Also be sure to see Rosemont's attractive cellophane drinking glass wrappers. They're open 9-6 weekdays and 9-12 Saturdays.

Photos by Rep-Dem. Staff Photographer Vince Blum

Household Hanna

By HANNA BENSON

DEAR HANNA:
I keep a phone book in my purse just in case I have to look up a number when I am visiting a friend. I don't like to tie up their lines calling information.
HELEN GOBBLES,
CLEVELAND

Good idea!

DEAR HANNA:
I found an easy way to open those detergent boxes. I keep a keyhole saw next to the washer and when I need to open a box, I just saw the top off. No more broken nails!
IRENE G.,
XENIA

Nifty suggestion! For readers who may not know what a keyhole saw is, it's the pointy kind.

DEAR HANNA:
A sanitary napkin tied to each knee sure saves a lot of scrapes and pains when you're doing floors!
MRS. JACOBSEN,
SANDUSKY

They also make dandy emergency potholders.

DEAR HANNA:
Here's a neat way to get a free lunch. When I shop, I go first to the deli section and have them make me a sandwich. I eat the sandwich before I check out and put the empty wrapper in my purse. It works like a charm.
IDA S.,
BARBERTON

Next time, bring a spoon from home and order some potato salad to go with your sandwich.

DEAR HANNA:
My husband and I have finally found a use for all those toilet paper and paper towel cores. We attached them together and make hamster tunnels which we give to the neighborhood children.
MR. AND MRS. FLERB,
HAMILTON

DEAR HANNA:
You can save a lot of cleanup work if you feed your children in the bathtub. When they finish, turn on the water.
MRS. F. R. BLACK,
TOLEDO

That reminds me of the woman who showered with her hose on so she would be sure to have a clean body and clean hose in the morning. Good thinking!

DEAR HANNA:
After throwing out dozens of pairs of my teenage daughter's underpants, I've discovered that there are men who will pay good money for them.
ELAINE KOVACK,
PARMA
Thanks for the tip!

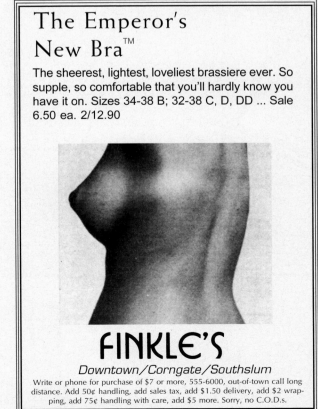

You'll adore these
Matching China and
Silver Patterns

Each Serving for Eight includes Fine English Bone China:
8 Dinner Plates, 8 Salad Plates, 8 Soup Bowls, 8 Cups and
Saucers, 1 Sugar Bowl, One Creamer, 2 Serving Platters.

And genuine Sterling Silver-Plated Flatware: 8 each of Teaspoons,
Dinner Knives, Dinner and Salad Forks.

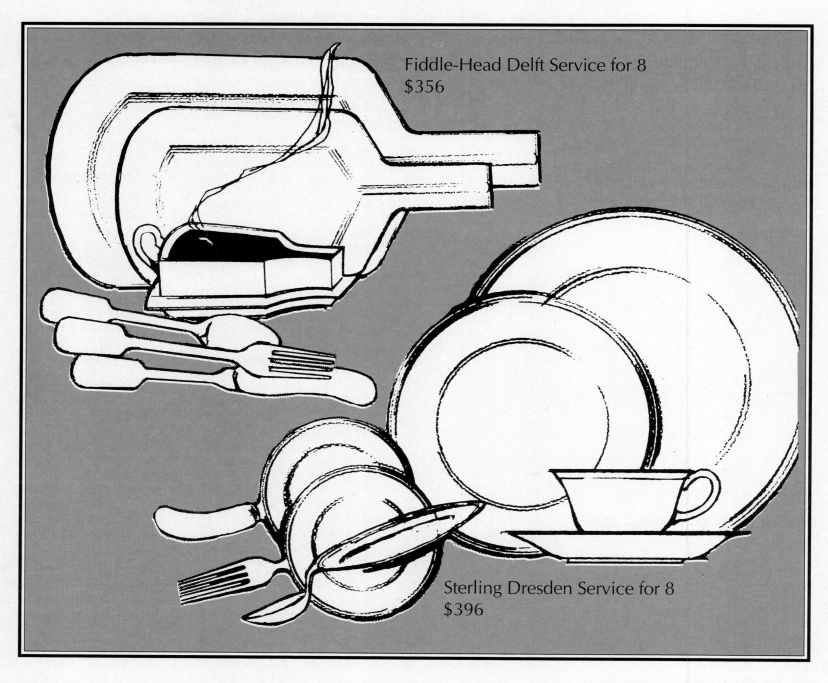

Fiddle-Head Delft Service for 8
$356

Sterling Dresden Service for 8
$396

FINKLE'S
Downtown/Corngate/Southslum

DEJC Coach Confident Of Dinosaur Walkover

By JED BENSONHURST
Special Rep.-Dem. College Correspondent

The Dacron Elementary and Junior College Dinosaurs are set for their annual cage clash with the Columbus College of Data Processing Army Ants this coming Friday night at 8:00, and Dinosaur coach Butch "Butch" Garmon doesn't seem too worried about the outcome. "When you size up an opponent," he commented, "you not only evaluate him on a skills basis but also on a psychological basis."

In this case, I asked myself as a sportswriter, what kind of person attends a data processing school.

Generally, it's a depressing mix of troll-like subsocial lowlifes, who, either because of some lower-middle class economic trauma inherited from the aggregate failure of unsuccessful and/or stupid parents, or a simple case of being too dull and unimaginative to keep up with the rest of the world, somehow end up, half in desperation, to succeed at any level, no matter how insignificant, and half out of an actual predilection for sterile, menial work that hasn't the slightest connection with the use of a human personality, lodged by default in a tragic and pathetic den of squirrelly creeps destined to process data for the remainder of their torpid little lives.

Typical Data Student a Zero

I visualize the typical data processing student in his youth, age 12, in the family basement, with his bulbous, bristly parabola of a head mounted on a limp, tubular neck that protrudes from a flare-collared, pebble-grained sport shirt manufactured out of some bizarre fiber unknown to normal science. And there he sits, hunched over his homemade crystal radio, hearing nothing but a faint murmur from the 50,000-watt station down the street.

Grinding along in the basement of life is he — a zero, nothing, nada, nihil, goose-egg who couldn't run more than ten yards without collapsing, much less take on an elementary and junior college basketball team.

This view is shared by the Dinosaur team members also, who feel that the peaked, sickly computer sissies will leave the gym crying, and probably in asthmatic fits.

Photo Courtesy Dacron Elementary and Junior College *Daily Dino*

CHECKING HIS SOFTWARE—Columbus College of Data Processing Army Ant Gerald Van Aken (right), fouls unidentified Dinosaurs guard, Gary Balkan, during last year's game. This brand of action is typical of the excitement generated at an Army Ant-Dinosaur encounter.

WHA Revises Player Draft Rules

FRIDAY, Feb. 10 (UPA)—The troubled World Hockey Association adopted a formula for signing up top level draft-eligible players today. The new system is designed to eliminate physical competition between owners and managers of teams, which last year resulted in a number of damaged restaurants and did "more harm to bridgework than good for teamwork," to quote league president Howard Baldwin.

Plans for the new draft system, which is designed to make the WHA more competitive with the NHL, were initiated after anonymous complaints reached the league offices that the Quebec Nordiques had signed the unborn child of Mark Howe, who as a player for the New England Whalers had previously signed away the child in return for locker privileges.

Other grievances were aired at a recent general league meeting including an accusation leveled by the Houston Aeros that the Edmonton Oilers were running a far-reaching illegal artificial insemination program and had offered substantial sums of money to Houston draft choices for "bottles of their 'fluids.'" The Edmonton club was also accused of signing up entire beer parlors full of potential hockey players for "a couple of rounds." The abuses will hopefully be stopped by the new system.

Contracts, Fists Waved

Also heard at the league meeting were complaints from several players that they had been signed to multi-year million-dollar contracts by various WHA clubs, some of which were gone when the players went to the stadium to look for them. The players' grievances were tabled after several complaints about their conduct at the meeting which apparently included shouting and waving contracts and, also, fists.

Under the new rules, each WHA team will be able to designate six players with whom they may negotiate, three of whom may be signed. However, there will be no limit to the number of teams that may designate any one player. The league hopes that this system will see more players signed than in previous years.

"I think our general managers are sensible folks, acting in the best interest of the league. If there is a situation where two or three of them are waiting for each other in the parking lot with tire irons or sledges and wedges, I'm sure they will stop short and say: "Why fight each other and the NHL?

"The intent of the rule is to make us something more than a bumper car league," says a hopeful Howard Baldwin.

Photo Courtesy Jim Bouton

Jim Bouton heaves the knuckler. A hard pitch to hit when thrown right.

Ex-Yank in Tarleg Talks

By LOU FLEMMONT
Rep.-Dem. Sports Writer

Jim Bouton, the world series winning pitcher formerly with the New York Yankees and many other baseball teams, has been in Dacron this week to talk with Dacron Blueberries manager Dick Sock about the possibility of play next season for the Tarlegs in the triple-D league. Bouton, whose family live somewhere else, has been working on his knuckle ball for the past year in Portland after having taken a year off to write the interesting TV series, *Ball Four*, which was seen once on area TV last year.

Bouton, whose knuckle ball can be devastating or dangerous depending on whether it's in the strike zone or the stands, says he thinks the Tarlegs have a good chance to turn around next summer and that he will not be asking for an outrageous hourly wage as long as he gets the job at the MacAdam plant generally given to full-time players.

If Bouton decides to join our team, it is sure his experience will be an asset to attendance at local games.

Rep.-Dem. Staff Photo

Vassily "The Russian Pogo Stick" demonstrates his famous "pogo" action against an unidentified Kokomo Kokonut, as other basketball players observe firsthand, while fans cheer wildly from their courtside seats.

Netster To Net More $

By FRANK GIANCONI
Rep.-Dem. Sports Writer

Dacron Trailers all-Bi-State semi-pro forward, Vassily "The Russian Pogo Stick" Vlademov, is reportedly quite happy with the progress of his contract negotiations for the 1978-79 season. According to Vlademov's personal sports representative, second-year law student Earnie Cardoze, the veteran player is demanding $40 to $50 a game, plus an additional bonus of 80 cents a basket, which I predict he's likely to get, given his "star" status on the team, and the phenomenal wages being paid professional athletes these days.

And, when you consider Vlademov's impoverished and oppressed background as a youth. One of two children born in the Russian Republic of Balukistan, he was forced to attend a state school until the 12th grade, after which the Soviet government forced him to play basketball for the Molshatsk Fastener Works in Odessa, where he was often required to work in the factory — all for 65 rubles a week! It's no wonder "The Russian Pogo Stick" is trying to cash in while he can.

I talked with the shrewd Trailer superstar recently at his well-heated Dacron apartment, and the feeling one gets is he's really an ordinary Joe. You'd never guess, unless you read the papers, that he's soon going to have an extra $75 to $80 in his pocket every week, all for the simple and, to him, enjoyable task of playing a game that to him is fun. I asked Vlademov if he'd given any thought as to what he would like to do with the money. He thought for a moment, and replied, "I might like to have a nice new coat. My wife has been telling me every so often that I am needing a better quality of coat, and so I believe this is what I will do. Also, shelves. I have for all of my time here in America been stacking things on the floor."

Pro Ball Good to Him

While talking to Vlademov, you get the impression he feels semi-pro basketball has been exceptionally good to him, and without it, he might still be just another factory worker. Of course there are some who contend today's prima donna athletes are more concerned with full stock portfolios than full court presses, but in the Russian Pogo Stick's case, you can't help but say to yourself — "Go ahead and give him the bonuses ... he's earned 'em."

Pigskin Preview
Losing Miners Train

By SANDY "SNAPPER' TRUDGE
Rep. Dem. Senior Sports Writer

With the football season over, players for the Dacron Strip Miners, who, although doing well in their last post-season match against an out-of-state Peruvian team, finished badly this year, once again punching out at the bottom of the Ohio semi-pro league, are looking toward improving their standing next year.

Although there is no regular off-season training for team members, many are able to keep in shape by doing hard manual labor.

Running back Jim Whichski keeps his back in shape throwing boxes off the many trucks that pull up to the loading dock at Rosenberg's Department Store and lineman Michael "Bull" Cheeser keeps himself in shape charging up tall poles (taller, even, than Muncies' dreaded "Warsaw line," which so devastated the Strippers this year) as a lineman for South Central Ohio Coal, Gas, Electric, Telephone & Telegraph Company.

Asked if he thinks it's funny he works as a lineman at both his jobs, Bull replies, "Not very."

Other players keep in shape in various ways, says coach Bill Task.

Double Loss Surprises Boxing Fans In Questioned Garden KO

NEW YORK, N.Y., Feb. 10 (UPA)—A Friday night fight in Madison Square Garden saw heavyweight fighters Beau "The Cracker Smacker" Williford and Goober Tyree knock each other to the canvas in the third round of what was scheduled to be a ten-round fight. The blow that dropped Tyree appeared to be a jab to the chest and that which felled Williford could not be identified at all as it appeared to have been loosed sometime in the previous round.

Twin KO or Dual Dive?

The double KO, one of the few recorded in boxing history, prompted cries of "fix" as well as the display of some dangerous looking knives by several Spanish-speaking men who appeared to have wagered upon the fortunes of Tyree.

Promoter Allan Braverman responded to allegations that the double KO had been the result of confusion in illegal prefight instructions to the fighters to "take a dive."

"That is absolutely ridiculous. That sort of thing might happen in Omaha where a lot of the fighters are Mexican and the promoters are Irish or something, but not in New York.

"The simple explanation is that both these fighters were terrific punchers but couldn't take each other's fire power." Braverman said he had no intention of promoting a rematch between the two, "not even in a parking lot."

UPA PhonePhoto

KO'd Williford felled Tyree with knockout.

When asked how he felt about the double KO, loser/victor Tyree said, "I feel good about winning, but I don't feel so good about being knocked out."

Nobody told him he didn't win.

Photo by Rep.-Dem. Sports Photographer Dade Jink

Practically all of the Dacron "Strip-Miners" semipro football team fans were out to see the miners whip Peru's National Soccer team in post-season exhibition play at the Mobile Home Bowl stadium.

NBA Tells Cops Hands Off Vestus

PHILADELPHIA, Sat, Feb. 10 (UPA)—NBA Commissioner Lawrence O'Brien told Philadelphia police yesterday that his office and officials of the Philadelphia Flyers and Los Angeles Lakers basketball clubs will deal with Vestus Tukwbu, the Philadelphia player who is accused of shooting and killing three players on the Los Angeles team during Friday night's game in Philadelphia The 7-foot-3 inch star center allegedly drew a small pistol from his trunks during a minor skirmish. He shot four Lakers, killing three and wounding one before teammates restrained him.

"We can settle our own affairs," Commissioner O'Brien told a news conference. "Tukwbu is an enthusiastic player. He has been fined heavily for his infraction and I am considering a suspension."

Cont., Sec. D, Page 30

Rockets Lodge Complaint

BOSTON, Feb. 10 (UPA)— Ray Patterson, president and general manager of the Houston Rockets, has lodged a complaint against the Boston Celtics with NBA commissioner Larry O'Brien. The complaint, lodged following the two teams' Thursday night meeting in Boston, alleges that the Boston Celtics and star "forward or forwards unknown" did deliberately and with malice "place or cause to be placed various annoying and noxious devices and novelties in and about the locker and shower areas of the Houston Rockets."

A Lot of Prank Stuff

Informed sources say that after the game, which the Celtics won 45-35, the Rockets returned to the dressing room area to discover "a lot of prank stuff. Ballroom cracker things on the shower floors, soap that turns black, itching powder on the towels and packages of juicy-fruit with rat traps in them."

Red Auerbach, president and general manager of the Celtics, denies that his team had anything to do with the boobytrapping of the visitors washroom. "That sort of thing isn't sporting. It's just a sick prank like in high school. I wouldn't be surprised if Rudy Tomjanovich had a hand in it."

Tomjanovich, whose nose and jaw were broken by Celtic forward Kermit Washington during the latter's career with the LA Lakers, has been advised not to comment on that affair pending settlement of the suit against Washington or until the wire is removed from his jaw.

Sources describe the scene in the Rocket dressing room as "pandemonium" and report that the itching powder on the towels was particularly effective. Some Houston players were also said to have sworn at the Boston team.

Commisioner O'Brien is expected to rule on the matter sometime next week.

Ex-Contender Wepner At Dacron's Golden Gloves

By LOU FLEMMONT
Rep.-Dem. Sports Writer

Mr. Charles "Chuck" Wepner upon whose fight with Mohammad Ali (Cassius Clay) the movie *Rocky* was based, was in Dacron Saturday for the Golden Gloves city finals.

After the fights, Mr. Wepner presented the winner of each division with a pair of boxing socks courtesy of Rosenberg's Department Store and a certificate good

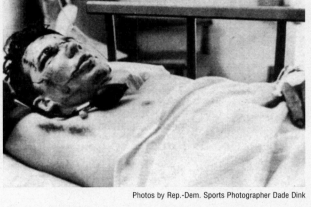

Photos by Rep.-Dem. Sports Photographer Dade Dink

Herring after being boxed by Nathan—He'd better get some steak on that "Glove Graffiti."

Plucky, tortoiseweight Sven Herring strikes pugilistic stance before father's camera prior to Nathan fight Saturday.

for $15 worth of health food from the Ra-Osiris health food grocery. After his presentation, Mr. Wepner took some of the older boys to the In-sole, which is a club frequented by sportsmen, to show them things they should as fighters always try to avoid.

The first fight of the evening saw plucky flyweight Ricky Stevenson fighting in the subnovice class battle a tough, cross-the-tracks opponent, Abraham "Hood Ornament" Jones. Both boys fought well, but the fight was stopped in the second round after Bo Silverfish, Jones's trainer, complained that Stevenson's father, retired Marine Colonel Mark Stevenson, had been "drawing his finger across his throat in a gruesome way" trying to intimidate Jones. The fight was called a draw and Jones a nigger by Colonel Stevenson.

In the dogweight open division, Kevin Doyle pounded Marcus Tyee to the canvas making use of his 15-pound weight advantage and one of his feet, according to Tyee. Doyle's victory came in the third round with the referee's back turned to listening to a low blow complaint from Doyle's handler. Doyle was declared champion of the division.

Exploded All Over Face

In the tortoise-weight open division, Sven Herring fought a long losing war as Bark Nathan's black bombs exploded all over his face, chest and ears, finally knocking him to the canvas with

the disaster running down his chin. Herring later missed his ride home when his father failed to recognize him.

Moving up to the pony-weight division, Mick Brennan and Jasper Filbert were victorious in the subnovice and open divisions respectively, Brennan winning on a knock down and Filbert when his opponent, as he put it, "cowarded out."

In the topweight division, the heiferweights, Stosh "Lunger" Croup hammered Otto Nillson into submission in the first round of their subnovice contest. After the ring had been toweled out, action resumed with Big Boy Hogan drilling and blasting the chest and top-knot of Alex "The Polish Sausage" Dumbrowski, the 279-pounder from East Dacron. Knocked out in the second round, Dumbrowski, when told of his loss, vowed to win if he had it to do it all over again.

The winners fully enjoyed their whole evening with Mr. Wepner and said they would revenge his loss to Mohammad Ali, if the champ and they should ever get old enough.

**MORNING LINE
At BLOWFISH PARK
St. Petersburg, Fla.**

By DUGAN O'NEILL
Rep.-Dem. Senior Sports
Writer (Ret.)

46th night of 52-day meeting.
Post time for the first race
7:30 (Dacron time)

506-FIRST RACE
6 1/2 Furlongs Virgin Claiming Purse $2,000

1-JEBREWS CALIENTE—Could be an upset—recently purchased by St. Pete police chief.

2-PAWN ME—Last ran well in Tijuana under different name.

3-JIMMY'S CART HORSE—Fits description of stakes horse stolen recently in Southern Calif.

4-TRAFFIC CITATION—Outsider, has broken wind and was recently refused entry into Mexico because of epizootic lymphangitis.

5-PORTUGUESE MAN O'WAR—Believed to be in foal.

6-DRAINAGE SLEW—Runs like it was on the deck of a freighter in a hurricane.

507-SECOND RACE
12 furlongs 3-year-olds and up.
Purse $2,500. Claiming price same.

1-SIR BARTON—Won triple crown in 1919—aging.

2-MAJESTIC DRINKER—Out of Northern Drinker—could last till closing.

3-HANDY JOB—Allegedly illegitimate foal of Nashua—owned by a groomer who moved to St. Pete some years ago with bottle of "seed."

4-THE FUELER—Good Chance—extremely long front legs and "special diet" will see a win.

5-COUNT FEET—History of leg problems.

6-AGGRAVATED ASSAULT—Related by marriage to '46 triple crown winner Assault. Owned by son of mayor. Likely.

508-THIRD RACE
Scarcoptic Stakes Purse $5,000
1 mile and 1/2. Open.

1-MONKEY'S FATHER'S BROTHER—Unknown.

2-VICTORIA PARKING LOT—Threw a hoof and a shoe last race out.

3-WAR CLOD—Runs best in mud as proved in Spanish American War.

4-HOMOGENIZED—Win disallowed on last race after jock "put down" favorite with .45 two lengths from finish. Determined.

5-BOLD DROOLER—Won special handicapped thoroughbred stakes held two weeks ago. Sympathy bets, anyone?

509-FOURTH RACE
3-year-olds and up. Allowance. Purse, an old Car.

1-JAIPUR WETTER—Owned and bred by a local syndicate known as "the syndicate." Good bet if anyone will take it.

2-VENUSIAN WAY—Might be a horse, might be another form of animal life. Allegedly has a manger full of crushed magnesium nodules and drinks kepone. A betting favorite with all-star racing fans.

3-INCINERATOR—Out of Kelvinator out of Carburetor. No.

4-HALE WHALE—Breathes thru tracheotomy tube. Outsider.

5-ANTHROPOID'S MOTHER'S BROTHER—Unknown.

510-FIFTH RACE
Swiss stakes 1 mile. Purse $4,000.
10 years and up.

1-TYPHOID II—Ran and fell last time out.

2-MACBREATH—Hobble home to win in similar company a week ago.

3-OLD PANT—Could foxtrot home to win—if so, will definitely win in a walk.

4-SIMIAN GRANDFATHER'S NON-CONSANGUINAL MALE OFFSPRING—Unknown.

5-MAJESTIC TORTOISE—Starts slow but sticks to it.

511-SIXTH RACE
Scheduled as "The Mayor's Stables Stakes" in which all the horses belonging to the mayor would race each other for a purse of $20,000. Race was canceled due to lack of betting interest.

**BLOWFISH PARK RESULTS
Saturday, Feb. 11, 1978**

FIRST—Mile; Pace; cl; off 8:00

6 Monkeys Uncle (V. Filth)	22.00	10.60	6.40
3 Duck Jam (Duncan Dickie)		7.20	3.80
1 Meat Bolt (Dickie Duncan)			3.80

Time 2:25

WINNER NOT PICKED

SECOND—Mile; pace; cl; off 8:21

5 Bull Face (A. Negroe)	5.20	4.00	2.60
6 Spovin (J. Meoff)		7.20	3.80
3 Scumby (V. Filth)			3.80

Time 2:15

DAILY DOUBLE (5-6) 15.00

THIRD—Mile; pace; cl; off 8:43

1 Blow Hole (D. Madrigal)	21.00	10.00	5.00
4 Horn Slammer (Souse)		7.20	5.80
2 Muck Eye (N. Groin)			6.00

Time 3:25 Scratched-Butt Fish

EXACTA (7-4).25

FOURTH—6F; pace; cond; off 9:05

7 Gleet Leader (C. Odour)	14.80	6.80	3.40
4 Sperm Tailor (No-Boy)		4.20	3.60
2 Pinhead (Grunter)			2.00

Time 4:00

FIFTH—Mile; pace; cl; off 9:30

7 Bumboy (Rathead)	7.60	4.20	3.20
3 Knocker (D Biter)		5.40	3.60
4 Cat Heart (No-Boy)			4.80

SIXTH—Mile; 70 yd. pace; cond; off 9:50

4 Chink Whiff (Duncan Dickie)		4.20	3.00
			2.40
5 Tar Hole (Dickie Duncan)		5.40	3.40
8 Bat Eye (N. Groin)			2.60

TRIPLE (142) 11.00

SEVENTH—Mile; cl; off 10:13

7 Monkeys Uncle (V. Filth)	21.00	7.00	6.00
8 Perisher (No-Boy)		5.60	3.80
1 Sashimi (Souse)			8.00

Time 1:59
No Scratches

They're Off And Sliding

By HOOT HEWETT
Rep.-Dem. Sports Writer

Photo by Rep.-Dem. Staff Photographer Dale Jink

Horse coming into clubhouse turn begins to falter before striking photographer. Littlefeather won, paid 4.25.

LAST NIGHT saw the first ever running of the 6 1/2 furlong Buckeye Stakes for maiden two-year-olds on the nation's only ice track for thoroughbreds. Doug Boghurp, starter at the new Silage Lake Downs racing facility, said the track was extremely hard last night although not exceptionally fast due to its being ice.

THE HORSES BROKE WELL from the starting gate in what was to be the second and last race of the evening, except for Littlefeather, a spooky bay who managed to get her tail frozen to one of the rear stanchions of the starting gate and after leaving the gate stayed behind by seven lengths while her tail stayed behind 6 1/2 furlongs.

THE BACK WAS CLOSELY bunched going into the first turn, although the time was not exceptional due to the tiny steps needed to maintain stability on the ice even with the specially studded aluminum shoes. Coming out of the turn, Lepages Stable filly Geronimo was in front by a length with Your Initials, Aunts Birthday and Favorite Color running a neck and a nose apart in that order.

COMING INTO the clubhouse turn, Geronimo improved her lead by three lengths while the rest of the back managed to enter the turn although not to leave it, coming along into the rail, through it, and into the grandstand area to be disqualified for leaving the track, falling down, and in some cases having to be destroyed.

GERONIMO ROMPED HOME to win with Littlefeather second by about 35 lengths. Protests by the betting public, however prompted a steward's inquiry, which led to the suspension of Geronimo's trainer Howard Boghurp and the confiscation of three empty fifty-pound sacks of cement which had allegedly been fed to the horse. Littlefeather was declared the winner and racing was suspended for the season.

O'NEILL'S PICKS

1—Jimmy's Cart Horse, Pawn Me, Jebrews Caliente
2—The Fueler, Aggravated Assault, Majestic Drinker
3—Homogenize, Monkey's Father's Brother?
4—Jaipur Wetter, Venusian Way, Anthropoid's Mother's Father
5—MacBreath, Old Pant, Majestic Tortoise
6—none

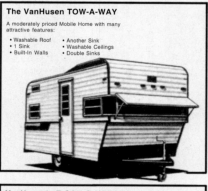

School Sports Spotlight

By SANDY "SNAPPER" TRUDGE

Friday night basketball action ... Tucker Tech Wingnuts dismantled Ezra Taft Benson, 110-76 ... Tucker Tech's Wayne Kozjac scored 40 points and sent Ref. Buck Petosky to the locker room with a groin injury ... Boss Prendergast's always hungry Lampreys sucked the life out of C. Estes Kefauver ... Vollo Bosdigian was the stand-out until thrown out for improper use of elbows during a timeout ... Warren Harding and Benedict Arnold played to a 21-21 tie in a napper at Harding ... The Sod Busters from Silage

Rural play a different brand of B-Ball as St. Vitus discovered in the first meeting of the two squads. Hank Pompk and Norris Stenson used a fancy move they call "thrashin' an' bailin'" to harvest a big 109-55 win ... In Post Game Action, Tucker Tech whipped Benson, lots of injuries, lots of cops ... C. Estes Kefauver held their team bus against tough opposition from Boss Prendergast ... A washroom melee cost Silage a cheerleader... Benedict Arnold topped Harding in their traditional parking lot punch out ... H.S. Grapplers met at Tucker on Saturday morning for the Mid-Ohio Regional Inter-Conference meet. It

was Tucker all the way with lots of injuries before, during and after the meet ... H. S. Diving meet at Benedict Arnold saw Jeff Keathcobb do a beautiful two-and-a-half gainer from the high board onto the low board ... Get well soon, Jeff! ... 26-year-old Tucker senior Walthus Marcus has been ruled ineligible for Dacron conference games ... The Dacron Urban Suburban and Catholic H.S. Conference loses a great competitor in the 7'2" center ... Sorry, Walthus, but congrats on the birth of your second son ... See you all at the Girls' Gymnastic Finals at Kefauver on Tuesday Eve. 7:30.

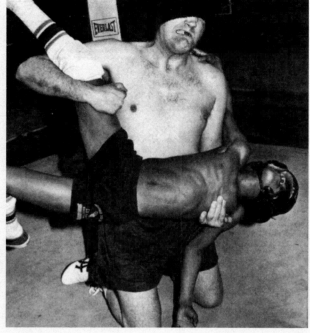

Photo by Rep.-Dem. Sports Photographer Dade Jink

Undefeated in Sacramento high school junior varsity wrestling, Chuck Scones was no match for The Human Meat Ax at the Mobile Home Bowl.

Toledo Teeth Are Cauterized By Motivated Dacron Skaters

By SANDY "SNAPPER" TRUDGE

THE PAST WEEK has been a remarkably successful one for the troubled Dacron Skaters. After losing to the bottom-of-the-league Ft. Wayne, Indiana, Madmen, they came back like squash balls to cauterize the high flying Toledo Teeth 9-8 at the Asphalt Forum Friday night.

IF THIS MIRACLE carried a byline, it would be that of Coach Cyril Plaid, whose wise words and bed checks may yet steer the Skaters out of the Sub-Canadian league's basement suite. Coach Plaid, who comes to Dacron from Manitoba, Ontario, said after Friday night's game that he confidently expected that the possibility of a turnabout in his team's fortunes might exist in the not too distant future.

PLAID CITED CENTER Derrick McChienery's recent return to the ice after a six-month suspension received in an early season game against the Sault Ste. Marie Siouxers as a possible factor in the team's success. McChienery, an aggressive player, was sidelined in a Michigan prison when authorities ruled that

Photo by Rep.-Dem. Staff Photographer Vince Blum

Deft stick-work by Skater's center Derrick McChienery opened door to victory goal over Toledo and penalty booth for half an hour.

the high-powered forward had deliberately skated off the fingers of Siouxers' winger Jacques Filthe-Be-ret.

THE SKATERS face a tough trial Tuesday night when they meet the hard-skating, high-sticking Niagara Falls Guys in Niagara Falls. The team is 0 for 2 against the Guys, though one previous away game was forfeited when the home team's Van-Husen Motor Motel suffered an unavoidable explosion in its number-2 engine hold. Team officials say there is no chance of a similar accident preventing an appearance in Canada Tuesday.

Teen Loses Pro-Am Debut

DACRON. Sat., Feb. 11—A California teen-ager, Chuck Scones, lost last night in his debut on the Winston Pro-Am Wrestling Circuit at the Mobile Home Bowl. The 13-year-old youth lost three straight falls to the 320-

pound, eight-time World champion Viktor Flozniac, better known as The Human Meat Ax. The match lasted just under two minutes as The Meat Ax took immediate control and crushed the 5 foot 4 inch high school freshman.

OHIO GAME LAWS AT A GLANCE

	Rabbit	Cow	Deer	Raccoon	Owl	Birds
Jan.	Night Rabbits only after the 17th. Buck rabbits may be taken prior to the 11th during the daylight hour with arquebus or un-modified Saxon bow. Hand knifing permitted hunters under 12.	None may be shot, trapped or wounded by accident to see how fast they run.	Doe week from the 1st of the month to the 7th after which only bucks may be taken with a seasonal limit of seven shots per hunter at the same buck. No deer may be hunted at night or with a weapon having a caliber larger than .50. Warning: Tree snaring, mine laying and drowning of deer are now illegal.	Pit traps illegal through '78 season. May be taken by any other means during daylight if for purposes of antenna decoration.	Baiting with poisoned mice permitted Ohio residents only during the month of January.	Birds not specifically covered by the "owl" amendment to the game and wildlife code of the state of Ohio may be destroyed for pleasure unless specifically protected by Federal legislation.
Feb.	During the month of February rabbits may not be shot from tree blinds nor may bait be employed as a lure.	Same as January.	Packs of dogs may be employed to chase deer during the club season (12-27) if the pack has not been starved more than three calendar weeks.	May be taken by bow only if calls are employed.	Club, bat and mallet hunting only. Evidence of sex must be preserved on all owls taken after the 12th until they are transported to the place of consumption.	As a result of certain January incidents, hunters are reminded that telephone insulators, which are the property of South Central Ohio Telephone and Telegraph Bell, are not birds.
March	Hares only may be taken in March. Very likely there are none left after last month.	Same regulations as February.	Deer are extinct in the month of March.	During the raccoon breeding season, March 10-21, two raccoons shot together count as one kill in the record book.	Hunting owl prohibited during March; shooting by accident OK	Absolutely no shooting of birds within one mile of any telephone, telegraph or power transmission pole or installation, which is property of South Central Ohio Telephone and Telegraph Bell.
April	Season ends 2nd of April. Rabbits shot between then and the end of the month are considered "sport rabbits." Under the terms of the State Conservation bill of 1975, every medical assistance must be given "sport rabbits" injured in taking.	Same regulations as March.	Restocking of forests with deer begins on first of the month. Stocked deer may not be taken until they walk steadily.	Raccoon are extinct.	Owl may only be taken in April by mink, marten, sable or white mouse ranchers seeking to protect their stock.	Bird maybe taken only with stones by children under 14. All previous regulations concerning S.C.O.T&T line insulators remain in effect.
May	**ALL SEASONS CLOSED**					

Which Fish Is Which?

By SANDY "SNAPPER" TRUDGE

NINE-EYED CARP

From 1' to over 5'. A vicious fighter, the Nine-Eye, found only in the Dacron area, makes use of its razor-sharp fins to slice lines and mar the finish on power boats in summer. Best taken on steel leader during winter. Bait: stick, bit of cloth, bolt.

BULLHEAD

6" to 2'. One of the most common fish taken in the Dacron area. It's sandy, pasty tasting flesh is much appreciated by cats and colored people. Bait: bacon, bullhead.

SMALL-MOUTH BASS

9" to 1 1/2'. Small-mouth are perhaps the best fish in the local waterways. They have been scarce lately, be-

ing on the winter grocery list of the Nine-Eye, but when caught (usually on a small hook baited with mosquito), make excellent eating. Bait: mosquito, ant.

SUNFISH

6" to 3'. A stubborn, slow moving fish, the sunfish is sometimes referred to as the "unemployed of the deep." It is quite good for throwing back or, if buried, of some benefit to roses. Bait: donut, chips, bread.

BLUEGILL

2" to 6". A popular fish in the area, the Bluegill puzzled lake and river biologists by failing to spawn for three years. It did spawn last year (although not in Ohio) and the fingerling stocked by the State show promise of providing much fishing pleasure in several years. Bait: worms.

A Record Catch In Reservoir

By SANDY "SNAPPER" TRUDGE

Earl Divens of Dacron landed the body of a 25-year-old Hamtramck, Michigan, man; Stanislas Slovaki, who apparently fell through the ice and drowned. Divens, who was fishing for perch Friday afternoon, landed the man with a Spell-White Arctic-Ace reel, Douglas 40-pound line and a Berkin fiberglass "Shorty" pole. He was using a "Slow-poke" ice lure. "I thought I hooked into a muskie," Divens said. "Man, it was tough pulling him in. My line broke just as I was getting my net down and I had to pull him in with a grappling hook." The 71" 185-pounder was taken to police headquarters, then to the morgue. The largest previous catch in the Licking Creek Reservoir was 33 pounds.

Snowmobiles Are Fun

By SANDY "SNAPPER" TRUDGE

Years ago when I was a boy, there wasn't anything like the "snow buggies" we have today. If a fellow wanted to go out through the hills in winter, he had to wear snowshoes and be darned careful he didn't get shot for trespassing.

Then about the time of the Second World War, a French Canadian fellow named Bombardier got the bright

Photos Courtesy VanHusen Mfg. Inc.

The VanHusen Snowbunny— a terrific machine.

idea of crossing a snowshoe with a scooter. Well, those first snowmobiles didn't amount to much. But it wasn't long before bright fellows like Woolworth VanHusen II got a hold of the early patents and made the idea into a business.

The VanHusen Yellow-Streaker—a great recreational vehicle.

Now it's a sport, too. The new VanHusen Snowmobile Home with the multi-auger attachment is just the thing for ice trawling and hardly a danger to skaters if they're careful about the trench. The smaller Van Husen Snowbunnies, Yellow Streakers and Snow Squirrels are just the thing for racers and no danger to the ecology as some suggest, for the trees they hit don't die.

No, the snowmobile is an excellent form of recreation. I was out last week on a new VanHusen Snowbunny. I drove around the lake about one hundred times and found the machine had plenty of reliability, in fact a bit more than I wanted, for when the throttle finally got unstuck, I felt like I'd ridden a pair of steel roller skates over a couple hundred miles of washboard. Pep, too. Top speed was enough to blow my glasses off my nose, go around the lake and run them over before I got my bearings back.

Hunters find the snow buggy invaluable for getting

The Van Husen Ice-Fox— beautiful and well-made.

into hard-to-reach areas, which in many cases would take hours to walk to. And, although most "game" are afraid of snowmobiles, they are not nearly so fast. More and more hunters are turning to this modern form of transportation both to run game down and to carry it out of the forest.

Eight Rules Of Bow Safety

1. Never keep a strung bow around the house.

2. Always keep a bow high on the wall out of your reach and others.

3. Never point a bow at anyone even if it is unloaded. It's not ALWAYS the unloaded bow that kills, but it has happened often enough to cause concern.

4. Never "horseplay" with a bow. There are enough people with their arms or hunting dogs stuck to trees every year.

5. Never shoot a bow unless you can see what you're shooting at. Most windows are broken by people who break this rule.

6. Set a good example. Don't go around drinking and shooting your bow straight up in the air.

7. Join an accredited Rod & Bow Club, like the one on Polk Street here in Dacron.

A Public Service of the Polk Street Rod & Bow Club.

Drowning Tips

By PATTY PLANT
Rep.-Dem. Feature Writer

EVERY YEAR we read, hear or see accidents happening around us. People we know or whose names we have seen in connection with hardware stores or the phone company are suddenly dead as a result of an accident. These are serious, competent people. People who run hardware stores or install phones have to be, so it goes to show accidents can happen successfully to anyone. Not just to silly children, not just to the old and feeble, not just to the heavy drinker. Anyone.

STATISTICS TELL US that people who don't know what they're doing are more than 2,000 times as likely to suffer a fatal accident than us. This goes for ice fishing and other forms of ice recreation just as it does for more dangerous sports such as bow hunting.

IMAGINE YOURSELF ice fishing with your wife one night. You walk by your ice hole. Suddenly your foot slips on the slick ice and you are plunged into the freezing watery ink of your own ice hole! Powerful currents tug you under the ice where buried logs threaten to tangle you, the hooks and lines of other fisherpersons threaten to snag portions of your coat and eyes. Above on the ice, your wife is screaming in the frosty air and repeatedly thrusting a large stick into the waters of your ice hole in the hopes you will take hold and be saved.

IF THIS HAPPENS, 90 percent of the time, you are dead. However, the other 10 percent of the time you can increase your chances of survival by taking a few simple safety measures.

1. Don't panic and scream. Screaming under water can't be heard and the lungs fill up with water.

2. Underneath the ice is a thin layer of air left for the Green Berets to use in wars. Swim under the ice and breathe it.

3. Try to find the hole you made or another hole in the ice. Don't just smash yourself against the ice over and over again like a policeman trying to get into a pot party.

4. If it looks like you're going to drown, be sure not to throw away your clothing, wallet and watch. This is very important to identify you later, especially a long time later.

THIS IS WHAT TO DO if you fall into the water. But if you are a woman, what should you do if your husband slips on some slimy ice and plunges into his own ice hole? First, scream to attract attention. Don't worry about attracting wild animals such as bears, as most of them have been killed by members of the Dacron Rod and Bow Club. After attracting attention, plunge a stick repeatedly in and out of the hole in case your husband is in the area and can grab hold of it. After ten minutes, you can assume the worst. Try and keep a grip on yourself. Remember he would want you to. Try and remember the name of your insurance agent, then phone him up and tell him. Many insurance companies no longer require estimates and a check can be in your hands within hours. Don't make the same mistake next time.

REMEMBER, with a little bit of caution and preparedness, accidents can be completely avoided. That's what we want.

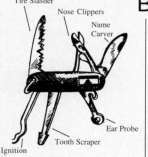
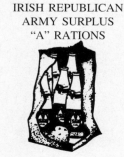

UPA News Photo

Two members of the Detroit Poles pro pole-vaulting team compete in an inter-squad game at the team's Tucson, Ariz., training camp.

Pro Vaulting On Tap

DETROIT, Sat., Feb. 11 (UPA)—The newly created National Pole-Vaulting League has announced that it will begin a full season of professional team pole-vaulting this spring. League President Buck McFinley explained the new sport at a press conference in Detroit on Friday. "Six men try to vault over the bar from one direction and six opposing players from the other direction," McFinley said. "The object is to achieve enough height to clear the bar and at the same time try to block the other players What we end up with is a dramatic battle between 12 men, 18 feet in the air." The bar is raised nine times after each "play" or vault. One point is scored for each player who gets across the bar. The seven NPVL teams, the Detroit Poles, Cincinnati Gazelles, St. Louis Louies, Milwaukee Jumps, Des Moines Crows, Minneapolis Leapers and the Kansas City Grasshoppers, will play a 56-game schedule beginning April 7 and ending September 3.

SLOPE DRIFTS

By JEAN LUC LAFFITE
Rep.-Dem. Ski Editor

As the current trend moves more steadily in the direction of downhill racing among today's amateur and leisure skiers, greater general interest has naturally arisen in the art of ski-tuning, to maximize the efficiency of the ski in relation to the skier's style, the terrain, and the conditions. This fine-tuning may be accomplished by a number of methods; however, Ulv Klenz of Chickenloaf Mtn. ski resort in Guysville favors the portable and precision gauged-veractor ski-tuning system manufactured by Tyroletron.

Keyed to the 30,000 mHz international ski frequency, the highly reliable unit performs a rapid Y-coupled molecular scan that electro magnetically sets a pair of skis in perfect synchronous tune. Discordant atomic ski structures, oscillating at divergent or improper levels, can disrupt critical elemental balances in most ordinary snow compounds, which in turn work to polarize the point of contact and possibly increase friction.

Rep.-Dem. Staff Photo

Ohio ski conditions continued to be far above average last week but occasional icy patches on top of the water made some slopes extra fast.

Skis generally vary by manufacturer and style as to the length of time they will hold, their tune. For particularly delicate skis, Klenz suggests a simple method of field-tuning, utilizing any of the higher register reed instruments and a small magnet. The procedure requires a good ear and some experience, however.

Parachuters Are Second

New Orleans, Feb. 11 (UPA)—The Ohio National Guard parachute team placed second here in international parachute competition after excellent showings in the four- and eight-man events. The Drifters, as they call themselves, moved up to second place from third after a plane carrying the Russian team overflew the drop zone and the Russian eight-man team landed in an alligator-infested bayou. The Russians, who had been in an excellent position to win first prize, were sent home in separate boxes, though some difficulty was had in identifying those remains which had been partly digested. President Carter has expressed regret over the incident and over increasing Russian presence in Ethiopia and Aden. First place, by default, was awarded to a California-based skydiving team, the San Diego Drop-Outs.

Top Bowler In Taiwan

By CHUCK DENT
Rep.-Dem. Foreign Sports Correspondent

Top-ranked bowler Pete Czerny of Dacron and 10 other U.S.B.A. bowlers were warmly received in Taipei on Friday night. The bowlers are touring 11 cities on Taiwan. The Taiwanese are great fans of bowling and it is not unusual for parents to name children after American bowlers, bowling equipment manufacturers and even bowling terms. Nearly 50,000 fans were turned away from Taipei's 25-story tall Bowling Palace high-rise bowling lanes. The Americans played on a specially constructed lane that met with U.S.B.A. specifications. The Taiwanese use a lane only 11 feet long, a ball the size of a 16-inch softball and pins made of rice paper over a wood frame. "They go ape for bowling over here," Pete Czerny said. "They just can't believe the size of our balls." In the first series of exhibitions, Anton Prozniack of Pontiac, Michigan, rolled three consecutive 300 games to place first. The Taipei newspaper devoted front page space to the exhibition. "天 柯 座 头" The *Taipei Evening Mail* headline said.

BASKETBALL
Small Ten Basketball

Rural Indian Ag-Tech Cows 85, Dayton College of Beauty and Cos. Mums 15

Zonesville Barber College Clippers 120, College of Lake Erie Bullheads 110

Columbus College of Data Proc. Army Ants 226, Toledo Danny Thomas Junior College Dannies 65

Steubenville Commuter Junior College Briefcases 89, Sandusky Air-Cond. Refrig. Repair Freezers 110

Semi-Pro Basketball
Bi-State League
MID-EAST CENTRAL DIVISION

	W	L	Pct.	GB
Chillicothe Dribblers	24	11	.686	—
Ft. Wayne Hoops	22	16	.579	3
Toledo Valve-Lifters	14	21	.400	9
Zanesville Zanies	11	24	.314	13
Dacron Trailers	9	28	.243	16

NORTH CENTRAL DIVISION

	W	L	Pct.	GB
Flint Arrow Heads	30	5	.857	—
Sandusky Bouncers	24	14	.632	7
Port Huron Huroners	19	20	.487	13
Kokomo Kokonuts	17	20	.459	14
Muncie Buckets	17	20	.459	14

EASTERN DIVISION

	W	L	Pct.	GB
Levittown Homes	12	31	.279	—

Saturday's Results

Flint 293, Dacron 17
Ft. Wayne 133, Zanesville 3
Kokomo 116, Sandusky 115 1/2
Levittown 66
Arrow Heads 293, Trailers 17
FLINT (229)—Janes 36 2-4 76, McPipe 21 3-3 45, Blackman 33 1-1 67, Tall 12 3-3 27, Greasham 3 0-0 3,Wonk 11 -1 23, Bubbs 13 4-4 30, Symantix 20 1-1 21, Oleo 1 0-01, Nekker 0 0-0 0 90-110-93
DACRON (17)—Glee 2 0-0 2. Simpson 3 0-0 3. Triangle 1 0-0 1, Scmautz 3 2-2 5, Anderson 0 0-0 0, Minsky 4 1-1 5, Soufle 0 0-0 0, Muffins 0 0-0 0, Wister 1 0-0 1, Thummyink 0 0-0 0 90-110-93
Total Fouls—Flint 233, Dacron 2
Fouled Out—Flint, Jones, , McPipe, Tall, Bubbs
Technical—Flint Coach Red Koonce 3, FSnt Assistant Coach Larry Harbourgass 2
Attendance—189
Fan Injuries—Flint 7, Dacron 33

HOCKEY
Sub-Canadian League

	W	L	T	GF	GA
Salt Ste. Marie Sewers	8	2	20	38	32
Niagra Falls Guys	6	3	21	36	33
Sandusky Boozers	5	3	22	35	33
Fort Wayne Madmen	5	5	20	35	35
Toledo Teeth	5	6	19	35	36
Muncie Powerglides	3	6	21	33	36
Dacron Skaters	3	7	20	33	37
Chillcothe Chilblains	2	5	23	32	35

Skaters 9, Teeth 8

Skaters	3	3	3—9
Teeth	3	2	3—8

FIRST PERIOD—3 Dacron, LeFrogg, MacChienery, MacChienery; 3 Toledo, LaFey, LaBlatz, LeFrommager; Penalties—LaFey (triple sticking)
SECOND PERIOD—3 Dacron, MacChienery, MacChienery, MacChienery; 2 Toledo, LaFey, LaBlatz; Penalties, Dacron LeGumes (eating on ice) Toledo Plunk (talking in face-off)
THIRD PERIOD—3 Dacron, MacChienery, MacChienery, MacChienery, 3 Toledo, LeFrommage, LeFrommage, LaBlatz; Penalties, Toledo (coach in net). Attendance—322

Powerglides 1, Dogfish 1

Powerglides	1	0	0—1
Dogfish	0	0	1—1

FIRST PERIOD—1, Muncie, Stompski (Fremd, Plotski) 4:22, Penalties—Muncie, Bumpers (street shoes an ice), Glimpsky (no shirt), Sandusky, LeFlame (talking with spectator during game)
SECOND PERIOD—
THIRD PERIOD—1, Sandusky, LeCar (LaFemme, Latrec) 8:13, Penalties—Sandusky, Hammershaw (leaving early), Muncie, Buttinski (hygiene foul)

Guys 2, Madmen 1

Guys	2	0	X—2
Madmen	0	1	X—1

FIRST PERIOD—2, Niagara Falls, LaPontoon 7:44, Mousse (LaFlame, Renault) 13:22, Penalties—Fort Wayne, Bortz (out of uniform) SECOND PERIOD—1, Fort Wayne, Kopskichez 2:27, Penalties—Niagara Falls, Citroen (not paying attention)

THIRD PERIOD—CANCELLED FOR AUTO SHOW SETUP
Attendance—110

Sault Ste. Marie Siouxers 0, Chilblains 0

Sault St. Marie	0	0	0—0
Chillicothe	0	0	0—0

First Period—0
Second Period—0
Third Period—0
Attendance—33

SKATER TALK

Forward Husky Burlow and defenseman Louge Fondue did not play Friday night. Forward Husky Burlow and defenseman Louge Fondue are short two uniforms ... After 30 games, the Skaters have two more victories than last year at the 30 game mark ... The Skaters will have their team bus painted red and green on Monday.

GOLF
Dacron Kiwanis Midwinter Ohio Celebrity Classic Invitational Open
Saturday's Results

Bill Cullen	334	434	301—1069
Kay Ballard	449	619	399—1467
Little Eva	660	614	803—2077
Clifton Fadiman	401	1190	630—2221

PONG
Saturday Night Results

DACRON TRAILWAYS BUS STATION PLAYOFFS
Willie Jackson d. Bo Lensky 11-3, 11-9, 11-10
Mohair Mohamet d. Lorry Dibbs 11-0, 11-1, 11-0
Perlaine Latice d. Greg Lurdle 11-8, 11-6, 9-11
Jorge Orantes d. Emanuel Fexiloro in overtime on Death Racer Game 3-1

BASEBALL
Triple D Pre-Spring Meeting Football
TRADE ACTION (FINAL)

DACRON TARLEGS sent catcher Russ Nixon to TOLEDO Mudhens for catcher Joe Pignatano and $75.

SANDUSKY HARD BALLS purchases SS Coot Veal from TOLEDO for $260. Sent pitcher Vinegar Bend Mizett to FORT WAYNE DUGOUTS for free.

ZANESVILLE CLEAN SOX sent groundskeeper Len Mumphrey to the KOKOMO KOKES for third baseman Pumpsie Green and 6 gross of balls.

NIAGARA FALLS NIAGERS sent reserve ourfielder, infielder, pitcher, bus driver, handyman, trainer Tickers Jeffers to the SOUTH BEND BUNTS for fingerball relief pitcher One-Leg Lempchick.

MEETING NOTES—Muncie Owner Charles O'Heck proposed triple headers to cut travel costs. The proposal was accepted. League President Hal Woodeshick okayed a plan to pull out of major league affiliations since no players had been called up since 1966. Semipro status will be adopted in 1979. Woodeshick also accepted a proposal to allow advertising messages on players' uniforms and outfield grass. Dacron Tarlegs owner Buddy MacAdam suggested six-man teams to lower payrolls. The suggestion will be voted upon Tuesday.

EXHIBITION
Football

DACRON "Strip Miners" 3, Peruvian National Soccer Team 0
Dac.—FG 15-yd. kick by Woodhuts
A.—322

TRANSACTIONS
College

Dacron Elementary and Junior College paid $3,000 to Columbus College of Data Processing for 6' 11" star center.

Basketball

Muncie "Buckets" and Fort Wayne "Hoops" exchanged coaches. Kokomo "Kokonuts" signed LaMarr Bunny to a 1.5 thousand dollar, one year pact.

Hockey

Charles "The Vending Machine" Amaretto bought a minority interest in the Dacron "Skaters" for a reported $4,000. Amaretto also owns an interest in five other Sub-Canadian League teams.

CARDS
Cleveland Invitational Tag Team Cribbage
Saturday's Results

Lyon Murray & Chas. Capone 3-0-4
Humphrey "Gauger" McMeerny & Prof. Reynolds 2-4-3
Newton Finn & Weatherman Quinn 3-4-4
Seedman Jackson & Little Larry Mole 0-3-0
Patty Reynolds & Flashie Voomer 4-4-0
Spivey Davidson & Louise Fletcher-Schmidt 3-3-4

SKIING
Dacron Area

Chicken Loaf Mountain (Guysville) 2-3 inch base, 1/2 new sleet
conditions—good to excellent

Rope Tow Mountain (Union Furnace)
no base, no new show
conditions—fair to poor

Alpine Flats (Tuppers)
1-inch partial base, 2-inches new mud, rocks and tire ruts
conditions—fair to good

Mount Barn-Top (Coolieville)
4-inch base, three inches new ice chalet burned down, chair lift broken, no parking, instructor in jail
conditions—fair

Winter Qualifying Trials
At Vail, Colorado
Saturday's Results

Body Skiing—Bidwell, Wyo. 3:33.988, Weeble, Colo. 3:36.772, Reddenbottom, Idaho 3:40.002
Giant Cot Slalom—Croop, Colo. 5:44.999, Spam, Vt. 6:01.099. Udder-Smith, Utah, 6:00.683
Mitten Removal—Toeth, Nev., 19:23.0445, Blizle, Colo., 20:01.435, Lidds, Calif. 20:18.453

SPECIAL OLYMPICS
Final Results Of Special Olympics V At Pasadena, Calif.

50-Ft. Dash—Unignner, Montana, Gold; Mesko, Mich., Silver; Potkin, NJ. Bronze
400-Yard Car Ride—SMITH, OHIO, Gold; Lemke, Fla., Silver; Shehab, Miss., Bronze
Head-Lifting Competition—Wheetie, Alabama, Gold; Mung Pang, Ha., Silver; Olinsky, Minn. Bronze
Hair Combing—Yistik, Penn., Gold; Thompson, Wisc., Silver; Hayhatts, Fla., Bronze;
Dry Surface Crawl—Tibbie, Fla., Gold; Cracker, Minn., Silver; Bosnigian, N.Y., Bronze
Free-Float—PIMLICK, OHIO, Gold; DURBROOK, OHIO, Silver; Shmpkin, Mass., Bronze;
30-Minute Nap—Beeker, La., Gold; ALL OTHERS DISQUALIFIED
Finger Wiggle—Hamilton, Nev. Gold; Moe, Ill., Silver, RECKLBERGER, OHIO, Bronze
Free-Fall Competition—Hifen, Tenn., Syzchucks, Penn., Gold; WAFFLWETZ, OHIO, Silver; Flogg, Ind., Bronze

TRACK AND FIELD
Pan-American Games Mexico City, Mexico Saturday's Results

Mixed Team Steeplechase—Peru-Gold, Bolivia-Silver. Mexico-Bronze
Six-Man Javelin Toss and Catch—Mexico-Gold, Brazil-Silver, Peru-Gold
Two-Man Pole Vault—Uruguay-Gold, Chile-Silver, Bolivia-Bronze
Three-Mile Dash—Cuba-Gold, Puerto Rico-Silver, Mexico-Bronze
Hurtle Throw—Panama-Gold, Columbia-Silver, Cuba-Bronze
Hammer Jump—Brazil-Gold, Paraguay-Silver, Chile-Bronze

PRO WRESTLING
Mexican Invitational Torture Matches '78

Mobile Home Bowl Arena, Dacron, Ohio
Bloodeater killed Judd Hymen by rupturing his heart and spleen.
? defeated ! in two falls breaking necks.
The Glove defeated Hemo Man in one fall with blood gushing from face and arm.

CBS CHALLENGE OF THE SEXES

Last Week's Results Boxing—Ken Norton vs. Billie Jean King: Norton - KO 1st
Baseball—Cincinnati Reds vs. Las Vegas Show Girls: Reds 112, Las Vegas Show Girls 0
Football Competition—Jethro Pugh vs. Sarah Baugh: Pugh 90 pts., Sarah Baugh 0 pts.
Slam Dunk Competition—Julius Irving vs. Dorothy Hamill: Irving 50, Hamill 0
World's Strongest Person Competition—Lou Feringo vs. Betty Stove: Feringo 2,280 lbs., Stove 120 lbs.

• *Old Sofas* • *Stuff That's Broken*
• *Junker Cars* • *Pole Lamps*

CLASSIFIED ADS

Use *Rep.-Dem.* Classified Ads to Sell Everything in Your House

• *Help Wanted* • *Used Bedding*
• *Second-Hand Clothes*

ANNOUNCEMENTS AND CLUB MEETINGS

Today, Feb. 12

DACRON CONSUMER ACTION COUNCIL meets to discuss marshmallows in children's breakfast cereal. 4:00, 565 Truman St., 556-0900.

DRIED DUNG ENERGY GROUP will hold a seminar on dried animal waste fuels at Kefauver High School 7:00 P.M.

WIVES OF JEROME WASHINGTON will meet to discuss alimony and child support payments. 8:30. SW Baptist Unity Jesus Assembly of God Hall.

WINDOW PEEKERS ANONYMOUS invites all window peekers to an introductory session at the Cocky Locky Motel. 9:00 P.M.

REBORN JEWS meet at Saperstein's Carpet Warehouse. 224 Polk St., 7:30. Bring your own refreshments.

Monday, Feb. 13

VETERANS OF DOMESTIC DISTURBANCES meets at Vernon Pullsok's house 399 Ginko St., 3:00 P.M.

RUBBISH SALE at Our Sweet Jesus 8th Baptist Church, 231 E. 11th St., 9 A.M. to 5 P.M.

OHIO TOASTMISTRESSES meet to discuss Enunciation in Auditoriums Where the Microphones Don't Work Well. At Yolanda Wukowiches, 990 Lindberg Lane. Dacron Glen.

LATE MODEL SEDAN OWNERS CLUB meets at Hirschs Gas 'N Go, 473 Roosevelt Highway. 8:00.

DACRON DIABETES FOUNDATION BAKE SALE at Forrest Lawn Hospital Emergency Meeting Room. 12:00 to 4:00.

Tuesday, Feb. 14

DEAF DACRONIANS meet at Sears Secor Ave. store to 'Speak-Out' with Councilman-person Olive Finch. 1:00 P.M. to 3:00 P.M.

KEFAUVER HIGH SCHOOL CONTINUOUS EDUCATION NIGHT SCHOOL continues today with non-stop schooling for adults. 8:00.

OHIO DEPARTMENT OF CONSERVATION offers a free course in non-destructive outdoor recreation. Strip Mine Refuge. Rt. 23 and Bituminus Highway. All day.

ARMCHAIR TRAVEL CLUB "visits" Miami Beach this week through the use of slides, movies and firsthand accounts. Mrs. Fulton Baxter Sr., 322 Chinese Elm Lane, Dacron Glen 272-7290 for details

Wednesday, Feb. 15

THE AMATEUR ORTHODONTISTS CLUB meets at "Dr." Dave Dweedle's home at 400 W. Condo. Apt. 350. Dacron Dells.

VICTIMS OF VIOLENT CRIMES GROUP meets at Sabos for lunch. 12:30. Security is being provided.

GREAT MAGAZINES CLUB meets at Gullet Library to discuss this month's magazine "Outdoor Life" - 2:30

THE RIGHT TO GET AN ABORTION IF YOU WANT TO COMMITTEE holds its annual Singles Supper fund raiser at Sacred Heart School Gymnasium. 7:30. Admission is $3.00.

UNEMPLOYED SHEET METAL WORKERS UNION holds its midweek all-day bowling championship and poker session at Roll 'n Bowl.

SEMI-PROFESSIONAL HOUSEWIVES OF DACRON will demonstrate the proper technique for two person wall washing at J.C. Penny. Corngate Shopping Center. 1-3 P.M.

DACRON SUPPER CLUB meets for lunch at Larry Becker's home. 909 Flowering Crab Lane Dacron. 835-1121 for details

Thursday, Feb. 16

LIARS CLUB meets at the Palmer House in Chicago. Free transp. leaves 3:00 A.M. from Cocky Locky Motel. Rm. 204. Knock on door and ask if Sid & Shirley are in there. Free food, entertainment, gifts and prizes.

POLISH-AMERICAN PICNIC will be held in Wright Brother Park. Food, games, softball game, beer. 9:00 P.M. Bring snow shovel.

OLD REPUBLICAN WOMENS CLUB will meet to complain about Democrats and people who leave their dogs outside all night. 7:00 P.M. Hazel Wentworth's home. 337-7968

YOUNG CRIMINALS OF DACRON hold their annual community dance and get-together at Dacron Boys Club. 564-2077 for reservations Admission $4.00

PUBLIC BEAUTIFULNESS RALLY. Buchanan St. Theatre, 2245 Buchanan St. 5:30 A.M., "Find the Beauty in Reverend Sun Myung Moon" free movie.

SILAGE COUNTY REPUBLICAN DINNER, 7 P.M. Chanticlier Room, Cocky Locky Motel. 413 Upton $3.35-a-plate. Speaker: Judge Jim Applebower. Subject: "Gun Control Nuts."

Friday, Feb. 17

DACRON ADVENTURERS leave for Colorado to hot tub down the Colorado River. Dacron Greyhound Bus Station 3:00 P.M.

DUMPA SOCIETY begins its annual membership drive. All persons with I.Q.s below 70 are invited to join. Contact Wonka Bullock at Rapid-Trot Messenger Service

FRIDAY YOGA MASS will be held at St. Christopher School. Directed by Father Frank Churchill. 8:30.

FIREPLACE GIRLS Hearth No. 81 Accepting membership applications from girls 6 to 12. 7 P.M. Christ Church of God. 4100 Secor.

Saturday, Feb. 18

DACRON BONE CANCER ASSOCIATION sponsors a week-long Marrow Drive. Phone 434-0092 for information. Donations taken at all area hospitals and McDonald's.

FRIENDS OF THE WEALTHY holds its annual Wealth Appreciation Night Dinner Dance at Chateau Frank and Alice. 8:00 to 1:00. $4.50.

DACRON POLICE DRUG SQUAD Corngate will hold a private drug inspection in the parking lot of the Food Clown supermarket. Citizens are invited to bring in their drugs for inspection and evaluations. 9:00 A.M. to 6:00 P.M.

THE DACRON PUBLIC LIBRARY WILL sponsor a BOOK-MOBILE DRAG RACE on Old Indian Scout Rd. and County View Hiway. 12:00 P.M. Admission is $3.50. Proceeds will go to the New Card File Fund.

Free INDOOR SCOUT JAMBOREE Sponsored by Mr. Rutgers Gullet. Well-scrubbed Scouts between 11 and 14, reserve space for your tent in bedroom or den now. Must come in person to 100 Polk St., Downtown

WW II 4F's meet for annual luncheon at Hi-Lo Grill. 344 Emily Dickenson 12:30

JOBS WANTED

MAN wishes job as male save/dog/pack-animal to attractive unmarried woman with red hair and long fingernails. Much experience, refs on request 445-3343

WOMAN seeks job as at person who watches tv and lays on the couch. Exp., willing to work full-time. flxbl. sal. range. Mrs. Bufford 545-0012

OLDER MAN seeks position as corporate V.P., board chairman or CIA operative in Hong Kong. Rome. London or Rio. No exp. Lrns fst, Eager. Call 667-8712

TEEN seeks work as drug tester for pharmaceutical firm. Has iron head and stomach, likes working with dangerous drugs. Parents cool. Low Salary. Has own motorcycle. 443-7671

LEGAL NOTICES

Annual Report of VanHusen Mfg. for the fiscal year ending Dec 31, 1977 is available for inspection at VanHusen Mfg. Consignor Affairs offices. 990 S. Woodrow Wilson Place, Scottsdale, Ariz., during regular business hours 8:30 A.M. to 4:30 P.M. by any citizen who requests it within 2 hrs of this notice; holds stock in VanHusen Mfg. and is not associated with or employed by any Federal or Ohio Regulatory commission and who will not use this report against VanHusen Mfg. in a court of law or in the preparation of legal proceedings against VanHusen Mfg.

NOTICE SMALL BUSINESS ADMINISTRATION

Willie's Community Bank And Loan Company Inc. Ltd.
Application No. 05/05-5122

Notice of Application for License to Operate as a Small Business Investment Company and Special Charter Lending Institution (Federal Minority Banking Exemption Amendment 0333)

An application to operate as a small business investment company and special charter lending institution under the provisions of Section 310(d) of the Small Business Investment Act of 1958 as amended (15 U.S.C. 661 et seq.) has been filed by Willie's Community Bank and Loan Company Inc. Ltd. (applicant) with the Small Business Administration, Negro Opportunity Development Division pursuant to 13 C.F.R. 107.102 (1978)

The officers, directors and stockholders of the applicant are as follows:

Dupress Robinson
President, Director
Rogers Walker The Second
Executive President
Lamar R. Jackson Jr.
Co-Executive President and Chairman of the Board
Irving R. Cohenberg
Assistant Vice Treasurer

Stated purpose of licensee:

"We is going open us up a bank where folks put they money in. We going make loans and charge us interest so the community, you understand, benefit. We gone do real fine in the bank business."

Dupress Robinson
Rogers Walker The Second
Lamar H. Jackson Jr.
Irving R. Cohenberg

Disclaimer of Debt

Responsible for my debts and signature only as of February 20, 1978. Fenton B. Sweater, 343 Lamb Lane, Dacron Estates, Dacron.

In two hours I don't know nothing about no debts. Hermann Speatzel.

I will not be responsible for debts and signature until I leave Ohio and change my name, file my finger tips off and get some plastic surgery. Bob Burke, 445 Creasted Bunting Road, Dacron.

Not responsible for debts incurred by my son, William, for purchase of autos, stereo equip., clothing, records, magazine subscriptions, camping gear, motorcycles, food or drugs. Carroll D. Shumdiggs, 90 Screech Owl Pl., Dacron.

LOST AND FOUND

LOST: Set of keys to 72 Lincoln Continental Sedan, nr. woods n. of Interstate 40 at Ketchums Swamp Exit in last 2 wks. Reward. Call Ajax Laundry Supply Co. After 2 A.M., ask for Bernie or Augie. No triflers pls.

FOUND: Businessman, about 55. 5' 8", balding, stoutish, 5-day growth beard. Wants to go home. For more info. call booth cor. Herm. Melville Ave. & Harding St. at 11:59 p.m. tonite sharp.

FOUND: six large sacks of garbage, near E. Hoover and Front Sts. Call 456-8239 after 6. ask for Len.

MERCHANDISE FOR SALE

Reichstag 400 Series Amp. 50,000 watts. registered with FAA. Like new, must sell quickly. Going away to military school this very afternoon. Larry Rendall 776-0078

PINT BOTTLE of Gen George Patton's Italy Invasion breath. Also Bogart snot. $400 for both or best offer. 688-4070

Half set of drum sticks for sale Ruby 440-9800

USED GYNECOLOGY EXAM GLOVES AND TABLE SHEETS. Completely soiled gloves and filthy disposable table sheets of high-grade paper. Gloves $15.00, sheets $7.50. Institutional Sanitation Service, 434 Dump Dr., Southslum.

ELDERLY JEWISH MAN free to good home. Knows charming stories, good with children, can do light work, eats small meals, receives tailor's pension and Social Security. 433-7609

MATTRESSES. 30 used mattresses, for good cause. $3.50 ea. Little Angel of Mercy Mission. 90 Riverwine, Southslum.

GIANT PICCOLO SALE now in progress at Music Mart. Corngate Shopping Center. Save up to 50% on name brand piccolo. Hundreds in stock.

PRISON ADDRESSES. Complete collections of names and home addresses of men currently serving time in prison, $95.00 331-6059

POLICE UNIFORM. Like new Dacron police uniform. Also service revolver and cuffs. $230. Call 544-7960

SNOW. Fresh, white clean, uncirculated. $4.50 lb. 332-8079.

ANTIQUES

Old Chair. Whatever. 255-0905

AUTOMOBILES

69 CHEV Impala 2-dr Hdtp, auto, a/c, ww. white/bl. top. Sacrifice - owner kidnapped, family needs ransom $. Best offer before midnite tonite sharp takes. Call 765-4567.

67 BUICK ELECTRA wagon, beige ext, bl int., AM/FM stereo, a/c, luggage rack, ww, V8, all power, 32,000 careful mi. exec's 2nd car, not needed as family perished in Beverly Hills Supper Club fire. Call Forrest Lawn Hospital Ext 432. 566-8345. Eves.

SE VENDE - Habla Espanol? B'no autobus. H'mlpg qulcbnma 427 mfg'ya Ford can rcbs y ldrms esta muy b'n. Qrmos mcho bnta fntsco grnde clnte. Cherrysimo. 2+2 y 4 en la rchta. Esteban Angeles telefono: 656-9670

72 LINCOLN Continental Mk V Sedan, blk ext & int,, all pwr access., ww, a/c, leather upholst., 45,000 chauffeur-driven mi. Runs good but trunk won't open. Reason for selling, leaving state. Call Acme Vending Machine Co. 245-3667 after 3 a.m., let ring 3 times, ask for Rocco or Vito.

65 MERCEDES-BENZ 230S Sdn, grey ext., red int., 6-cyl, 4-spd manual, 65,000 mi., fanatically maintained. Owner relocating in S. America. Call 643-2333.

BUSINESS OPPORTUNITIES

GROW INDUSTRIAL PISTACHIO NUTS Send $3 to NUTS. P.O. box 405 Cleveland Ohio for info.

HOW TO MAKE A DOLLAR - Send $1 to Box 34 Dacron, Ohio.

HAVE WE GOT AN OPPORTUUUNITEE 4U Own your own pathology laboratory. We send u all the dope, teach u all the ropes. It's a cinch to be a pathology lab owner. Profits-Profits-and-more-Profits can be yours for being on the ball rite now Call FAS-PATH LABS 255-0908

EDUCATIONAL

NOW REGISTERING Adult Education Course in Blacklish (the Afro-American English language). Dacron Elementary and Junior College. Campus at Rt. 404 and Three-Corner Rd. Call 272-4610.

"WOMEN'S LIBERATION" Living proof that Jewish women want to mate with dogs to make more niggers? LEARN ABOUT NATIONAL SOCIALISM IN THE SAFETY OF YOUR OWN HOME Writer to the National Socialist Party of America and Dacron. 3100 E Grant Dacron, Ohio.

EMPLOYMENT

Help Wanted

ARMY MEN-3,443,540 positions open. U.S. Army Opportunities 223-4000

APPLE SORTER Full-time position, good wages sorting apples. Work in your home. 333-4242. United Apple and Peach.

BATON AND DRUM INSTRUCTOR Wnt. man or wmn. to tch btn and drm inst to cripld chldrn nghts, wknds. Mrs. Brn. 722-9658.

BARMAID - woman, attractive, lrg. breasts, dependable. Angelos Spaghetti-Ville 434-6509.

BANK PRESIDENT - Good salary, benefits, apply in person FIRST OHIO FEDERAL SAVINGS AND GUARANTY AND BANK

CARPET SALESMAN - If you can think BIG and sell HUGE you can make ENORMOUS wages at CARPET UNIVERSE. Call BIG BUFF BARKNIAN 434-5600

CHILDREN - pay top dollar, two weeks per year, all expenses paid, benefits, no qualifications, boys or girls. Contact R. BOX 332, Atlanta Georgia

CONSTRUCTION WORKERS WANTED
DUMP SLABBER
TWIST BEATER
NIPPLE WACKER
GROUT BLOWER
MONGER
IRON DRAPER
LUMMOX OPERATOR
FRAG SETTER
CUPPERS
GLUTTERS
GRAPPLERS
CALL 347-6691
FOR INTERVIEW
AMERICAN UNITED PLACEMENT INTERNATIONAL

CONSTRUCTION - I'm building a mirror universe in another Dimension. Need carpenters, sheet metal workers, electricians, plumbers, framers, astrophysicists & people who grow real good dope. Must be willing to really get into it. X-pedition leaves Mar. 1. Contact: Groovey Straub. 268-8808, after school.

COMPANION for elderly woman, must enjoy physical and verbal abuse, cats, birds and TV. Wges paid 221-3323

COOK - Grill, broil, sandwich. Must be clean, free from sores, lice, disease, no long hair, nails. Dirty Mac's 332-5409

NATUROPATHIC CUT-MAN Modern, health-conscious boxer has immediate opening for top-flite cornerman skilled in all forms natural healing. Herbal styptic, kinetic stitching techniques a must. Write: Cleveland "Kid Kelp" DeFrance, Box 52, Dacron. Ohio.

TIRE DENTISTS
Experience Necessary
DENTA-TRED INC.
Apply in Person. 355 Polk St. Suite 408

DISH WASHER
BUS HELP

We're looking for a few good men who are interested in a career in restaurant sanitation engineering. We will train you. Good wages, benefits, vacation, meals. We speak Spanish and Black. Danny's All Night, Melville & 8th.

Nuclear Waste Disposal
HI PAY
LO DEATH RATE
Apply in Person
S.C.O.C.G.E.T. & T.
Suite 220, Coal Building
Monroe and Cooper

AUTO SEAT SALES - looking for experienced well-groomed man experienced in door-to-door auto seat sales to work in local area. Good wages. Work your own hours. Be own boss. Fee paid. 221-5454.

DONUT POLISHER 10 P.M. - 6 A.M. Apply in person Jelli's Donut Shoppe.

DRIVERS. - Wanted 18 yrs. or older to drive here and there and all over, up and down, in and out, and way out there and right back here for local firm. Must Have License. 443-5454

EVANGELIST CABLE TV TECHNICIAN - Experienced, salary open. Resume to Box 7211, Dacron.

EXECUTIVES - needed to add class and help with clean-up. House of Chili. 442-4345.

FAT PEOPLE to model line of shoes for catalogue photos. Pigs Feet Shoe Co., Box 32234, Cleveland.

FEMALE WANTED - Female of Species from earth wanted for experiments. Will pay many Xzlotoids to female of species from earth. Apply by waiting near large hole at streets of Truman and Bycrus.

FRONT DESK HELP - experienced front desk person to work at front desk. Will train willing back room person. $120 wk.

GENERAL OFFICE - general office work, general filing, typing, taking dictation, and phones. Generally easy. Good Wages. General Office Equipment Co 332-5451

GENERAL - experienced U.S. Army General for light housework, sewing and cooking 242-4421.

HAULERS General hauling, some dumping, occasional tossing 966-9904

HOMEMAKERS to make 30-40 homes in Dacron area United Homes Inc. 444-8895.

HOG INSEMINATORS - prestige job. Easy work impregnating champion hogs. Benefits, good wages. 334-5546.

INK SALESMAN - reliable man wanted to sell name-brand ink, all colors 883-2231

IDIOT non-professional non--union idiots wanted for local theatre production. Call Player's Playhouse, 323-2214.

SELL QUAALUDE INSURANCE IN YOUR SPARE TIME - Dynamic, growing co. is looking for pt. time agents in Dacron area to write the hottest new coverage in town. Protects policyholders from losses occurring from rug burn, stairs, silverware, and cars. Oppty+ 688-4119.

JANITOR - light maintenance, good hours, good pay, very little vomit to clean up, for hard-working Polish man. Mr. Trumble. 443-0095

JIG BORE/JIG GRINDER OPERATOR - Must be good with all types of jigs. Must have 5 years exp. boring and grinding jigs JigCo 223-3221.

KIDNEY MACHINE REPAIRMAN - Good pay for man with interest in kidneys. No exp. nec., will train. Dacron Kidney Co. 332-4543

LABORERS - Must have H.S. diploma, references, polygraph and psycho tests $12 per day. 665-6523

LIFT TRUCK OPERATOR - Were looking for a college man who wants to start at the very bottom of firm that isn't growing at all. Must be willing to work hard for low wages. 232-4413.

LATINOS - Latino males with dance training needed for elderly ladies' ballroom dance class. 332-5456

Wanted: Guided Missile and Atomic Bomb Mechanic. Call: Bob McKeronski, 1420 E. Coolidge, 676-4312.

MUNG SLINGER - 5 yrs. exp. slinging mung a must. 225 per week. United Mung. 443-5540.

POODLE FRIDAY

Sml. est. pack wild dogs need brite poodle friday for errands, minor denkeeping. Good barking (60 bpm), nice appearance nec'y. Arfitunity + Paving Park Area.

PRINZE LIFE & CASUALTY OF HOLLYWOOD Send confidential resume to: MG-300

HOW BAD DO YOU WANT A JOB GALS? New in town? Divorced and broke? Put that "thng" of yours to work on some of the stiffest, most tume cent johnsons ever. We want to fck your eyes out, secys. So get over here. MIIDDLE STATES BOLT, NUT & FASTENER. BOX-F. Dacron.

SECRETARY TELEPHONE OPERATOR/CLERK/TYPIST/RECEPTIONIST/NURSE - large local firm seeks woman with complete office skills $38O per month.

VAN HUSEN MFG.
TRailer-5-5555

ATTN YOUNG GALS We're fcking secys and doing it like there's no tomorrow. Interest'd in boffing our front-line execs 'till you're catatonic? Then get the fck over here & apply. MIDDLE STATES BOLT, NUT & FASTENER BOX-F, Dacron

UNREGISTERED NURSE wanted for person who's not sick. Call: 561-6271 after 5 p.m.

Pets

MEXICAN HAIRLESS SHEPHERD PUPS. Cross between German Shepherd and Mexican Hairless. Small body, large ears and teeth, long tail, hairy legs, smooth body. Gentle but mean. Good for guarding your lap. 12 weeks old. $35. 223-7986.

SCOTTISH TERRIER PUP. AKC registered. 7 yrs old. $45 564-7968

Burmese Cat, two yrs. old, beautiful, semi-neutered 333-9878

FREE DOG PUPPIES. cute 100% dog puppies to good home. 332-6869

FREE RESEARCH MONKEYS. 50 Rhesus monkeys used in medical research. One per family. Suffer from cancer and have metal plates in head, but otherwise healthy and lovable. Discount Pharmaceutical. 5655959

GUPPIES FOR SALE. Must sell 50,000 guppies. 5¢ each 3 for 25¢. Midwest Guppie Distributors, 332-5647

MUST GIVE AWAY OR WILL DROWN. 12 kittens must go either to your home or to heaven. 332-7960

ST. BERNARD STUD SERVICE: Champion St. Bernard available for stud. $25 per 1/2 hr. Semen. $58 per pint.

BEAGLE FOR FREE. Must get rid of family dog. Attacks children, killed family cat and passes gas. To a good home. 272-7548

AFRICAN WABUUDO DOGS. Very rare dog from Somalia. Does not bark, shed or run. Screams instead of barks. Eats only flies and horse dung. Only 12 in entire country. Wabuudo Kennel, 232 Polk St., 212-6050.

RABBITS FOR SALE. Cute cuddly rabbits. $2.50 per dozen. Good for children or dinner.

MUST SELL TRAINED CROW: Brilliant trained crow has requested larger home with two stories. I can't deliver, perhaps you can. Speaks two languages, can answer phone and crack nuts $30. 272-3131.

RUBBER SNAKES. Ideal pet for shut-ins. $15. 272-5069.

ARABIAN HORSE Exc. cond., low miles, light eater. $330. 272-6079.

GREAT DANE. Big, clean, gentle well-trained, likes to please. Like having a man around the house. Perfect for mature single woman. $79. 272-4443.

DOG FOOD: Special blend of meat and bone meal. $23 per pound. Dacron Dog and Cat Pound.

DOBERMAN: Vietnam vet. Lethal bite. Strictly a one-man dog. Will not respond to commands of new owner. $120.

Services

BOB's LICKETY-SPLIT PRINT SHOP 1556 Harding. Bob Roberts Prop. "Well print anything and we mean ANYTHING!"

SEPTIC TANK PUMPING I will pump your septic tank completely full. No tank too big. Jim Dandy. 767-8979.

Professional Magician: Have been on Gong Show. Children's parties. entertaining, clubs and business meetings Low fees Call Magic Pete at 324-8979

OFF-DUTY POLICEMAN: Dacron police officer will provide child discipline for reasonable fees. Call Bert 234-5678.

BED WETTERS, NAIL-BITERS, EAR/NOSE PICKERS, BITERS, KICKERS, ILL-TEMPERED Children and Adults cured. Call Russ. 332-7960.

DEWORMER will Deworm your children or pets Call Mrs. Rhodes 435-9709.

PHYSICAL THERAPY: Attractive single girl therapist works out of her home. Evenings. Specializes in male problems. Low fees. Call Rhonda 232-8880.

MALE ESCORT Will accompany single women evenings to and from social occasions, work, appointments. Or will entertain at home R.B.M. P.O Box 33.

BABYSITTING: I will take care of children your home for very low cost. Maria c/o Work Release Program. Director of Rehabilitation. Silage County Women's Correctional Facility.

EXECUTIVE DISCIPLINE: To be a more effective executive you need professional discipline training. You will be taught to work harder, play harder and get more out of life. It's painful but worthwhile. Equipment supplied. Lisa 545-7698.

COUNSELING SERVICES

PREGNANT?
Come In & Visit Our Clean, Spacious Offices and Abort Your Baby. Se Habla Espanol.

Welfare Accepted Bank Cards Welcome

"Helping Women Be Who They Are"
Concern, Inc., 243 Harding St.

KILL YOUR BABY AND GO TO HELL Spend Eternity in Hell If You Want. Babies are people. Babies are life. GOD LOVES BABIES. GOD LOVES THE UNBORN. DAMNATION AWAITS YOU IF YOU HAVE AN ABORTION. DON'T DO IT! 272-9911
Jesus Loves Babies Association

END EMBARRASSING GAS SEIZURES A No-Baloney Cure for Excessive Gas CALL 272-4424. DON'T WAIT FOR A FRIEND TO GIVE YOU THIS NUMBER!

WANTED TO BUY

HUMAN BABIES Successful manufacturer of novelty throw pillows, purses, and bags will pay top $$$ for your extra babies. Act now. Box d-14.

DEE & PEE AUTO RE-PAINT & PAIR Cash for your car or anybody else's. 661-3140. 75 East Coolidge.

I WANT YOUR LAWN—I will pay you more than what you could get for it anywhere else. Cash on the spot. Arrange to show me your lawn by calling me at 223-8907.

WANT TO TRADE

Oak desk, wall unit, shelves, oak storage cabinets for a drawer. Call Jim 565-5959.

Men's Large toupee. Like new, dark brown, husband died, for tropical fish tank. Call Doris Alport. 475-0096.

Civil War sword and hide-a-bed, like new, for blue area rug or hair dryer. Call Bud and Betty Alright. 342-0798.

Wheelchair, crutches, walker and leg brace for 10-speed bike. Call Don Aldunne, 576-9877.

Complete chain saw, ever-sharp carbide-tip blade for rides to and from market and church. Call Red Bean, 342-8097.

3/4 hp bench grinder (no face shield) and Norelco elc. shaver for Braille typewriter. Call Howard Wurst, 454-9870.

Wife who can cook for wife who can dance, one day per week. Call Les Moore, 435-9721.

Will trade my laundry for your laundry. S. Lefky, 342-5748.

Will trade attic fan for large living room painted in blue. Call Gloria Davis, 463-7999.

PERSONALS

Thank you Jesus Christ for helping me win the Publisher's Clearing House. Bless you. - DB

Come home, honey. I shaved the beard off and threw out all those magazines. I love YOU. - Butterball

Repent! Cleanse your soul with Amway Hand Detergent. Margret Plank 786-7968.

Will the owner of the blue Buick with Ohio License plate B-7478 please go to the Corngate Center parking lot Your lights are on.

Caroline, come live with me in rose-covered trailer. - Ed

Melvin Pernik, remove your possessions from 4243 Polk St. by Feb. 13 or they will be smashed, broken, crushed, burned and thrown in the alley.

Jim, call me please please please please. - Laura

Honey Pie, I love you but I cant afford to see you anymore. Can we make some kind of deal?, - White Socks.

Jim, I can't stand it without you, call me, come see me, write me, do something, anything. -Greg

JIM, call me after nine. If you don't I will kill myself. - Pookie

Loren Blenk, call your grandmother.

Betty, look, I enjoy it. I don't know what else to say. - "The Sniffer."

You want to know what the goddamn foreman of this linotype shop can do? He can go eat fuck, snot batshit, pig assholes, sperm, piss, farts and his own cunt hair. I quit.

Karen. HAPPY VALENTINES DAY even if no boys sent you any cards. - Dad

Anyone witnessing an accident at Cooper and Madison between a green Chevy and a black women, call Irv Sheperton. Attorney at Law. There's a bottle in it for you.

If you want a good time, call my ex-wife. She'll treat you right. She's clean and its free All comers are satisfied. Call: 272-4394.

Bob, either you give me the $20 or I blow the whistle on your restaurant. Especially, the hamburgers. I'm sure the Health Department would love to find out about Fido. - Vic.

IN MEMORIAM to the 6 graduating Seniors (and their dates) from C. Estes Kefauver Class of '64, killed in a car wreck on the night of the prom. We know that you all would have been successful by now.

Prissy V. - I really am sorry about the "prowling" but I just can't help myself. Someday I'll be all right and we'll get back together again. Please believe me and happy Valentine's Day. - Bobby McA

HAPPY VALENTINE's DAY to Mary, Dotty, Susan, Cleo, and Alice from your ex-husband Bill.

Mary N., Call me before 5 a.m. this morning. I have something wonderful for you but after 5 a.m. it will be too late. - Richard

LEGAL SERVICES

DIVORCES
THIS WEEK ONLY!
$250, two for $400
(uncontested and court costs)
DAVID R. GOLDSTEIN
Attorney at Law
25 years experience
340 Taft St.
272-9932
By Appointment

PRICES THIS LOW SHOULD BE AGAINST THE LAW!
DIVORCE - $89.99
BANKRUPTCY - $129.99
REAL ESTATE - from $39.95
WILLS - $59.99
PERSONAL INJURY - NO FEE
(75% of total take in lieu of payment)
KREPSTEIN, SHEPSTEIN, WEINSTEIN, FEINSTEIN & SMITH
455 Harding St 332-6875

SUE THE *&$!"!& JERK!
Let's GO TO Court!
MEYER "THE RABBI" SAPERSTEIN
DIVORCE - INJURY - CONSUMER FRAUD - ANGER
TOP DOLLAR SETTLEMENT GUARANTEED.
Lets Get Together!
675-9978 Out-of-towners call collect.
SEE YOU IN COURT!

HOUSES TO SHARE

One bedroom house to share with clean, employed, white, Lutheran male with no pets or foul habits. $235 per month. Heat paid. Must keep house clean

RESORT COTTAGE On Lake VanHeusen. Cheap winter share. Beach, boathouse, raft, diving board, water skis and bike path.

To Place A
Classified Ad In
The Classified Ads
CALL THE
CLASSIFIED AD
HOTLINE
555-4070
and ask for "Classified Ads"

TO PLACE YOUR CLASSIFIED AD
Outside the Metropolitan Exchange Area Call
(614) 555-4070 and ask for "Classified Ads"

The Rep. Dem. Classified Ad Department located at 100 Polk St. at the back of the second floor, is open all day Monday thru Friday and closed all day Saturday and Sunday.

THE DACRON REPUBLICAN DEMOCRAT CLASSIFIED ADVERTISING RATES
and information

Weekday and Saturday mornings and double on Sunday (applicable to all residents of Ohio.

49¢ per line per day	31 days
59¢ per line per day	8 days
68¢ per line per day	5 days
80¢ per line per day	2 days
$1.00 per line per day	1 day
$1.09 per line per day	0 days

Ads must run consecutive days with no change of copy or raising the price on things just because you had a lot of calls in order to qualify for the above rates. Account due and payable three days before receipt of 1st statement so when we bill you, you are already late. $1.00 per line per day lateness surcharge. In case of typographical error, especially of an extremely embarrassing or financially disastrous nature, the Republican-Democrat, a wholly-owned subsidiary of S.C.O.C.G.E.T. & T. Communication Group. Inc., is responsible for only one incorrect insertion and this strictly to the extent that you hire several expensive lawyers and spend years suing us for the cost of the ad. Don't forget to send Ohio State sales tax to the governor if you sell anything. Minimum advertisement 40 lines.

Ads cannot be canceled or changed until after the first day's insertion, especially personal ads. If you have an especially good personal ad, we may keep running it for months, regardless of the disruption it causes in your life. The Dacron Republican-Democrat reserves the right to edit, reject, laugh at, and misspell any advertisement.

YOUTHADELIC!

By VERN SCHAUB
Rep-Dem. Teen Critic

In case you haven't heard, the newest musical sensation that has teens "flipping" is called the Disco. Discos feature the pulsating, rhythmical sound of today's chart-topping disco music, where the emphasis is on a beat to dance to. And "wow!" are teens ever dancing to it! Exciting new disco dances like the "Hustle," or the "Bump" as insiders call it, are really popular at schools and "Y" dances, as well as at Dacron's own discotheques such as "Ludes" and "Poppers," or the city's newest spot, "Irv's 'The Place'," for those teens who are over 21.

Although most of today's disco music is being recorded by black people, Dacron's own popular group, The Driveways, has captured the disco feeling in its new recording, "Suck My Homework," where the band has mixed a theme of teen confusion and hope for the future with a sophisticated instrumental background of electric guitar, drum, bass, and other electronically synthetic instruments. I talked with the members of the group backstage at "Poppers" about all the attention they have been garnering, and the boys say it's "O.K.!"

I couldn't agree more, but what does the disco scene mean in terms of today's to-tal teen philosophy? Before, when there were teen resentments against war and society and rules, we had music that sang about those feelings. However, on the contemporary wavelength, it looks like today's youth have "mellowed down" to a level of inner peace and satisfaction; thankful for the privileges they have, and content just to dance the night away in their youthful innocence.

The order of the day is, as the Beach Boys used to say: "Fun, fun, fun" — and the non-stop, "cookin' with gas" beat of the disco craze, that has teenagers as far away as England clowning it up with fake pins through their noses and the put-on horseplay in the disco halls, is just the perfect mood setter. It's disco-mania forever, and you can believe it.

Photo Courtesy WEED staff

Dacron listener-supported radio station WEED disc jockey, Ira Haden, tells. the 3 a.m. R & B audience how important their contributions are to the success of meaningful alternative media in the Dacron area. Such popular daily features as "What Did We Learn from the Viet Nam War?, 1978," "How Much Did We Learn from the Viet Nam War?, a Perspective," and "The Rock and Roll of International Arms Limitation" are only made possible through the donations of an interested public, as well as "Afro-American Firing Line," WEED's new gun auction program for Blacks.

MARCH of HITS

1. **LOVE SIEVE**
   FUCACIOUS
   Principal Records
2. **CRISCO DISCO**
   THE QUEERS
   Pacific Records
3. **FLY LIKE A STONE**
   LYNARD SKYNARD
   Atlanta Records
4. **DO IT TILL IT HURTS**
   THE PIMPS
   Motown Records
5. **LOVE ME LIKE YOU USED TO LOVE ME WHEN YOU LOVED ME, LOVE**
   FLAMEOUT
   Ringling Brothers Records
6. **FRATRICIDE**
   CHUCK BERRY COSTELLO
   DDT Records
7. **NAKED WOMEN DETECTIVES THEME**
   THE GLAD BAGS
   Epic Records
8. **DO WHAT THE SNIPER SAYS**
   THE DIGRESSIONS
   Polymer Records
9. **FAT ENOUGH TO LOVE YOU**
   BARRY WHITE
   Darktown Records
10. **SUCK MY HOMEWORK**
   THE DRIVEWAYS
   Mel's Record-Your-Voice Records

The MARCH OF HITS Top 10 List is compiled from sales figures at Dacron record and music stores everywhere.

TOP 10 Country & Western HITS

1. **MY HEART HAS THE FLU**
   PATSY LOU FLETCHER
   Stumptime Records
2. **DON'T SHAKE MY APPLES IF YOU DON'T WANT MY TREE**
   MEX PEARSON
   Acne Records
3. **YOU'RE A REAL GONE GAL (AND I'M GLAD YOU WENT)**
   THE CAROLING COWBOYS
   Okie Records
4. **SIX-PACK OF LOVING FOR YOU**
   THE FILLING STATION BANDIT BAND
   Cornkissed Records
5. **OLD ENOUGH TO BLEED, OLD ENOUGH TO BUTCHER**
   GEORGETTE GEORGIA
   Yokel Records
6. **DON'T NEED MARIJUANA TO MAKE ME CRAZY ('CAUSE I'M SMOKING WHEN I LOOK AT YOU)**
   BIG DITCH PRESTON
   Hayseed Records
7. **LOVE ON TAP, BLUES IN A BOTTLE**
   CONALRAD HILTON
   Stockyard Records
8. **PA'S GOT CANCER, MA'S GONE BLIND AND ME—I'M JUST PLAIN MISSING YOU**
   SKEETER JUGGS
   Fillemup Records
9. _____
10. _____

TOP 10 Country and Western Hits List is compiled from sales figures at Lee's Ohio-Billy Records Store, 2770 Cindertown Highway in East Dacron.

Toots Arnold's TV Mail Pouch

By TOOTS ARNOLD
Rep.-Dem. Television Reviewer

Q. I have heard that the fella who plays Ripp on Quarrel is leaving the show because of big movie offers. Is this true? Jim Drimble, Dacron.

A. We didn't hear that. What kind of movie offer? Is he going to finish out the season or what?

Q. I made a bet with my girlfriend that Murk Dubbleston on Grogan's Hose used to date Don Derby on Indiana 4-0-4. If I win, I get something real far-out. Bernie Tarpins, Dacron.

A. We don't remember Don Derby although we remember Indiana 4-0-4. Was he the real tall blond guy with the motorcycle? Or was that Clint Busby?

Q. Has there ever been a television program about a fella who did terrible embarrassing things to women and who wanted to stop but couldn't? Bob, Dacron Estates.

A. There was a program called McGurfs Joint and in that show there was a character who liked to slap his wife's hat with a fish. Is that the show?

Q. Are Lee Majors and Farrah Fawcett-Majors related? Sue Weilson, Dacronview Hills.

A. To whom?

Q. I am in love with Donna Durr on Money Farm. Is she married? I have to know. Phil, Dacron Glens.

A. She's not only married, Phil, she's dead. Donna was killed in a car accident three weeks ago.

Q. How come the Mr. Whipple Show is so darned short? I just love it, but by the time I get comfortable, it's over. Also how come it's not on a regular time? Mae Jenks, East Dacron.

A. We love Mr. Whipple, as does just about everybody, but unfortunately that's not a show, it's a commercial. Maybe, if enough people wrote the networks, they might make it a show.

Stuntman Don Starling in make-up.

Q. Who plays Lassie on The New Lassie Show? Is it still Lassie or someone else? Ted Blisco, Dacron Hills.

A. Lassie is played by the stunt man Don Starling.

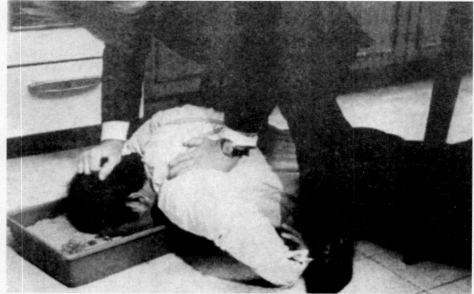

Ripp (Todd LaCrosse) and Jeff (Geofry Fenton) scuffle on QUARREL. Channel 4 at 8 PM.

Eustus Donald, member of Trout People's Council of Elders

Wednesday night at 9 P.M. on Channel 2, David Brinkley narrates a special NBC documentary, "The Trout People of Chippewa Lake," which explores the beliefs and customs of a little-known Christian religious sect who inhabit a remote area of Wisconsin and believe themselves to be reborn lake trout. The documentary contains many never-before filmed scenes from daily life at Lake Chippewa, where members of the community support themselves by catching bugs in their teeth for money. Included is actual footage of a Church of Trout baptismal ceremony with a total immersion baptism lasting three days.

Radio Sidelights

MORNING

5:00 WONK—Around-the-calendar news and weather till midnight.

6:00 WOIO-AM—"You and I and Him" Rev. Mundale discusses you and God and how you can make Him like you.

7:00 WOIO-AM—"Radio Tot" Stueben the Clown and his pal Oinky entertain with noises and laughing.

8:00 WOIO-FM—Easy listening—one continuous 24-hour-long performance of a single Mantovani composition by the Hollywood Strings.

9:00 WEED—"Ad Libitum" Latin students trade unrehearsed witticisms.

11:00 WOIO-AM—"City Forum" Hereford Black hosts. Topic: 'Do we need a subway or just a couple of underpasses and a new bus?'

AFTERNOON

12:00 WEED—"Boss Party" Three hours of contemporary music as drawn from the collection of Tom Dumphrey, a local student. This Week: The hits of Question Mark and the Mysterians.

12:00 WOIO-AM—"Music From Duluth" A selection of music from the Duluth, Minnesota, area.

1:00 WOIO-AM—"Art and Grace Remember" Art and Grace Lippe talk about the past. Today: War-time rationing of automobile tires, Truman and polio.

3:00 WEED—"Ohio Poets" Jeffery St. Christopher reads the works of Appling Dirksen Generalstone including 'The Crop Duster' and 'Sponge Cakes and Brown Hats.'

3:00 WOIO-AM— "Armchair Doc" Dr. Dumont talks about bunions, corns, cysts and sore behinds.

4:00 WEED— "Our Crazy Heritage" In Vietnamese and English.

EVENING

6:00 WAKY— "Hit Attack" D.J. Blitz Kreeg hosts six hours of rock hits, teen talk and screaming.

9:00 WOIO-AM— "The Sounds of Industry" The VanHusen Trailer Company Accordion Orchestra plays Bach and The Beatles.

	AM	FM
WOIO	880	101.1
WONK	1130	
WAKY	1290	
WEED		90.7

TV Pull Out Section
TV FOR A WEEK
February 12-18, 1978

TODAY
February 12, 1978

MORNING

6:00

2 LIVING BIBLE Religious chatter with a minister or two.

6:30

2 BIBLE LIFE Talk about religion with a priest.

4 THE BIBLE AND YOUR LIFE Priests and ministers chat.

13 THE LIFE OF YOUR BIBLE Ministers discuss things with Priests.

6:45

4 TRUTH OF TRUTHS True stories about real life experiences.

7:00

2 WHEN JESUS WAS A TEENAGER - Cartoon. Savior helps a lonely widow take care of her yard.

4 DOO-DOO - Children.

13 ANSWERS ANSWERS ANSWERS Dr. Beaumont raises religious questions.

81 GUCZKFOOESTOE-PARAZIMBWA Special-interest ethnic program in Spanish, German, Japanese, Italian and Swahili.

7:30

2 MORNING AFTER MATINEE "A Gift Greater Than Money" (1969). Heather Menzies, Bill Delgrado star in a story about a blind millionaire and the woman whose love he buys and then sells for a profit.

4 BIBLE BOYS Baptist adventure series. Del Medgars guests stars as a born-again fireman who saves arson victims two ways at once.

13 THE BRAIN BOWL Local high school students compete for sports equipment in games of intelligence. Scheduled: Pendergast vs. Tucker Tech.

81 FACE THE ANIMALS Milton Perkins host. Platypus, antelope, bison, manatee and peacock are this week's panelists.

8:00

4 NAZI DEATH CAMP - Cartoon.

13 BIBLE BINGO - Inspirational Game Show.

81 SLUM SCHOOL - Children. Counting to eleventy and spelling "ain't."

8:15

13 TEMPORARY TECHNICAL DIFFICULTY There is nothing wrong with your set.

8:30

4 SOOPER DOOPER DYNA-PIGS AND THE KIDS FROM FLIPPITY HONK HONK - Children.

13 KICK AND PUNCH Kick and Punch try to build a house but wind up in the hospital when the house falls on them.

9:00

2 HIS MASTER'S MOUTH - Religion. Cardinal Terrance Cooke talks about sitting right there in a TV studio and speaking to America live (taped).

4 MASS FOR SHUT-UPS Father Angelo Umbert conducts the Mass in sign language accompanied by the Youngstown Deaf Boys Choir.

13 CAPT. STUPID - Children.

81 WORLD OF WORMS Educational

9:30

2 GOD DAMN IT - Religion.

4 BOWERY BOYS They detonate a nuclear device.

13 CHILDREN'S WEATHER

81 KUKLA, FRAN AND JOHN KENNETH GALBRAITH Principles of Keynsian economics portrayed with hand puppets.

10:00

2 WACK! - Children.

4 DEEP THOUGHT - Religion. This Week: An allegorical comedy about five people who must either confront reality or sit in a ditch all afternoon.

13 FACE THE FLOOR

81 TREASURES OF IRELAND - Documentary. Special: A look at exhibits from a collection currently touring the U.S. The artifacts, which date back to the 11th Cent., include a lump of dirt, several large stones and a mummified potato (60 Mins.).

10:30

2 ARE YOU NUTS? Teen daredevils perform feats of bravery. Jodie Foster joins the gang in climbing into discarded freezers, jumping down chimneys and provoking mean dogs.

4 THE ROCK HOUNDS - Cartoon. The Hounds' record goes to number one, but Boozer gets fleas and Mitzi has to spend the night chained out in the yard.

13 BLUBBERBUTT - Cartoon.

11:00

2 HOW'S YOUR LIFE? Peter Ustinov talks about his career as a big fat person.

4 POND SCUM - Cartoon.

13 WHILE YOU'RE IN CHURCH - A prominent rabbi tells why it's all right for them to play golf on Sundays.

81 KLASSICS FOR KIDZ - King Lear. Lear regains his sanity only to find out that his car has been stolen.

11:30

2 THE SUPER HEROES PUPPY GHOST AND

MUSIC COMEDY DRAMA CARTOON BLAST-OFF - A haunted house is the scene of Fungo's birthday party but the Fang intends to crash it ... with a hydrogen bomb.

4 MOVIE SHOWCASE "Two-Party Doll" (1967). Washington is in an uproar after an angry scientist turns the President into a cocktail waitress. Fleece DuBois, Necker Goodlook. Angela Brackket.

13 WHAT'S GOING ON? Chase Manhattan Bank President David Rockefeller is interviewed by a panel of 12 college students drunk on beer.

81 CARTOONS FOR THE BLIND Dr. Phyllis Hough reads cartoons scripts while her husband Ted supplies the sound effects.

AFTERNOON

12:00

2 ISSUES AND EVASIONS

13 DATELINE: YOUR HOUSE Very local news.

81 PATTY PLANT'S PLACE Popular journalist interviews coal miners with black nose disease.

12:30

2 COLLEGE HOCKEY TODAY Coach Leon Poole of the Columbus College of Data Processing talks about his teams upcoming Very Small Ten League meet with Dacron Elementary and Junior College.

13 SUB-CANADIAN LEAGUE '78 Skaters' Coach Cyril Plaid discusses coming game with Niagara Falls Guys.

81 CLIFF'S THEATRE NOTES: Brief theatrical summation of "A Farewell to Arms" by Ernest Hemingway. With study questions.

1:00

2 THE LAST BOWL OF ALL Injured players from eight NFL teams take on the Harlem Globetrotters in the Astrodome.

4 WORLD SERIES Yankees meet the Dodgers in the second game of the World Series at Yankee Stadium. (Rerun).

13 SUB-CANADIAN LEAGUE '77 Skaters' Coach Cyril Plaid discusses last year's game with the Niagara Falls Guys.

81 FIRING LINE The conclusion of a debate on welfare reform between host William F. Buckley and a 4 lb. 3 oz. small mouth bass.

1.30

81 PROS AND POLS - Sports. Konrad Dobler of the St. Louis Cardinals vs. William Eastland of the U.S. Senate in benchpress competition; pending trade regulation spot quiz; pass, kick and punt contest, and tax shelter debate.

2:00

81 MULATTO CHEF -

Cooking. Today's Meal: Hog Jowls Marsala with corn bread and artichoke hearts.

2:30

13 RAP IT UP Teen sportscasters discuss the week in Dacron High School fights after basketball games.

81 SNIVELING LIBERALS

3:00

4 THIRTY-MINUTE MATINEE "One Is Plenty" (1970). Made for radio movie.

13 EMERGENCY ACCOUNTANTS Drama.

81 RICH MAN, DIRTY GIRL Part XII (Rerun).

3:30

2 MIDST OF THE TAME Close-up look at cows. This large herbivore is seen in its natural habitat, the barn (60 Min.).

4 MANS WORLD Bruce Jenner and Don Meredith shave, do yard work and fix autos.

13 HIGH SCHOOL BASKETBALL TODAY Silage Rural Farmers vs. St. Vitus Penguins.

81 CONTACT CHESS Semi-Finals from Spain: U.S. vs. Italy.

3:45

81 SPPPEEEECHCHCH TTTTTTTTTTTODAY Speech problems and their treatment with Dr. Evan Reynolds.

4:00

13 ACCENT ON ADVENTURE Flyfishing for bottle-nose whales.

81 HAMMERS AND NAILS Home handyman Mike Burrows tells how to dispose of household nuclear wastes and answers questions about open hearth blast furnace repair in your basement.

4:30

2 POPE! - Comedy. (Rerun).

4 MOVIE - Adventure. "Attack of the Giant Kitten People" (1961). Enormous kittens terrorize a Japanese train layout (90 Min.).

81 POPCORN CINEMA - Movie. "Calling All Nuts" (1973). Five lunatics pass the police exam and are assigned to a SWAT team. Richard Shark. Courtland Bourgand. Brace Tightpants, Hat Feeny (90 Min.).

81 ALISTAIR COOKE'S POCKETS (Rerun).

5:00

2 RERUN NEWS News broadcast from last month.

EVENING

6:00

2 NEWS

4 NEWS Channel 4 "On the Air News Team"

13 NEWS - Lunch/Doberman.

81 SLOW NEWS News for the hard-of-thinking.

6:30

4 CBS NEWS

13 ABC NEWS - Comedy.

81 DULL NEWS News for people with heart conditions or problems with their nerves.

7:00

2 DISNEY Original Mouskateers are the special guests. They

discuss their embarrassing failures in later life (60 Min.).

4 60 SECONDS New fast-paced, magazine-format news and information program.

13 WORLD WAR SEVEN - Documentary. Israel invades New Guinea. Brazilian Marines land in Greenland (60 Min.).

81 MABINOGIAN - Drama. Part XLVIII of the BBC's dramatization of the famous Welsh myth cycle. In this episode, Gwetlyngnndyltmynne and Mllrynnddnnme symbolize fertility in the ancient Celtic cattle worship ceremonies. Gwetlyngnndyltmynne - Sally Struthers; Mllrynnddnnme - Richard Chamberlain.

7:01

4 THE B.O. GERTZ SHOW B.O. and Miss Columbus look at Triple-D League baseball pre-spring training. How are the Columbus BlueNoses going to do? And what about those Dacron Tar-Legs and Toledo Mud-Hens? Miss Columbus wants to know.

7:30

4 QUEMOY, THE FUSE ON A BOMB UNDER WORLD PEACE - NBC Special Documentary. (Rerun).

81 INDOOR TENNIS Six local Jewish women play tennis for half an hour, indoors.

8:00

2 C*R*U*T*C*H* The C*R*U*T*C*H* team stops an epidemic of the 24-hour bug. Johnny Semple, Sue Backer (60 Min.).

4 QUARREL - Comedy. Rip accuses Beth of getting fat. Beth argues with Jeff over his religion, Lester chews out Uncle Don.

13 BELLY-UP The Pollution-Fighters save a buffalo who has eaten a whole box of red dye No. 2. Warren Oates, Shawn Dobbick.

81 SHUT-IN NEWS News for folks who don't get out much.

8:30

4 HAW HAW HAW Gospel artist Bobbi Lee Collins sings songs about Jesus and makes fun of colored people.

81 VICTORY AT HOME - Documentary. Part 6. Andy and Linda battle to save the airing deck while Bill enters the war on the side of the upstairs maid (60 Min.). B&W.

9:00

2 BOMB SQUAD - Drama. Rod and Lola defuse a bomb in a massage parlor. Lola is raped and Rod has to explain homosexuality to a child. Julie Trench, Matt Hummer (60 Min.).

4 SPIN-OFF All of Norman Lear's high school classmates who are still living get prime-time television comedy shows of their own.

13 BEST SELLERS FOR TV - Movie. Two-hour

dramatization of Dr. Benjamin Spock's classic "Baby and Child Care." Henry McCoon, Tyro Espafadio, Lee Benz.

9:30

4 PHYSICS PHENOMENA: EXPLORING THE KNOWN - Special. Physical power used to bend metal and move objects is among the physics phenomena explored by host Clint Eastwood.

81 THE SALVATION ARMY AT WAR - Documentary. Newsreel footage of Salvation Army Battles. Episode 7: The UNICEF Challenge.

10:00

2 CROSSING GUARD - Drama. Officer Friendly faces danger when he has to cross the child of a famous gangster. Bennet Burke, Vito Fabmosa (60 Min.).

10:30

2 TWO GUYS, ONE GIRL AND A DOG - Comedy. Julie has the itches but doesn't know if it's the fellows or poochie.

81 YAKKITY YAKKITY BLAH BLAH BLAH Panel discussion of local issues.

11:00

2 NEWS

4 MORE NEWS

13 STILL MORE NEWS

81 MORE NEWS YET

11:15

2 SO MUCH NEWS THAT YOU WOULDN'T BELIEVE IT

4 ALL THE NEWS IN THE WORLD

11:30

2 TORTURE CINEMA - Movie. "Eat My Guts You Devil B'at'rd' (1965). Two men go berserk in a hospital with machine guns, killing everyone but a woman who is carrying Satan's baby. Suko Tumaki, Iko Noki, Priscilla Price.

4 HATRED THEATRE - Movie. "Slaughter the Toddlers" (1970). Woman sells her children to a band of maniacs for money to buy nail polish. When she changes her mind, there's trouble. Sczchz Trcfmzck, Lrfkch Frzcdk.

13 PAIN CLASSICS - Movie. "The Nun Puked Blood" (1975). A gang of killers mutilate nuns and wear their clothes. Yetti Cornin, Erin Burtle, Hose Dinkmeier.

81 BEEP! BEEP! SENORITA - Spanish. Comedy. A lot of Mexicans shout and laugh and eat and go to church.

12:00

81 MASS FOR DRUNKS

1:00

2 ZIPPER TALK - Adult. Mature topics are discussed.

1:15

4 SERMONETTE

1:25

13 SERMONERRA

1:30

2 SERMONELLA

FRIDAY
February 17, 1978

MORNING

6:00

4 BARN YARD LANGUAGE

6:30

2 LAMP ONTO MY BRAINS - Religion.

4 BLACKTALK Franklin D. Truman discusses combing your hair into narrow rows and tying hundreds of tiny knots in it.

7:00

2 FASHIONS FOR CHRIST - Religion. Rev. Irving A. Smith talks about dressing good on Sunday.

Buck Mackenzie (Pierre Defoe) tries to get a threesome going with his wife and a mop-wielding 15th Century Cavalier on LOVE CANADIAN STYLE. Channel 13 at 10:30 PM.

4 MORE BLACKTALK Franklin D. Truman spends more time discussing things that are important to black people.

13 BIBLE COOKERY With Mrs. Monson. Today: Leviticus Casserole.

81 GUITAR TALK Faun Rosenberg instructs on the folk guitar. Today we select a good guitar case. (60 Min.)

7:30

2 GET OUT OF BED AMERICA - News. News features and what time it is. Host Bill Beadle.

4 WHO SLICED THE CHEESE? - Children.

13 BOOBIES - Cartoon.

8:00

4 FRIENDLY NEIGHBOR Tom borrows a nail. (Rerun)

13 THE UGLY DUCK CLUB - Children.

81 NIGGER RAP Black public service program with Ossie Foote.

8:30

2 DIRK CORVETTE - Talk. Dirk interviews unknown celebrities.

4 SIBLING RIVALRY - Game. People compete for their parents attention.

81 VIRGIL WITH VITTLES Classic cookery instruction in Latin by Dewey Fingerhuth.

9:00

2 EMBARRASS YOUR WIFE - Game. Contestants tell terrible personal things about their wives to get their dander up. With Buck Williams.

4 THE POOR HOUSE - Game. People are given one last chance to clear up their debts. Bill Cullen hosts.

13 UP LATE TO WORK MATINEE - Movie. "Are We Dead Yet?" (1964) Exciting thriller about three people who come back from the living. Albert Ray, Duff Skelter.

81 SUNRISE CINEMATOGRAPHY SCHOOL Francis the Talking Mule Retrospective. "Francis in the WACS" (1952) Donald O'Connor, Piper Laurie. Francis the Talking Mule joins the Women's Army.

9:30

2 $50,000 THEFT - Game.

4 SNEAK ATTACK! - Game.

10:00

2 DARK IS THE NIGHT - Serial.

4 CHEAT YOUR PARENTS - Game.

10:15

13 WHIP IT OUT - Game.

10:30

4 EDGE OF THE BED - Serial.

4 WHO'S TALLER? - Game.

13 THE $40,000 PILE OF MONEY - Game.

81 MOVIE "Francis in the WAVES" (1953) Donald O'Connor. Francis the Talking Mule joins the Women's Navy.

11:00

2 CELEBRITY HOUSEWIFE Ann Southern cleans behind the stove and Florence Henderson scours a lasagne pan.

4 LINDA'S TV TEA PARTY Linda Blossom welcomes Lucille Ball, Elizabeth Montgomery, Elinor Donahue and Sheldon Leonard to her tea party, but everyone's busy except Elinor.

11:30

2 SEARCH FOR A HOSPITAL - Serial.

4 GENERAL DISTRESS - Serial.

13 ALL MY PROBLEMS - Serial.

AFTERNOON

12:00

2 WORLD OF WOE - Serial.

4 ALL OUR GRIEF - Serial.

13 AFTERNOONS OF OUR DAYS - Serial.

81 MOVIE "Francis Joins the D.A.R." (1954) Donald O'Connor. Francis the Talking Mule finds out that his great-great-grandmother was eaten at Valley Forge.

12:30

2 THE GATHERING BUMMER - Serial.

4 WHAT GIRL? Mary recognizes her mother in an old magazine ... a girlie magazine. Denise Poole stars.

13 THE FILTHY AND THE RICH - Serial.

1:00

2 DROP DEAD - Game. Celebrities threaten regular people until they "drop dead." Bob Cumbles hosts.

4 WHO CARES? - Game.

13 THE OLD MARRIED PEOPLE'S GAME - Game.

1:30

2 YOUNG AND PREGNANT - Serial.

4 WHY ME? New game show features cancer victims versus Hollywood stars.

13 D.O.A. - Cartoon.

81 MOVIE "Francis Frees Seoul" (1955) Francis the Talking Mule fights in the Korean War.

2:00

2 BOWLING FOR DONUTS - Game.

4 ARCHY'S AUSWITZ - Comedy. (Rerun)

13 PUBLIC INFORMER Col. Tom T. Pockets Jr. of the National Free Rifle Party Hosts.

2:30

2 LITTLE HOUSE IN THE DITCH - Drama. Everyone goes blind and bleeds out the ears. (Rerun)

4 TIMEWASTERS THEATRE - Movie. "Hercules Unzipped" (1963) Steve Reeves, Paul Lynde.

3:00

13 DEATH WISH - Cartoon.

81 MOVIE "Francis Founds the Franciscan Order" (1958) Popular talking mule becomes a saint.

3:30

2 LET'S PUT IT IN OUR MOUTH! - Children.

4 THOSE BAILEY KIDS - Comedy. 14-year-old Suzi wears halter top and gives male viewers blood pressure problems.

4:00

2 NAME THAT FOOL - Game.

13 THE LICKING AND SUCKING GAME.

Starship Doorprize grows hair all over it. Kink: William Slop, Spiggot: Laurence Bellbouy (60 Min.)

13 THE PUS-SUCKING BRAIN WORMS - Cartoon.

4:30

2 MIKE WALLNUT Joining Mike are Jill Havershamp who was the first woman to contribute to a sperm bank, several postmen and a bond salesman who served as 1st Lieutenant in World War II.

4 PRO WIFFLE BALL - Sports.

81 OUR UNENDANGERED SPECIES - Educational. The sparrow (60 Min.)

5:00

2 BIG BLUE BRUISE - Children.

4 LOST PEOPLE - Drama. Capt. Palmer finds a boy but loses Nippy. Era Blackman, Earl Teems. (Rerun)

13 MISTER ROGER'S BEDROOM - Children.

5:30

2 ODD COUPLE - Comedy. They finally kiss. (Rerun)

4 HEY MEEES (SMACKING NOISES MADE WITH THE LIPS) WON TO FOOK? - Spanish.

EVENING

6:00

2 NEWS

4 NEWS

13 NEWS - Lunch/Doberman

81 NEWS FOR EGGHEADS

6:30

81 NEWS FOR DOUBLEDOMES AND FOUR-EYES

7:00

2 NBC NEWS - Chancellor/Brinkley.

4 CBS NEWS - Walter Cronkite.

13 ABC NEWS - Harry Reasoner, Barbara Walters, Bobo the Clown.

81 NEWS FOR COMMUNIST SYMPATHIZERS

7:30

2 THE 77 DAUGHTERS OF JOSH McKAY - Drama. Daughters 12 thru 19 have babies, daughter 56 gets captured by Indians and daughter 63 runs away. (60 Min.)

4 GROGAN'S HOSE - Comedy. Grogan has to spend the night with a streetwalker to convince Hamm that he's been in the service.

13 GONG SHOW - Game. Vladimir Horowitz, Michael Barishnikov, Beverly Sills and Pablo Casals perform.

81 IT'S AN ADULT'S WORLD - Children.

8:00

2 ZITS - Comedy. Zits gets sick in homeroom and cuts his hand in shop. Mr. Blogett finds Camilie a boyfriend ... Zits! Todd Flanket, Maloney Onus. Felice Trogg.

13 DONNY AND MARIE Members of the audience, cloyed to the point of insanity, rush the stage and beat Donny and Marie to death with their seatbacks. (60 Min.)

81 THIRD WORLD OF MUSIC Tanzanian National Opera Company performs "Ungo-Bungo Binga-Bangs Ugga-Bugga-Boo" (90 Min.)

8:30

2 CHICO AND THE WORMS AND BACTERIA - Comedy.

4 MY NAME JOSE JIMINEZ CBS Special pre-empts regular programming. Guest Stars Geraldo Rivera and George Hempert (voice of the Frito Bandito) join host Bill Dana for an evening of stripping cars and picking tomatoes. (90 Min.)

9:00

2 SWITCH - Crime Drama. Meredith MacRae turns out the lights. Chuck McCann shuts off the air-conditioner and Bill Bixby guides an entire freight train onto a siding. (60 Min.)

13 AN EVENING WITH FRED FISHSTONE - ABC cartoon special features prehistoric fish characters. (90 Min.)

9:30

81 FARMING THE CITY This week: A closet full of sheep.

10:00

2 THE NAKED WOMEN DETECTIVES - Crime Drama. Kari and Penni pose as nymphomaniacs in order to catch a prostitute murderer. Heather Nolan, Keena Poy.

4 STAR ROAST - Comedy. Eight stars roast the late Elvis Presley.

81 LIVE LIKE THE INDIANS "The Dog" A combination beast of burden, electric blanket and brunch.

10:30

2 LAVERNE AND SHADMOUTH - Comedy.

13 LOVE CANADIAN STYLE - Comedy.

Patty Jo and Frenchy accidentally mix up mackinaws.

11:00

2 NEWS

4 RUMORS AND NEWS

13 BAD NEWS Suko Takamura, Dent Dankford.

81 NO NEWS AT ALL.

11:30

2 TONIGHT David Brenner is stand-in for Steve Martin substituting for guest host Joey Bishop. Guests include Johnny Carson.

4 WRESTLING Slippery Dick vs. The Teat.

13 MOVIE "Our Wonderful F.B.I." (1959) How the Federal Bureau of Investigation made America completely free of all crime except an occasional case of shoplifting by teenagers on a dare. Broderick Crawford, Jack Webb.

81 HUH? Loud news.

12:00

4 DAYLIGHT ZONE - Drama. Traveling salesman (Richard Dean) runs into some perfectly explainable problems while driving through a small town.

81 OHIO THE BEAUTIFUL Dayton's elm.

1:00

2 LAST NIGHT Myrna Banks recaps the day that just passed.

4 THE NEXT DAY Host Bill Snerp talks with a two-headed bounty hunter and a myna bird once owned by Jack Ruby.

13 LAST NIGHT TODAY - Talk. What host Kurt Kutis talked about last night.

81 LACK OF FUNDING ETV Station closes down until some checks can clear the bank.

2:00

2 LAST LAUGH - Comedy. One last giggle before bed. With Jackie Gayle.

4 LAST NEWS OF THE EVENING First news of the day with Herb Bennett.

13 FUZZ AND STATIC

Contestants vie to see who can feed the most hippies to a flesh-eating perodactyl on the WHO CARES? game hosted by Red Fluven. Channel 4 at 1 PM.

SATURDAY
February 18, 1978

MORNING

6:00
- **2** SLEEP SCHOOL College Calculus lesson IV.
- **4** ILLUSIONS
- **13** THOUGHTS

6:30
- **2** FARM NEWS Today: Lottie Hutchinson, from out to Dartown, had a 9 lb. 8 oz. boy and the widow Bensons old sheepdog died.
- **4** CARTOON COMMUNION - Religion.
- **13** THE DIRTBALLS - Cartoon.
- **81** TEST PATTERNS IN ITALIAN

6:45
- **4** PASSOVER PIG - Religion.

SCREW YOU's Mrs. Dill (Denise Bush) and her daughter Toots (Kathy Persky) discover that Bump (Paul Markum) killed their priest. Channel 4 at 8:30 PM.

7:00
- **2** THE GUTTER KIDS Huntz Hall kidnaps the Lindbergh baby.
- **4** PUFFY THE SHREW - Cartoon.
- **13** FLUFF THE CARP - Cartoon.
- **81** MENAGE A TROIS - French.

7:30
- **2** UNCLE GROPE - Children.
- **4** MUDDY MOUSE - Cartoon.
- **13** STREET COLLEGE Today's Lesson: Breaking antennas off cars

8:00
- **2** FACECRUSHER - Cartoon.
- **4** LITTLE MANIACS - Children.
- **13** THE EGG SUCKERS
- **81** WHAT'S WITH THIS COUGH? Health.

8:30
- **2** BOOM! - Children. This week the Boom! kids blow up St. Patrick's Cathedral in New York.
- **4** LET'S EAT LIKE RABBITS Health.
- **13** CHILD'S PLAY - Children. The Gang plays with matches and drain cleaner.
- **81** VIDEO GARDENER Jeremy Compton Blockett plants snow begonias.

9:00
- **2** CARTOON NEWS
- **4** MOVIE "The Bug That Sucked the Earth" (1959) B&W.
- **13** MR. DODDERS' NEIGHBORHOOD Mr. Dodders gets boys to play with dolls and acts like a big silly.

9:30
- **2** OOPS! BOING! - Children. The kids talk about how being fat is okay if your parents have lots of money and you have a go-kart and a pool table.
- **4** EIGHT IS TOO MANY - Comedy.
- **81** THE DIRT Scientists prove that things live in dirt.

10:00
- **2** CAPTAIN FLEA - Children. Capt. Flea visits a hospital and watches people get shots.
- **4** OHIO SAFARI - Adventure. Bill Brucker safaris into Corn Belt country in Northwest Ohio and encounters pheasants and hogs.
- **81** EYE ON: EARS - Educational.

10:30
- **2** JIGABOO JIVE This week guest dancers are from the Columbus Boys and Girls correctional facilities. "Jive-Band" is the Burrheads who sing their current hit "Fug Yo' Face."
- **4** MADE FOR TV MOVIE PLAYHOUSE "Death Moped" (1977).
- **13** KAMIKAZI KIDS - Cartoon.
- **81** BOOK SNOOZE

11:00
- **2** LARDMOUTH - Cartoon.
- **81** LETS MAKE A MESS - Children.

11:30
- **2** CHIPPER'S OLD MAN Chipper shortens his Dad's golf clubs, paints the sofa and finds something interesting in big brother's dresser drawer.
- **13** MOVIE "Abbott and Costello Go to Hell" (1949).
- **81** JEWS! JEWS! JEWS! - Religion.

AFTERNOON

12:00
- **2** GILLIGAN'S GHETTO - Comedy (Rerun).
- **4** MANNY MOOSE CLUB - Children. Old cartoons, old movies, old jokes.
- **81** LUNCH TIME Half-hour break

12:30
- **2** NFL HOTLINE What cornerbacks gave their wives for Valentine's day.
- **81** A NEGROID LOOK AT THE NEWS

1:00
- **2** NATIONAL BASKETBALL ASSOCIATION AND HOCKEY LEAGUE ICE-BALL Scheduled: Chicago vs. Detroit.
- **4** CANADIAN BANDSTAND The Flannels do "How's Your Cold?"
- **13** THE EXPLORER'S Bob and Betty discover the basement.
- **81** LARGE BOWEL Dr. Entwhile takes phone-in questions about large bowel problems. 344-7860.

1:30
- **13** POLICE DENTIST - Drama.
- **81** POLITICAL POOP DECK

2:00
- **4** MOVIE "Disease Takes a Holiday" (1935) Fredric March, Claire Trevor.
- **13** POLACK BOWLING - Sports. Wzchzych vs Wchechzchz for the Polack Sausage Company's Gold Trophy Championship
- **81** WHAT THINGS ARE MADE OF This Week: Mud (dirt and water), Dirt (dust and filth) and Dust (tiny particles).

2:30
- **81** COMMERCIALS IN REVIEW 60 minutes of uninterrupted TV commercials with adman Dick Duffy.

3:00
- **2** THE BIGGEST JERK IN THE WORLD COMPETITION - Sports. Alex Karras, Otis Sistrunk, Arnold Schwarzenegger and Bob Lily talk loud in restaurants, push in line, smoke cigars in a hospital and try to cheat each other out of money.
- **4** YIP AND YAP Ida and Rose try to return a half-eaten coffee ring at the new grocery in town.

3:30
- **4** BEMUSED Ertha knows she's forgotten something but can't remember what (Rerun).
- **13** SMALL WORLD OF SPORTS Puff Billiards, Spit in the Ocean, Jacks, Authors, and International Slides and Ladders semi-finals. (90 Min.).
- **81** MEET THE MUCKRAKERS

4:00
- **2** SPORTS OF THE WHOLE WIDE WORLD - Sports. Kayak racing in Nevada, bullfighting in Greenland, stock car racing in Tanzania, Chinese checkers in China (90 Min.).
- **4** HOLY SMOKES! The Finkletters buy a haunted pie factory (Rerun).
- **81** THE SEWERS OF PARIS Narrated by Neville Chamberlain (60 Min.).

4:30
- **4** MISSION: UNMENTIONABLE Leader of an important free world power likes to "dress up."

5:00
- **4** STEP ON IT - Adventure. Mark speeds away from a supermarket. Dolly squeals out of a driveway and guest Alex Karras lays a patch of rubber as he flees a posh hotel.

13 THE HAT MAN - Drama. Irv is forced to make a deadly hat for a terrorist. Monte Tripoli, Donald Crossley (60 Min.).
- **81** SOMALIA The exotic land of Somalia is discussed by people who have never been there.

5:30
- **2** BURNS AND ALLEN Gracie is dead and Ronnie's career has never amounted to much, so George says the hell with it and fixes a drink.
- **81** PREJUDICE AMERICA Vance Packard and Shirley Chisolm discuss why Jews whine all the time and make so much noise when they eat.

EVENING

6:00
- **2** SPECIAL CBS DOCUMENTARY - "Zeppo - the Lost Kennedy Brother" (Preempts regular programming).
- **13** STAR TREK Four Hollywood stars retrace the route of migrating Dutch settlers with South African President Johannes Vorster. Lindsey Wagner, Paul Lynde, Soupy Sales and Connie Stevens.

6:30
- **2** ABC'S CBS NEWS
- **81** NEWS FOR PETS

7:00
- **2** MEAN KINGDOM Animals eat each other and go to the bathroom on plants.
- **4** SING ALONG WITH BUTCH Butch Bummerbecker leads band in merry renditions of "On a Bicycle Built for Two," "By the Banks of the Ohio," and "Take Me Out to the Ball Game." Guest stars: Lou Reed, Kiss.

7:30
- **2** EMERGENCY CLOWNS Rollo and Biff get an emergency call to cheer up a troubled world leader. Buddy Ebsen, Don Grady (60 Min.).

8:00
- **2** CANDID TYPEWRITER The "F" key is upside down.
- **81** AN EVENING WITH THE INDIANA STATE SYMPHONY ORCHESTRA It's their night off.

8:30
- **2** HIDE AND GO SEEK - Drama. Nick falls in love with a waitress but has to leave her when Dunnigan picks up his scent. Vess Lorry stars, Peach Davies and Hector Neggle costar.
- **4** SCREW YOU - Comedy. Bump cheats Mrs. Dill out of $5 and gets 30 days in the county prison where he kills a priest. Paul Markum, Denise Bush, Heinrick McDonald.
- **13** ROOTS! - Comedy. The Kintes try to pay for a mobile home with goats. Wayne Marshall, Donna Hellman.
- **81** YOU WEREN'T THERE The Peace of Westphalia is signed and you weren't there.

9:30
- **2** SPACE 1968 Everything is "A-OK" as Wally and the crew conduct first manned test of the Apollo command module and encounter no problems (60 Min.).
- **4** TANNER'S TAXI - Comedy. Tanner's got a hooker in his cab so he makes his move, only the big black guy isn't a hooker.
- **13** FLIT - Comedy. Troy and Brent get into a tiff with Jody over his snubbing Jason at the disco. Ricky and Buff decide to get "divorced." Tim Considine, Moochie Corcoran and Billy Mummy star.
- **81** THE FOLK MUSIC OF FISH (90 Min.)

10:00
- **4** BAD DENTIST - Drama. Dr. Tishman deliberately drills through a man's jaw and sews his cheek to his gum, Nurse Roy overcharges the welfare patients. With Bennett Ross, Nancy Dusalt (60 Min.).
- **13** SEE LONDON Richard Dawson, Jimmie Walker and Jamie Farr try to see up Sally Struthers's skirt (60 Min.).

10:30
- **2** WHERE THE HECK IS BABY SUE? - Comedy. This week, Delores leaves Baby Sue in the dry cleaners by accident, Shirley Jones guest stars.

10:45
- **2 4** FLASH NEWS BULLETIN Huge explosion in Indianapolis. Details at 11.

11:00
- **2** NEWS
- **4** NEWS
- **13** NEWS
- **81** NEWS

11:00
- **2 4 13 81** NEWS

11:15
- **2** NEWS
- **4** NEWS
- **13** NEWS
- **81** NEWS

11:30
- **2** SATURDAY NIGHT LIVE Guest host: Chevy Chase. Skits poke gentle fun at pentagon generals and the Nixon Administration. Tony Orlando and Dawn perform.
- **4** MOVIE CINEMA - Movie "Oh! Boy!" (1968). A white man and a black woman marry, divorce and get married

again to Chinese people. Paul Pringle, Harvey Baker Jr.
- **13** MOVIE FOR A MIDNIGHT - Movie "To Hell on a Bus" (1948) The story of a bus crash in Peru and the survivors who kill each other over a woman who died in the bus when it fell off the mountain. Connie Humphreys, Sheldon Plummett, Hack Branway.
- **81** MOVIE CLASSIC FOR YOUR VIEWING ENJOYMENT - Movie "At First the Tender Touch" (1960). Jean Du Fey lends a sensitive hand to the story of a stormy relationship of a woman torn between philosophies, a man who has witnessed the hell of war, and a circus clown who is crying beneath his greasepaint. A confrontation between woman and clown is performed in symbolic freeform dance with an Eno Frisch Japanese gourd score. Claude Pissoui, Simone Sucre, Paul Ovarie.

1:00
- **2** BIFF SLURPSLIME'S WEEKEND WOODSTOCK Performers: DumpTruck, Dead Idiots, the Queers. Songs include: "Don't Wave That Thing At Me" and "Throw-Up."

1:15
- **2** IT'S A DOG'S WORLD Stunt dogs are interviewed.
- **13** J. B. ROOSEVELT'S BIG CAR SALES HOME DRIVE-IN MOVIE "Destructo" (1963). A giant goldfish terrorizes the sewers of Kyoto.

1:30
- **4** EVENING SERMON Rev. E. Marshall, "Early to Bed and Early to Rise."
- **81** THE POOR SPEAK OUT Poor people beg for money.

1:45
- **81** NATIONAL ANTHEM (Spanish)

2:00
- **2** THE SIGN-OFF SHOW - Variety. Guest performers: U.S. Marine Corps Band do "Star Spangled Banner."

2:30
- **13** J. B. ROOSEVELT'S BIG CAR SALES HOME DRIVE-IN MOVIE II "Scum" (1951). Gooey substance raises havoc.

4:00
- **13** EDITORIAL REBUTTAL

4:05
- **13** MASS FOR MILKMEN

World's first outlaw golf tournament on SPORTS OF THE WHOLE WIDE WORLD. Channel 2 at 4 PM.

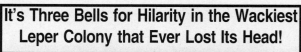

Rep.-Dem. MOVIE REVIEWS

By ELAINE HUSBERT
Rep.-Dem Movie Critic

BLAZING JEWS

A Film by Mel Brooks

Well, Mel Brooks has done it again! This time he's turned World War II upside down and injected his brand of outrageous, "go-for-the-throat" humor into one of the darkest chapters in mankind's history. Brooks plays a moneylender who, along with Marty Feldman and Gene Wilder, are rounded up in the middle of the night by mincing, effeminate storm troopers and sent to Treblinka concentration camp. Brooks and Company manage to save their lives by putting on hilarious shows for the Nazis. Finally, after everyone but Brooks, Feldman, and Wilder have been killed, the camp is liberated — by the Japs. "Better a Japanese Jew than a dead Jew," Brooks cracks at the end as he and Wilder and Feldman lounge by the pool at the Beverly Hills Hotel decked out in traditional Japanese garb as messages in Japanese are broadcast over the P.A. Mel Brooks has scored a hit and has managed to find the big laughs in a holocaust in which his own cousin was injured.

 "1/2"

Mini Reviews

Earth Wars

In a place not very far away, there is a war as good faces evil. Lots of rifles, mortars, and fistfights. A young boy, a pretty girl, and a pair of amusing walkie-talkies steal secret plans and blow up a supply dump.

Outer Space Mafia Sharks

A school of giant white sharks lands on earth and joins forces with the Mafia to terrorize California coastal regions, and there is no way to stop them.

Oh, Christ!

God comes to earth as the adopted son of a poor bemused Jewish carpenter and ends up getting nailed.

Tong Sung Street Murders

This is another Eastern-Western cop gang film from Hong Kong. It was filmed in Real-O-Rama, which is a new technique that gives you the feeling that you are actually on the screen.

A series of pain-inducing sounds and vibrations during violent scenes creates the effect that you are being wounded. You should be warned that Real-O-Rama can damage some synthetic materials.

The Polack Who Fell From a Ladder in Spain

A seething, sexy film about a Polish house painter who tries to make love to a woman whose husband was either killed in the war or isn't home from work yet (the film is unclear about this), but ends up instead giving the wainscot a second coat. The woman's child observes the incident through a keyhole, then goes outside to play with his friends.

Flu Bug!

A Russian medical research team accidentally gives the whole world the flu. Everyone feels terrible for 36 hours and then feels much, much better, but stays in bed an extra day just to be on the safe side.

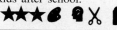

The Housewives

One of those sensitive films that makes women weep and men fall asleep. It's the story of Kerry and Doris, who enjoy being housewives, and their relationship with Vicki and Katherine, who are lawyers but would love to be housewives, except they can't stand cleaning diapers, cooking dinner, and picking up kids after school.

Rep.-Dem.
RATING GUIDE

MOVIE TOO LONG, REFRESHMENTS PLENTIFUL, REST ROOMS CLEAN

MOVIE IS DIRTY WITH EXPOSED BOSOMS, NO CARTOON

ULTRA-VIOLENT TRIPLE FEATURE FROM JAPAN

COLOR MOVIE THAT DOES NOT MAKE SENSE, OCCASIONAL GUM ON FLOOR AND SEATS

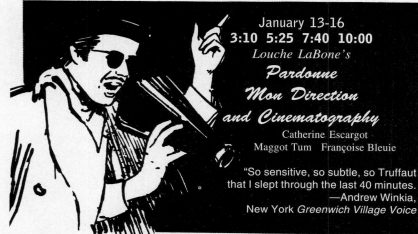

Forrest Laughan's
HOLLYWOOD DEADLINE

Seen huddled at **Irv Korn's** plush **Steer 'n' Beer** t'other eve—pulchritudinous (pardon our French!) Inger Stevens & new throb **Dan ("Ross") Blocker**, still beaming over U.S. Fat Institute's **Mister Cholesterol of the Year** award **La Stevens**, between bites of rave fave Belladonna Salad, reports inking pact for new **ABC-TV** bio of Aussie thrush **Grace Moore**. La Moore's tragic death in 1945 plane wreck sadly coincided with passing of beloved film funnyman **Rags Raglan** in Julie Gold's posh **Dregs o' the Deep** eaterie deluxe, where **Freddy ("Chico") Prinze**, just in from pistol range, confided to pals he'll take up Sufi priesthood after May 2-10 date at **Mel Swindler's** ritzy **Silver Slug** in Oo-la-Las Vegas. Sign in Palm Springs mortuary window: *"You Don't Look So Good Yourself!"* . . . Dose two De's, **Billy De Wolfe** & **Brandon De Wilde**, no longer on speaking terms . . . and **Jean ("Singin' in the Rain") Hagen** not singin' in the shower; *"Is my throat sore!"* croaks La Hagen.

Overheard at **Lou Korn's** sumptuous **Celebrity Shack**, comic **Andy Devine** to actor-singer **Jack Cassidy**: *"Say, you don't look too good yourself!"*

Among lucky guests at Italian director **Vittorio de Sica's** cocktail bash for recent earthquake victims: the Ol' Groaner himself **Bing Crosby**. Der Bingle to 87-year-old crony **Groucho Marx:** *"You don't look so good yourself!"* Quipped eaves-dropping 93-year-old Longhair **Leopold Stokowski**: *"And you don't look so good yourself!"* **Bing's** squelch: *"And you don't look so good yourself!"*

Bing Crosby

Answer to Yesterday's Puzzler: Cocoanut Grove Fire, 1941—236 Dead.

• **Der Bingle** told our spy he'll take golfing holiday in Spain, where admirers include **Hizzoner Francisco Franco** . . . which reminds us, **Hizzoner Richard Daley** among first-niters applauding warbler **Mary Ford**, preeming at Chitown's flossy **Pump Room** . . . birthday bouquets to **Mack Sennett**, 96 years young today, and Silent Screener **Ramon Navarro**, 88, who still works out with the boys!

• B'way chums set for June roast of Screen Queen **Joan Crawford** at **Toots Shor's** in N.Y . . . **Joan** said to be cold to idea . . . Meanwhile, **Marilyn Monroe** look-alike **Joi Lansing**, dining at **Julie Swindler's** swish **Check & Receipt**, excited about role in upcoming made-for-TV bio of **Jayne Mansfield**. *"I haven't been able to get excited about anything in years,"* purrs Joi... Broadway Buzzings: **Larry ("The Jolson Story") Parks** as Hizzoner **Joseph Stalin** in **Sol Rurok's** big-$$$ B'way musical based on idea by **Leon Trotsky** ... **Sebastian Cabot's** recent weight loss has friends worried ... but chum **Arthur Treacher** going ahead with skedded **Ed Sullivan CBS-TV** stint.

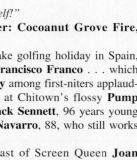

Inger Stevens

• **Hot Off the Hollywood Hotplate:** What's this a li'l birdie hears about an **Elvis** comeback? Pals say **The Pelvis** has finally licked the weight problem once and for all, but doubt he'll make a comeback soon. **Elvis**, per usual, not talking.

• **Frank Sinatra** telling intimates he's buying another plane—explains mom **Dolly Sinatra** wants to take up flying . . . **Laughan Mowings:** Song Stylist Supreme **Jim Croce** knockin' 'em dead at **Irv Roth's** famous **El Rancho Maitre D'** . . . Kooky rockabilly group **Lynrd Skynrd** bum's-rushed from **Mel Korn's** lavish **L'Overcharge** t'other early a.m. after throwing food at Chantoozie-doozie **Hildegarde**.

• Original Italian Stallion, Director **Roberto Rossellini**, not taking overseas phone calls these days . . . Overheard at **Lou Gold's** tres-elegant **Menus 'n' Things**, English teen idol **Marc Bolan** (in town for preem of new **Jimi Hendrix** flick) to guitarist extraordinaire **Brian Jones**: *"You don't look so good yourself!"* . . . Well-wishers hoping sultry forties star **Veronica Lake** finally off the hard stuff, though **La Lake** still not up & about . . . **Totie Fields'** amputated leg to surviving leg (according to Comedian **Fred Clark**): *"Say, you don't look so good yourself?"* . . . Sci-Fi writer **Rod Serling's** lucrative TV commercial career maybe ended—seems **Rod's** lost his voice.

Sal Mineo

• From the Hollywoodpile: Actor **Sal Mineo**, mum on rumored **Buddy Holly** celluloid bio role... **Sal** not dating **Ann Sheridan**, as gossipers allege. *"He's not involved with anybody nowadays,"* reports a spy.

TILL NEXT TIME, A FORREST LAUGHAN FAREWELL...

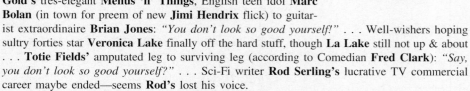

Restaurant Review
Szechuan Suey

**By ARTHUR and
DEVINA MORISS**
Rep.-Dem. Restaurant
Reviewers

A new restaurant has opened downtown on Truman St. It's called Szechuan Suey and it features authentic Szechuan food. The Szechuan province is the Mexico of China and its native food, like that of Mexico, is hot! It is delicious food, if you can eat it.

We began our meal with spring rolls, which are a Chinese version of our egg rolls. They were very good and very different from what was to follow. Next was Hot and Sour Soup. It was delicious, then got extremely hot, and we had to go on to the main dishes.

I ordered the Beef with Cashews, Devina had the Lobster with Sizzling Rice. Boy, it was hotter than the soup. I separated the cashews from the rest of the dish and cleaned some of the sauce off and was able to enjoy the nuts very much. Devina said her lobster tasted like a lobster tamale with lots and lots and lots of peppers. Even

with plenty of ice water, Devina had to take her sweater off. It was quite an experience. But if you like hot, hot, hot food, you'll enjoy Szechuan Suey.

AN APOLOGY... Devina and I are very sorry about the unfavorable review we gave The Top of the Building in last Sunday's *Rep.-Dem.* The food was actually (now that we think about it) outstanding. At first my steak seemed tough, but now that I think about it, it was cooked to perfection. Devina's crab legs were not old, they were marvelous as was the salad, the dessert and the wine. We highly recommend The Top of the Building and give it four Forks.

Rep.-Dem. Restaurant Review Rating System

Fair
Pretty Fair
Better
Real Good

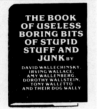
STAMPS

New Issues

By MORRIS STEINPT

There have been a variety of interesting and unusual international issues lately, many of which will doubtless become items of great collector interest in the not so distant future. Rumania's new 20 Lei special edition, for instance, is printed upside down. Its design, numerals, and incidental copy are all upside down but be careful: this one is tricky because if you happen to have the stamp itself upside down, it will look just like it's right side up and you could mistake it for a regular edition 20 Lei stamp.

France has a new set of 15 franc "ground-mail" issues commemorating important aspects of French culture such as five-foot bread loaves, Charles de Gaulle, and the topless bathing suit.

Dahomey's new airmail stamp is as large as a bed

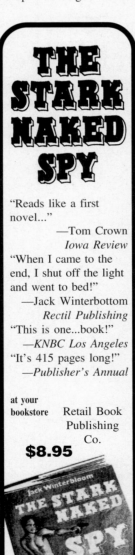
sheet. It's designed to be applied directly to the wing of the plane that's carrying the airmail. It costs the equivalent of $860 U. S. but will allow its purchaser to send 2,000 airmail letters all at once.

The British pound is so weak these days that the U. K. 10p stamp doesn't cost anything anymore in most countries—a definite boon to bargain-conscious uncanceled block collectors.

Exotic, tropical Haiti is now employing 3 percent of its population as postage stamps. They cost 20 U.S. each and the Haitian government expects to cancel three or four thousand of them

New French 15 franc issue.

next year.

Three different. African countries (Mali, Rwanda,, and Transkei) have postage stamps with nothing on them because no one in those countries can read or count.

And here's one more newsworthy foreign stamp note: Bulgaria's efforts to cut down on postal cost deficits are being lead by a super-effective new poison glue stamp-backing!

BOOK REVIEWS

GRINGOS IN A STRANGE LAND
By Mark Marischino
Brown & Co. $12.50, 372 pages.

Reviewed By ANATOLY BARNYARD

When a witness named Mark Marischino, claiming to be a former CIA operative, attempted to reveal in Congressional hearings that the United States was engaging in massive, covert programs in New Guinea, spookwatchers were puzzled. Their bewilderment turned to anger and alarm when psychiatrists and doctors, doubtless in the thrall of the intelligence community, tried to discredit his testimony. Finally, the CIA itself branded the man a "weirdo."

It took the publication of Marischino's Gringos in a Strange Land to publicly reveal at last the labyrinthine strands of what may well have been one of the most bizarre operations in the history of this country's discredited intelligence efforts.

According to Marischino, he was approached by two CIA agents in 1973, just after his graduation from New York University's prestigious film school. At the time, Marischino was taping a video documentary called "A Street Life Slice of Street Life" While working from a frozen yogurt truck in Greenwich Village. "They said I was a genius," Marischino writes.

Marischino was quickly put in charge of an operation called "Operation Chunks of Real Fruit," which employed large numbers of Spanish-speaking people who had been trained to scrutinize and analyze everyday life in third-world countries. In Gringos, Marischino charges that between 1974 and 1977, the CIA sent more than 2,700 "frozen yogurt trucks" into New Guinea, all equipped with raspberry and strawberry yogurts—and hidden video cameras.

"Then," writes Marischino, "came the dirty deed." In a particularly moving passage, illuminating the author's courageous sensitivity and honor, "Operation Chunks of Real Fruit" reached its bitter conclusion: "We were told to rendezvous at a hidden airstrip. While thousands of trucks flooded the runway, I mingled with my men. They told me of the hideous poverty into which their people had fallen since the revolution. Even with my faltering knowledge of Spanish, I knew what they were trying to say: they felt they must set their people free. Tension was growing; shouts began to fill the air. Finally, in one enormous, anguished eruption, the cry went up: 'Yankee Si! Fidel No! Forward! To Havana!' It was then I realized what had happened. The CIA had chosen the wrong island. I quit on the spot."

Marischino documents his misadventure with many interesting handwritten notes of his own. According to his account in Gringos, the CIA had planned to either rid Miami of anti-Castro Cubans or slip exploding yogurt cups into the hands of high government leaders in Havana. For Marischino, it was a severe disillusioning process. For thousands of homesick Cubanos,, it was the last chance to liberate their country that turned into a permanent vacation in Papua. And for the CIA, it was just another gruesome chapter in the agency's shameful past.

ROOTS AROUND HERE.
By Bob Melwood.
Dacron Elementary and Junior College Press.
$8.50, 128 pages.

Reviewed By LAWRENCE SILHAUSER

Mr. Silhauser is a professor of local history at Dacron Elementary and Junior College.

Roots Around Here is the fascinating book by Bob Melwood, of 1109 North Cove Blvd., who has painstakingly traced the history of his family and how they came to Dacron and what they did when they got here and before they arrived. It took Bob more than a year and a half to find all this out, but it was well worth the effort to get all the insights into our own local history that we get from this book.

Mr. Melwood begins his saga with the story of his grandfather's boyhood in old Cleveland, telling us about the skills his grandfather, Jeff Melwood, was taught in preparation for manhood, such as fence-painting and trimming the hedge, and about the cultural and spiritual things that Jeff learned growing up. Jeff Melwood was baptized a Methodist and he would pass the lore of Methodism down through all the generations of the Melwood clan.

When Jeff was still very young, he was forced to come to Dacron—his parents having moved here. But grandfather Jeff does not forget his heritage of being from Cleveland and often tells his son Lou, Bob's own father, about the Cleveland of his boyhood so that none of the Melwoods will forget where they came from.

This is a valuable historical book that belongs on the bookshelves of every family in Dacron that lives here.

CHESS

Countering The Gambit

By HYMAN BREMSTEIN

One of the many good reasons for meeting an opponent's Sicilian countermating open file back-threat castled Lubbovitch middle game with the classic Ombloski Pawn and Bishop Gambit to Queen's Knight 6 is shown in this excellent example—a match between International Masters Yatchsokovallovic Gullumbiaschevsky and Chuptzavan Bologonorvech in Prague in 1911. Gullumbiaschevsky opened with a Queen's Pawn to King's Carport 3, Bologonorvech countered with a Bishop's Shoe-Bag to Rook's Afterbirth 2. Then Queen's Dumptruck to

**GULLUMBIASCHEVENSKY
BLACK**

**BOLOGONORVECH
WHITE**

Knight's Bullflop 4. Because nobody on this newspaper bothers to proofread the shit I write here. "Just turn it in by Thursday," that's all they ever say to me. I hate chess. Chess stinks. Only a total queer would even think about playing chess. You know that crap about how ancient Teutonic knights invented it to sharpen their warrior skills? Right. I'm sure that's just exactly what ancient Teutonic knights did to sharpen their warrior skills—sit around and play dolls on checkered tablecloths all day. They were out killing Jews and raping peasant girls and you know it. I get $35 a week to write this. I teach high school. I need the money. I have a family to support. But I hate it. And I hate you. And I would like to take your souvenir Mexican onyx chessboard and smash your shitty skull with it. I would. Yes, I would.

BESTSELLERS

FICTION

This Week		Last Week	Weeks on List
1	**THE POTATO BIRDS,** by Patricia O'Tottle. (Large and Brown, $9.95.) Follows a rollicking, brawling Irish immigrant family from the time they evolved out of slime mold until their eldest son becomes king of the world.	4	27
2	**HEM OF FIRE, HARPOON OF ICE,** by Rebecca Crash. (Ham Press. $6.95.) Saga of an Eskimo seal hunter struggling to succeed in New York's Fashion Alley.	3	6
3	**THE POLICEMAN DIED BLEEDING,** by Eric Frack. (Classic Press, $8.95.) Cop killer kills cops; killer cop kills cop killer.	2	19
4	**DITCH OF VENUS,** by Elizabeth Barrett Browning. (Bound Books, $10.00.) Lewd, filthy pornography which is all right to read because it was written by a famous female poet	9	3
5	**THE DUMMERILLION,** by J.R.R.B.B.T.S.E.D. Bonkbrain. (Charnel House, $10.95.) Muffets and Tuffets and Trivits and Droolers and Retards and Gnats and Garden Gnomes attempt to retrieve the Fairie Queen's Silver Fox Ranch.	1	37
6	**THE BIG WINK,** by McDonald Gunbutt. (Permanent Press. $7.98.) There's murder afoot and a detective steps in it.	5	15
7	**FISH AREN'T PEOPLE,** by Griff Graffew. (Lippincough-Muffin, $7.95.) Hilarious fish stories from steam, lake and fish bowl by the author of *People Are Dogs.*	7	3
8	**THE SPAYED CHEERLEADER,** by Monte Liffits. (Bench Press. $6.95.) A beautiful co-ed with a shameful secret helps Dirk DuRango track down a homicidal cornerback.	10	6
9	**THE GRASS IS ALWAYS GREENER OVER THE WILDLY MASTURBATING DE-FROCKED CATHOLIC PRIEST,** by Erma Bombeck-. Phillip Roth and Graham Greene. (Muddle, $9.95.) Three popular writers team up for a joint effort in fiction.	6	17
10	**DEATH TAKES A BATH,** by Lady Agnes Rumplte (Tenniscourt, Barce and Yarmulke, $9.95.) Lady A's last and most ingenious. The young niece did it.	8	50

NONFICTION

This Week		Last Week	Weeks on List
1	**THE SCHNAUZERS FLY TONIGHT,** by Wilhelm Veruckt (Spaetzel Press, $7.95.) True story of the Third Reich's secret canine air corps.	1	7
2	**LESBIANS, HOMOSEXUALS AND PEOPLE WHO HAVE TO GO TO THE BATHROOM A LOT,** by Dr. Felix Fipisetter. (Short Books, $12.50.) Sexual problems explained with drawings, photos and free-form poetry.	9	30
3	**THE BOOK OF USELESS BORING BITS OF STUPID STUFF AND JUNK,** by Irving Wallace, David Wallechinsky. Amy Wallenberg, Dorothy Wallstein, Tony Walletto and their dog Wally. (Pummel and Duff, $19.95.) Wallace family's grocery lists, grade school report cards and some things the neighbors told them.	9	30
4	**MAKING PEOPLE GIVE YOU ALL THEIR MONEY,** by Arthur Cooz. (Obst Books. $11.95.) Aggressive road to success through threats and physical intimidation.	2	5
5	**GO RAPE YOURSELF!** by Sgt. Irene Buttice. (Wayne and Schuster, $9.95.) Ex-Detroit policewoman takes a tough stand on rapists and their victims.	4	24
6	**THE JESUS JAR,** by Father Frank Fowler. (Revival Press, $12.95.) TV preacher talks about saving goodness for a sinful day.	6	65
7	**IN THE BEGINNING THERE WAS A HOLE WHERE WATERGATE WOULD BE BUILT,** by Tony DiFleppo with Byron Trussett. (Dill, $10.) Bricklayer DiFleppo gives first-hand account of building the Watergate Hotel.	5	29
8	**LOOKING OUT FOR #4,** by Raymond Marchell. (Pig and Whistle, $9.95.) That third-best friend may hold the key to your entire life.		
9	**WE ACTUALLY LIVE FOREVER AND HAVE THREE LEGS,** by Dr. Aaron Humpstetter. (Dump, $6.95.) Remarkable scientific revelations about the common facts around us.	7	54
10	**ROOTS AROUND HERE,** by Bob Melwood. (Dacron Elementary and Junior College Press, $8.50.) Dacron's Melwood clan and their origins in Cleveland.	10	1

PAPER BACK BEST SELLERS

1 THE PRESIDENT SHOOTS WHORES, by Victor Dal-Green. (American EZ Read Press, $1.95.) Sex-crazed killer in the White House.

2 LOVE'S TORRID WATERS, by Felice Edmunds-Platte. (Minora Books, $1.75.) The 67th Jessica Thebes romance takes place in a 17th-century French fish pond.

3 THUNDER BENEATH THE QUILTS, by "P". (Perfume Classics, $1.95). Romance between a lovely Countess and a dirty Italian slave pirate.

4 THE MASHED POTATO COOKBOOK, by Delores Diggmont. (Mum Books, $6.50.) Over 700 new recipes in this fifth volume of the popular "Potato Cookery" series.

5 FEELING OUR BODIES, by The New York Women Person's Female Collective. (I AM ME/Womanstrong, $4.75.) Tips on the location and use of various parts of women's selves.

6 BELLE OF THE BENWA BALL, by Ward Ransem. (Black Pants Press, $1.95.) Two samurai fight for the hand of a Southern belle.

7 LEAKS, DRIPS AND LUMPS, by Dr. Jerome Feingers. (Pocketbook Books, $2.25.) A famous Ladies' Doctor explains the complexities of women's bodies.

8 PASSION'S PURE PILLAGE, by Dorinne DuDaphne. (Lipstick Books, $2.75.) 2,000-page epic saga of a woman who likes men in three states.

9 THE JOY OF SERVING OTHER PEOPLE, by Grace L. Chitchat. (Ranch House, $1.95.) True story of a woman who found her sanity at the end of a mop.

10 THE FILTHY, DIRTY WOMAN WHO ATE WITH HER HANDS, Jack Dock. (Stuttgart Books, $1.25.) Private Eye Bus Warren gives a female terrorist just what she needs, then just what she deserves.

The listings above are based on weekly sales at the Dacron area bookstores.

Windsor, Detroit's Canadian Cousin

By BURT AND HELEN BURL
Rep.-Dem. Family-On-The-Move

IT IS HARD TO BELIEVE that another country can be so close to the U.S. and still be another country, but a mere one-third mile from Detroit is Windsor, Ontario. Although Canadians seem to try very hard to be American, Canada really is a foreign country and Windsor is, technically, a city with the romance of a foreign port.

WE TOOK THE WINDSOR TUNNEL that travels beneath the Detroit River and as we came back up into the sunlight, we knew we were in another country. Everything was written in French and in English, which is very quaint although annoying.

OUR FIRST STOP was the magnificent Convention Hall. A convention was in

Hotel Postcards Ltd.
Our hotel room was clean and courteous.

progress so we had to settle for a self-guided visual tour from our auto. Then we were off to the V. O. Historical Museum, where we learned just about everything there is to know about Canadian whiskey. A quick stop at the riverfront Dieppe Garden and some interesting riverfront wildlife. Then on to the Hotel Industrial.

WE TOPPED THE EVENING with dinner at the Queen's Dinner Diner: exquisite ground sirloin patty,

mushroom caps, mixed vegetables, sherbet, and beverage.

THE NEXT DAY we went to the Willistead Art Gallery. We enjoyed the paintings as much as is possible to enjoy paintings, then on to the University of Windsor. It's really some college! There we learned that Windsor was established in the middle of the 18th century by French farmers. In 1935, we were told, Windsor was united with East Windsor, Walkerville, and Sandwich and things have been just great every since.

WE CLOSED OUT our brief foreign weekend with a quick tour of the riverfront factories and a shopping spree in downtown Windsor, where we stocked up on maple sugar candy, fireworks for the kids, and commemorative spoons.

THE NEXT DAY we were home in Dacron.

Burl/Kodak Instamatic Photo
Industry is what makes Windsor get up in the morning.

Our Twin City, Dacrõn, Pakistan

By WILFRED ARNOLD
Special Rep.-Dem. Travel Correspondent

IF YOU CLOSED YOUR EYES, ignored the odor of animals, and pretended that the strange language you heard was English, you could almost think that this City thousands of miles away on the other side of the globe is our own city of Dacron. Yes, you guessed it, it's our twin city—Dacrõn, Pakistan.

PAKISTAN IS LIKE OHIO in many ways and Dacron, on the Indus River, is like our fine city. The weather in both cities can be warm or rainy or chilly. Bricks are everywhere as are dogs and small gardens. Dacron is twice as large in land size, but Dacrõn's population is six times as big.

LIKE OURSELVES, Dacrõnites are hard-working people. Unfortunately, there is not as much work to do in

Pakistan as there is in Ohio. Many Dacrõnites are wonderful craftsmen and masters of the art of hand-painting party favors and toy doll faces. Dacrõn is the worldwide center of doll face painting. Other important industries include carrying wood, digging trenches and sweeping.

THE PEOPLE SPEAK a language called Urdu, which is not their fault. Few go to school to learn English. Public education in Dacrõn is free, but the only schools are private and far too expensive for most Dacrõnites. A program to teach the people to read was undertaken several years ago by the United Nations, but it failed because none of the people who needed to learn to read could read the announcements for the reading classes. But the lack of education doesn't seem to bother the Dacrõnites. When they need any important thinking done, the U.N. or the Peace Corps volunteers will do it for them.

LIKE OUR DACRON, Dacrõn has a town hall, police and fire stations, hotels,

Photo by Wilfred Arnold
We would call it a desert, but the Dacrõnites know better—It's a farm!

restaurants, and businesses. These are all in one building, which is indicative of the economical nature of the people. Everywhere you look you can see frugal people doing frugal things. No food or water is wasted. Products are used and re-used to get the most out of them.

THE MAIN RELIGION is Islam, although it is not uncommon for a Dacrõnite to convert to a regular religion if given an incentive like a radio or a harmonica. The Dacrõnites frequently go to a large domed building called a mosque. It looks somewhat like a Mr. Drippy

ice cream cone. The people go there to pray although what it actually sounds like is wailing and making noise.

THERE ARE DIFFERENCES of course between Dacrõn in Pakistan and Dacron in Ohio. Dacrõn has no sanitation facilities. We have no monkeys. Dacrõn has few roads and sidewalks. We don't have desert just outside of our door. Despite the differences, there is a common spirit that we share with our small brown brothers and sisters so many thousands of miles away. If you ever get over to Asia, drop by our twin city and say "hello" for everybody.

Photo by Wilfred Arnold
The life expectancy in Dacrõn is only 39 years, so these two teenagers have to do a lot of living in a short time.

Michigan's Upper Peninsula

The Water Wonderland's Proud Bonnet

By GRIFFITH VAN KEMP

WAY UP NORTH In Ishpeming the folks wonder why Michigan is called the "Auto State." From where they stand in the rich, rolling snow-covered pine forests of the Upper Peninsula, it should be called the "Crisp, Fresh Northern Air State" or the "Snow-Covered Pine Forest State."

THE UPPER PENINSULA is a wonderful place to visit and right now is the most budget-conscious time of year to enjoy Michigan's beautiful and historic "Upstairs."

THE UPPER PENINSULA of Michigan is located directly north of the Lower Peninsula of Michigan and is accessible by auto across the stunning four-mile-long Mackinac Bridge, which spans the deep, ice-filled Straits of Mackinac.

THE REGION was first discovered by the French in the early 17th century. It became British, then American, and then British again and finally American, and there are plaques where

Michigan Water Resources Board

Billions and billions of gallons of fresh and frozen lake water help Michigan earn the name "Water and Ice Wonderland"

several forts used to be that attest to this.

OF PARTICULAR INTEREST to the family travelers is the beautiful Tahquamehon Falls near the paper mills in Newberry. The falls rise to a height of 48 feet with a 200-foot-long crest of paper-colored water. In Munising there are 12 more waterfalls that fall

round the clock all year long except when they're frozen in the winter. As you drive along Lake Superior's shore you will see—or would, if the weather were warmer—ore ships laden with ore from ore mines which, as you travel west, will be on the driver's right, although covered with snow this time of year.

ACCOMMODATIONS ARE COMFORTABLE and reasonable. Gasoline and auto supplies are in great abundance. The food is famous locally. Restaurants like the Cedar Chip Inn at Germfask and the Potawatomi Lodge on the Yellow Dog River have been visited by countless travel-

Michigan Ore Board

The mighty tracks of the lake carry ore from the rich mines of the Upper Peninsula as soon as the ice is cleared in the spring.

ers. "Lakefood" is especially good, and whatever you do, be sure and try the gooseberry relish!

MICHIGAN'S UPPER PENINSULA is a pine-and-snow-covered paradise and a travel bargain that's hard to beat, especially in January and February. As the Upper Peninsula of Michigan state regional motto says, "Si quaeris peninsula amoenam circumspice" (If you seek a pleasant peninsula, look around you).

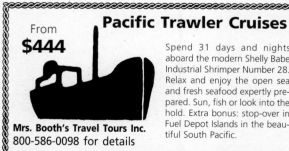

Local Travel Agency Offers Laetrile Tour

By NORA BUGBAUM
Rep.-Dem. Travel Writer

Homing Pigeon Tours of Dacron is offering a two-week vacation to Acapulco, Mexico, with a laetrile treatment every evening (the drug is legally available in Mexico). The trip includes round-trip air fare, accommodations at a first-class hotel, theatre and dinners. Acapulco is famous for its beaches. "There are quite a few people in Dacron who are suffering from cancer who would like to take advantage of laetrile and get some sun and surf at the same time. There's no sense having a boring time during a disease when you can swing!" Evelyn Rogg, owner of Homing Pigeon Tours, said. The first charter leaves next Friday. There are a few openings left, so sign up soon if interested. "A word of caution," Mrs. Rogg warns. "Don't drink the water. You could cure your cancer and pick up the you-know-whats!"

The Garden

By Doris Preavey

Winter Gardening Questions Most Frequently Asked

Rep.-Dem. Staff Photo

The Winter Garden has a special beauty all its own.

Q. What should I be doing about my rose bushes this time of year?
A. Nothing.

Q. What can I do to help fruit trees survive the cold?
A. Leave them alone until spring.

Q. Which garden vegetables can be set out during February?
A. None.

Q. Do forsythia shrubs need any special winter care?
A. No.

Where the "SKI AREA" is!

Mt. Barntop is the ski resort where every day is a Winter Blizzard of fun. From the frosty, snow-frosted, snowy slopes by day to our all-log, wooden "Chalet Nook" by night where the flaming log fire is warm as well as the kioke coffee, and girls. What a "snow" ball!

ON PREMISES —
· Snow Skiing · Snow Making · Snow Riding ·
· Snow Rolling · Snow Dancing · Snow Coloring ·
· Snow Crafting · Snow Club · Snow Shopping ·
· Snow School ·
· And "Snow" Much More! ·

OUR SPECIAL WASHINGTON'S BIRTHDAY GIFT TO YOU!
No cover, no minimum (to guests) at Professor Snowski's Sno-mo-jo, our all new horse-drawn disco sleigh, featuring the latest in big-name popular recordings.

Phone for your reservations today:
3486 Old Bridge Rd., Coolieville, Ohio

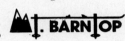

PET OF THE WEEK:

Duffy

Duffy needs a home. He is 14 years old. He's part sheep dog, part Great Dane and all lovable. His owners gave him up because he bites children and wets in chairs. Wouldn't you like to adopt Duffy?
Call 8352384 and ask for "Duffy."

Controversy Leads to Dog Fighting At Kennel Show

By DONOVAN GROAT
Rep.-Dem. Feature Writer

A CONTROVERSY over the selection of top dog at the Second Annual Dacron Dog and Kennel Klub Dog Show sparked a large fight between dozens of champion dogs.

WHEN A GERMAN MINIATURE PINSCHER, "Erhard," owned by Mr. and Mrs. Dex Rexall of Dacron Dells, was selected "Best of Show," members of the North Dacron Kennel Club accused the dog of being a small, imperfect Doberman Pinscher. During the loud, heated argument that followed, two German Shepherds broke free and attacked a Polish Otter Hound. Moments later, a group of Japanese Terriers surprised an American Water Spaniel as if slept in its cage and caused a contro-

Cont. Sec. F, Page 21

Rep.Dem. Staff Photographs

41 dogs, 9 people and a Rep.-Dem. photographer were injured in the half hour dog controversy.

Before the dog fight began judges Hermman Bakker and Don Sairari carefully inspected each of the 128 dogs in the 2nd annual Dacron Dog and Kennel Klub Dog Show.

INDIVIDUAL CATEGORY WINNERS

Sporting Dogs—"Babe," California Tennis Terrier, Whitaker Kennels, Dacronville.
Hounds—"Jeb," Alabama Prison Hound, Dacron Dales Dog Society.
Working Dogs—"Terry," Temporary Office Dog, Dacron Dales Breeder's Guild.
Toy Dogs—"Thimble," German Wallethound, Silage County Kennel and Muzzle Club.
Non-Sporting Dogs—"Paddy," Irish Lounging Setter, independent entry.

NOT AN ADVERTISEMENT NOT AN ADVERTISEMENT

Open House Trailer

Photo Courtesy Presidential Court Trailer Pant

It's open house all this coming year at the picturesque, new, just-opened, Presidential Court Trailer Park on North Shakespeare at 140. Let the friendly people at Presidential show you why your next home may not even be a house. The Presidential Trailer Court is conveniently close to the dump and only seconds from 140, city water is available and the Interstate is only moments away. Plus you'll love strolling or driving down Presidential Trailer Court's broad avenues lined with sturdy oaks about forty or fifty years from now.

House Sense

Increase the Value of Your Home

By HERMAN HEMMING
President, Silage County Board of Realtors

WITH A LITTLE PAINT, a little plaster and a little good sense, you can make sure your house sells quickly and at the price you want. The secret to increasing the resale value of your home is to highlight the good points of your home. If one area of the home is particularly unique and attractive, stay there and chat. When you show the house, hurry through the small rooms and concentrate on the larger. Keep basement visits short and discourage close examination of furnaces and water heaters. Offer detailed explanations for all problem areas. For example, if you have a badly stained wall caused by a leaky roof or water from a broken pipe, hang up an empty frame and call it "modern art."

USE YOUR HEAD AND STUDY THE FOLLOWING SIX TIPS:

1. BUY AN inexpensive rug to cover basement cracks.

2. IF THE FOUNDATION is cracked, plaster it over.

3. PAINT YOUR asphalt driveway black. It makes the grass and weeds growing up through it look neat and clean.

4. RENT NEW appliances, furniture and plenty of plants.

5. NEVER SHOW your home during the day.

6. WALLPAPER OVER any major structural flaws.

NOT AN ADVERTISEMENT NOT AN ADVERTISEMENT

Home Of The Week

Photo courtesy of Plumb Construction

"Home of the Week" is this little gem of a colonial built by Plumb Construction, 2320 N. Washington Irving. It's pretty, practical and loaded with options and, best of all, the folks at Plumb say this beauty can be yours for only $23,000 exclusive of lot and options. For more information give a call to Otto Plumb Construction at 549-9100.

3600 W. Taft

LUMBERLAND

Hardware and Lumber
"Lumber in to Lumberland"

**Mon to Sat
Open 9 to 9**

Masonic
Cement
Drivets
99¢ doz.

Pipe Fitters
Chain Pliers
$7.90

C-Clamps   A-Clamps
M-Clamps   B-Clamps

$1.05 apiece

Hi-Quality
Miter Basket
$10.00

Pine Knots
19¢ doz.

$3.78
Sakrete Lawn and
Shrub Sealer
5 gal. pail.

For Windows,
Picture Frames.
Glazier's Plate-Glass Wacker
$3.99

Electric Hammer   Black and Deckshoe

$22.20

Precision
3/8" Jewelers
Jack
$9.99

Nail-Making Kit   Baseball Bat Ash Trees
$2.99   ## $33.99

100 Feet of Wire, Heavy Duty Snips Makes 200 6" nails
Two by Four Trees
$49.99

Coarse-Toothed
Rip Saw
$14.49

50% Off Rustic Shelves WERE 6' by 12' NOW 3' by 6'   Saw dust ## 11¢ lb.

SPECIAL LUMBER BARGAIN BUYS

per piece	6'	8'	10'	12'	14'	16'
2"x8"	2.24	2.99	3.73	4.48	5.23	6.19
2"x4"	.96	1.28	1.60	1.92	2.24	2.88
2"x0"	.80	1.07	1.33	1.60	1.87	2.14
2"x1256"	3.59	4.79	5.99	7.19	8.39	9.80

Drywall Kit. Includes plaster,
heavy paper. Makes 12 sheets   ## $39.88
of plaster board.

Flooring Oaks

$110.00

Wood Slivers
29¢ dry qt.

Hickory-Handled Leaf
Spoon

For Yard
or Garden   ## $12.00

Wall Stretchers
$5.99

Ball level
     ## $11.98

Left-Handed Finishing Nails
$1.49 lb.

Circle Wrenches
Made in U.S.A.
Set of 12

$14.99

Double-Handle Screwdriver
Set of 3

$5.49

Electric Power Brush
Paints, Varnishes,
Shellacs

$19.99

LUMBERLAND

3600 W. Taft   Open 9 to 9 Mon to Sat   Charges Accepted

Fill 'er Up — With High Test Comfort

"A tamper-resistant door and being close to the curb is something we really enjoy about our home," notes John Devish.

had an abandoned filling station for $7,600, Donna and John said they'd take it. Donna Devish, who is a self-taught interior designer, added a homey touch to the large auto bays that serve as the main living area. Hydraulic lifts keep the family auto and a kingsize bed and dresser out of sight until they are needed. The office has been converted to an all-electric kitchen. When spring arrives, John plans to sod the front apron and use the gas pumps to hold water for the new lawn. "It's really a great little home," John says proudly. "Someday I'd like to put our name on the revolving sign out in front."

Photos by Rep.-Dem. Staff Photographer Prissy VanHusen

"A gas station really had everything we needed—including two bathrooms." Donna Devish remarks.

Ex-Service Station Is Extra Terrific Home

By DOTTY SCHWIMMER
Rep.-Dem. Home Editor

WHEN AN AUNT DIED and left him $9,000, John Devish knew exactly what he would do with the cash. "Donna and I planned to buy our first home," John says with a smile, "but for $9,000 all we could get was a small tree and a patio." So when a realtor friend joked that he

The Devish's relax and have a morning cup of coffee in their "breakfast bay", as they call it.

NEXT WEEK
In The Sunday
Rep.-Dem.
Home Section
Rustic Conversion

The story of how a young Dacron couple took a run-down old ranch house and turned it into a charming barn.

Before

After

REAL ESTATE

HOUSES FOR SALE

DACRON–4 BR, 3 bedrooms, 2 1/2 bth, 1 bathroom, gas ht, electric heat, 2 car gar, 1 car garage, fin bsmt, unfinished basement, hi 40s. $78,000 541-3253

DACRON–3 working bdrms, in-grnd bath, fin LR, 2 car fplc, gourmet bsmnt, by owner $69,000 678-4248

DACRON–Brick split, floor split, crack in foundation & another split in the driveway. $9,600 378-1713

DACRON
Handyman's Dream

You'd have to look far and wide to find a home with as many possibilities for the handyman as this gem in the rough. It's a beautiful 3 BA 2 bath that's just waiting for the man who likes to work with his hands to add the 2 bedrooms and that other bath. PRICED TO SELL

SWINESTEIN REALTORS
837-6600

DACRON-Just listed 3BR col. LA w/ fplc, Wright Br Pk area, immed poss, nudist lady neighbor $86,900

DACRON DALES
MUST SELL FAST

Here's a beauty that must be sold quick, 3 bedrooms, 1 1/2 baths, sun room, garage Owners have moved out so you can move right in. This one won't last long! Hurry! $33,900

MORRIS GRABUKS
4410 Monroe 378-4740

DACRON DALES

Lg 4 BR Colonial, 2 1/2 baths, LR w/ fplc, lg fam rm, 1/2 acre treed plot. Owned by an elderly widow who only used it to live in until the mortgage was foreclosed.

CITY COUNCIL REALTY
BUD MUDROE 343-1399

DACRON–7 rm Neanderthal, w/cave bears, maint-free, wlk to flint pits $52,500 978-6578

Dacron–8-story Colonial Octoplex w/7 units for in-laws or rental income.

WALLIS SLOPT
Home Builders

6000 N. Shakespeare
883-5200

DACRON–2 rm abandoned car, $1,200. by owner 475-4325

DACRON–lg hole in ground, attractive neighbrhd, close to schools $9,900 766-8234

DACRON GLENS
HISTORICAL HOUSE

The famous Fazullo Murder House is on the market at a price that's too good to pass up. This three bedroom 2 1/2 bath home has been in newspapers and on tv statewide. Formerly owned by Vito Fazullo, reputed Dacron "underboss of underbosses." A real conversation starter. Hi 90's

CITY COUNCIL REALTY
BUD MUDROE 3431-399

Dacron Estates

New lux homes cust. built to order. Brick and stone construc. Slate roofs, hard wood flrs and paneling, tile baths, hi ceilings, plaster lath walls, 14 roms and up From low $Zillions.

WALLIS SLOPT
Home Builders

600 N. Shakespeare 883-152l

DACRON VIEW HILLS–Mint brick cust. 5 BR, 4 1/2 bath, excell loc, all appliance, wlk to everything, fin bsmt, ten ct, ingrnd ht pool, o'sized lot, w/fplc in all rms, maint-free, 3 car gar, fam rm, parq flr, view, A/C, w/w cptg, patio, dead end st, sunny kitch, many extras not for sale.

DACRON VIEW HILLS AREA–3 BR, 2 bath, 2 ft of water in bsmt can be used as pool, large rms, only 87 blks from fashionable Dacron Vw Hills $83,000 938-6057

DOWNTOWN
Ideal For Growing Family

This is a big one you can grow into. 140 bdrms, 162 baths, cent A/C, crpting thruout, huge mod kitch, din rm seats 300, many extras, mail chute, elevator, gift shp. A special buy $220,000

SWINESTEIN REALTORS
837-6600

DOWNTOWN–Ski Chalet, Winter spoils retreat right in the heart of downtown Dacron. $51,000. 334-7766

EAST DACRON
CONVENIENT TO
TRANSPORTATION

Charming home, convenient to all trans, 3 bedrooms, 1 1/2 baths, rebuilt truck engine, $54,750. 272-3194

NORTH DACRON is where the sonofabitch foreman of this typesetting shop lives and if that motherfucker gives me any more shit tonight I'm going right up there to his house while his wife and kids are asleep and set the fucking place on fire.

WEST DACRON
OUTASIGHT VALUES!

WEST SIDE BLOCKBUSTER SALE

4BR. 2 1/2 bath, cent a/c, lg gar w/room for plenty of old Cadillacs and Buick Electra 225s

5 BRrms ranch, fin base, w/fplc, room for many illegit. children

#BR brick ranch, den, extras, white school nearby full of kids w/lots of lunch money

Brick Cape Cod, 7 rms, 2 bths, formal DR. full base, nice neighborhd to spoil

MORRIS GRABUKS
4410 Monroe 378-4740

NO MONEY DOWN

REST OF YOUR LIFE TO PAY

NORTH DACRON

6 rm Call mch

6 rm split cust Col

7 rm gin Mnch drk

9 rm rd nrk mgt lm

9 dm rgkjl wk sqy

Q gbx imnld Mr. Mxyzptik

From $80,000

PLUMB CONSTRUCTION

2320 N. Irving 549-9100

CONDOMINIUMS
ROOM CONDO

Buy into new home, all privileges incl. bath and kit, laund, prkg. Large rm w/ view. Hi re-sale value potential. Lo monthly fee takes care of all maintenance. Rms in this house go fast! $12,750 Call 5337980 today

COMMERCIAL PROPERTY
DACRON
Investment Property

Sixteen flat in prftable Southslum area. 32 apts, maint-free, full rented, moneysaver cold air heating system, painted 1962, rents can go up immed, a must see for doctors or other investment types.

SWINESTEIN REALTORS
837-6600

SOUTH DACRON apt houses up to 12 units, will burn to suit. $75 536-7971

SILAGE CO. Mink Ranch. 3000 mink bedrmns, w/minks, must sacrifice due to smell. $98000 492-0929

SILAGE CO. Attractively strip-mined farm land, 2/acre contact S.C.O.C.G.T.T.& E 458-1000

DACRONVILLE

Negro Church, excel loc. for gogo bar or auto body shop if cleared of negroes. By owner, no reasonable offer refused 1-244-7205

RENTALS

COLLEGE AREA–Ruined home ideal for 20 or 40 students to share 498-3433

DACRON ESTATES–inexpensive rms for rent to runaway boys call H Gullet 433-5000

DACRON GLENS–Student or bachelors, board with fanatically religious family that doesn't smoke, drink, wear makeup or hum. $70 Mo. 983 Glenridge 437-7229

EAST DACRON–Dirty places for single men. $50 ma. 456-9233

QUAINTOWN–Authentic N.Y.C-style lofts. No heat, no elec, no appliances, no bathrms, illegal. Fr $200 Call 340-3675

Q-TOWN–Freezing Garret, ideal for promising poet. $60 no deposit no fee 688-4595

QUAINTOWN AREA–Luxurious converted livestock pens, 2 & 3 rm. fr $190. 11 NW 7th St. 459-2573

SOUTH DACRON–rat-infested firetrap to clean church-going family only $180 mo. 2 yrs deposit. 1181 1/2 S Emily Dickens See Super

SOUTH DACRON–Efficiency apt in middle of the street. Roomy. $90 436-8792

SOUTH DACRON–Attractive apt. with 4 exits. Ideal for drug dealer. Frm $150 1009 S Melville

TRAILER HOMES

PRESIDENTIAL TRAILER PARK–1 BR 48 ft sacrifice sale by owner, have to move 475-2122

PRESIDENTIAL TRAILER PARK–2 BR 60 ft lowlow price must leave 475-3437

PRESIDENTIAL TRAILER PARK–58 ft w/cabana, extra lo price owner has to leave fast 474-7294

PRESIDENTIAL TRAILER PARK–54' 2 BR, you name the price, owner moving at any cost 475-9473

PRESIDENTIAL TRAILER PARK–62 FT 1 1/2 bath 3 BR really have to get out of here 475-8942

OUT OF TOWN

SILAGE CO. Quiet country setting surrounds this elegant 4 bedroom stone house which is completely under water. $41,000 1-441-3600

SILAGE CO. Attractive pigsty, could be cute second home, needs work. $97,000 1-441-3507

LICKING CRK RES

Licking Creek Reservoir Nuclear Cooling Pond lakefront lots $2000 as. Lots without lake frontage $6000

MORRIS GRABUKS
4410 Monroe 378-4740

East Coast Midtown Beauty

Sits on 18 acres with 12 rooms, 20 baths, 5 elevators, cent. A/C, all elec.

kit, formal ding rm. indr pool, ten ct, bwling alley, prof landcape, close to schools, churches, transp. UPPER BRACKETS (202) 456-1414

HAMMERS 'N NAILS

By MIKE BURROWS

DEAR MIKE:

My heating bills are ridiculous. I think my problem is that the north side of my house is all windows. What can I do? JIM TRAVERS, DACRON HILLS

JIM—You have to get rid of that northern exposure. I suggest that you cut a 10' trench all around your foundation to a depth of about 8'. Winch your 14-ton biped bridge lifts into the trench and with a Doolittle connecting bar, raise the house. When you get her up about three feet, slide your screwcore excavation elevator in and take her up. As she comes up to ground level, hook your lock braces around the frame, connect that to your dozer and slowly rotate the house until the north windows are facing south. Lower the house and rearrange the landscaping.

DEAR MIKE:

I've got raccoons in my walls. They came in through a vent in my chimney and now I can't get them out. Any suggestions? LARRY TRAINER, SANDUSKY

LAR—Listen for the raccoons in the walls. When you locate them, put your shotgun right up to the wall and unload. Patch the hole.

DEAR MIKE:

I want to put a second bath in my upstairs, but I can't connect into the existing system. What should I do? HARRY WEMBLE, DACRON

HAR—Put in a new system. Just bust through the ceiling, run a 6" soil stack down to the basement and through the foundation, and hook into the sewer system.

DEAR MIKE:

My fireplace is very dirty and sooty. I heard that tossing a couple of aerosol cans in the fire will do the trick. True? HOWARD VENUS, PETOSKEY, MICH.

HOWIE—Try it and see. But cover your face and eyes.

DEAR MIKE:

I have an old upright piano that needs refinishing. It is all pebbly and rough. HERBERT KLAMM, TOLEDO

HERB—Look in your Yellow Pages under "Refinisher-Wood." Load the piano into your half-ton and take it in. Be sure to ask how much it will cost, when it will be ready and do they need a deposit.

DEAR MIKE:

I got your book on building a home for $15,001) and I'm about halfway done, but I have a problem. The house is leaning about 60 degrees to the south. I followed your instructions perfectly. What's wrong? VICTOR BAGDAGIAN, DACRON

VIC—There's nothing wrong with you. That book got all messed up in the printing and everything's off a foot or so. I'm really sorry about it. Please accept my new book, "Building Your Own Indoor Pool," as a gift. Sorry Vic.

See Mike Burrows every Sunday afternoon at 4 on Channel 81.

snail daley
by merv drucker

OH, PRIVATE DALEY, IT'S NOON...TIME FOR BREAKFAST IN BED!

PVT. S. DALEY ESQ.

TAP! TAP!

MOST PRESENT AND PRETTY WELL ACCOUNTED FOR, SIR!

THEY LOOK SO NICE...THEY CAN ALL HAVE A WEEK'S LEAVE

EUROPE HAS BEEN INVADED!

HOW MANY ARE IN FAVOR OF DEFENDING FRANCE?

EEEEK!!!

WHAT'S THE MATTER, SARGE?

I DREAMED WE HAD AN ALL-VOLUNTEER ARMY!

WE DO...

!

2-12

...AND I HAD TWO YEARS OF COLLEGE!

BAM!

WACK! BASH!

SLASH!

SLUG!

CRUNCH!

STAB!

POW!

SLICE!

CRACK

MERV DRUCKER

FRANCINE
by ami

I'LL HAVE A TURKEY WITH A SIDE ORDER OF CHILI DOGS!

I HEARD YOU WENT OUT WITH ALVIN!

YOU SAID YOU'D NEVER SEE HIM AGAIN AS LONG AS YOU LIVE

AND A PIE

YOU SAID HE DEGRADED YOU AND MADE FUN OF YOU! YOU HATED HIM!!

ALL HE DID WAS CALL ME A FAT, UGLY SLOB.

YOU CAN'T LET HIM GET AWAY WITH THAT!!

IT DOESN'T BOTHER ME.

HE HURTS YOU AND YOU GO RIGHT BACK!!!

WHY? WHY? WHY?!!!

HIS FATHER OWNS A BAKERY!

Smarm
by Bicycle Cards

Mind your P's and Q's.

The early bird gets the worm.

The good die young.

the EYES HAVE IT

2-12

"Is there anybody around here who can read a hold-up note in Braille?"

"Oh, sure...Just stumble down four blocks until you smell the gas station. Turn left at the barking dog. Keep going until he's out of earshot, make a right onto the gravel path until the overhanging branch knocks your hat off. You can't miss it."

"Get this. There's a blind guy on the phone who says he just _heard_ a UFO!"

"Senator Bighorn just appointed me to keep an eye on campaign fund expenditures."

"Are you sure you want to see Butterflies Are Free again?"

"They did a great job on ol' Bagboy. Feels like he's just resting."

Prince Belligerent
IN DAYS OF OLD WHEN KNIGHTS WERE BOLD
by Hack Foister

Our Story: PRINCE BEL'S DAUGHTER KAREN HAS JOINED THE CHILDREN'S CRUSADE TO THE HOLY LAND LED BY THE MONK PEDRASTUS. AFTER TWO WEEKS OF MARCHING, THE CHILDREN HAVE YET TO SET EYES ON AN INFIDEL.

BEFORE SHE LEFT ON THE CRUSADE, THE PALACE LIBRARIAN HAD TOLD KAREN THAT JERUSALEM WAS A COUNTRY MADE OF WOOD, RULED BY A HIDEOUS INFIDEL WITH THE BODY OF A SNAKE WHO ATE COAL AND WHOSE NAME WAS THIRTY-THREE.

A FEW DAYS LATER, WHILE PRINCE BEL WAS ENGAGED IN COMBAT, KAREN STOLE AWAY TO JOIN THE HOLY MAN PEDRASTUS ON THE CRUSADE.

WHEN KAREN WAS DISCOVERED MISSING, BEL AND URN SET OUT IN HOT PURSUIT OF THE PRINCESS.

PEDRASTUS HAS AT LAST ARRANGED TRANSPORTATION TO THE HOLY LAND FOR THE CHILDREN.

BEL AND PRINCE URN FEEL KAREN IS TOO YOUNG TO VISIT THE HOLY LAND. THEY HAVE ARRIVED TO PREVENT HER DEPARTURE.

KAREN WATCHES THE SHIP PULL AWAY WITH A WISTFUL LOOK. PERHAPS BEL WILL LET HER GO TO THE HOLY LAND NEXT YEAR WHEN SHE IS OLD ENOUGH.
2011

NEXT WEEK— Auto dé fe in the Musty Isles

CAVEMEN
BY BOB HECK

WE'RE CAVEMEN WHO HAVE A WRITTEN LANGUAGE...

...STOVES AND REFRIGERATORS...

...TELEVISION...

...AND GAS-GUZZLING AUTOMOBILES...

OKAY, OKAY...WE'RE CAVEMEN WHO HAVE A WRITTEN LANGUAGE, STOVES AND REFRIGERATORS, TELEVISION, AND GAS-GUZZLING AUTOMOBILES...SO WHAT'S THE JOKE?

I DON'T KNOW...WE DON'T HAVE PUNCH LINES YET!

HILLY BILLY by TED GLASSOW

I SEED THEM GOVERNMENT MEN A-HEADED UP THIS-A-WAY, JAKE---DID THEY FIND YORE MOONSHINE STILL?

HECK NO, BILLY--WHY, THESE DAYS, MARY-WANNA'S GONE AN' TOOK ALL THE PROFIT OUTTA MOONSHINE STILLS

WELL, WAS THEY AFTER YE FER CHICKEN THIEVIN'?

NAW--WHY WOULD I THIEVE CHICKENS WHEN THAR'S FOOD STAMPS YE KIN GIT FER FREE?

THEN I GUESS THEY'S CAUGHT YE FEUDIN' AGAIN--

I DECLARE, BILLY, YE SURE AIR BEHIND TH' TIMES--THEM THINGS IS ALL TOOK CARE OF IN COURT NOWADAYS

WELL, DURN IT, WHAT DID THEM GOVERNMENT MEN WANT YE FER?

'CAUSE I JEST BEEN APPOINTED FEDERAL D.A. O' PHILADELPHIA!

OFFICIAL WHITE HOUSE COPTER

HORRID THE HUN by RIK GREENE

MY HUSBAND HORRID...

"...CARVES UP KINGS AND KINGDOMS..."

"...SLICES THROUGH WILD BEASTS..."

POEMS

"...SLASHES THE THROATS OF NEWBORN BABES..."

"...AND CHOPS OFF HEADS OF PRIESTS..."

SO HOW COME I CAN NEVER GET HIM TO CUT THE LAWN?

RIK GREENE 2-12

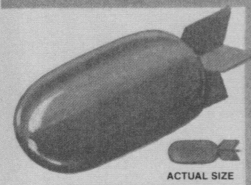
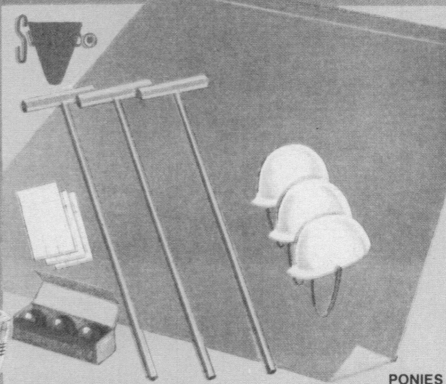

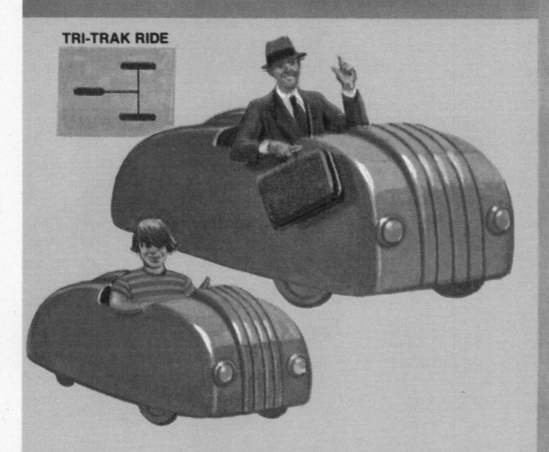

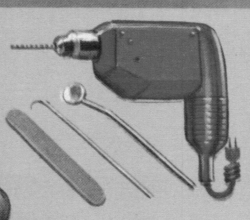
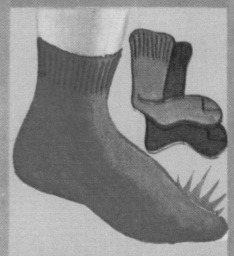

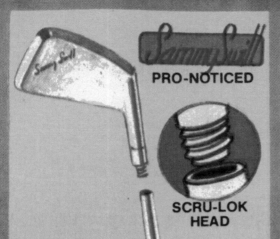
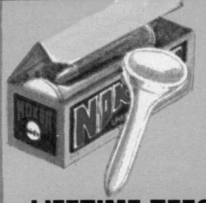
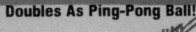

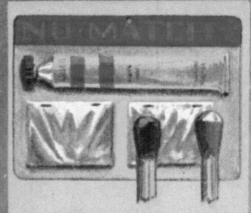

Dacron Republican-Democrat

February 12, 1978

pomade

Trailer Parks—Suburbs for the Space Age
by James R. Bland

New Hope for the Plump
by Paul Swift

America's Love Affair with WEEKENDS

SIR WALTER SCOTT'S

Personality Pomade

Want the facts? Want to learn the truth about prominent personalities? Want informed opinion? Want wild speculation? Weird lies? Write Sir Walter Scott, Pomade, 635 Madison Ave., New York, N.Y. 10022. Your full name and embarrassing things about your body will be used unless otherwise requested and sometimes even then.

Q. *Is Al Pacino a genius or a madman?* —Ellen Sparks, Clear Lake, Ind.
A. Neither. Al is a gifted young actor of Italian extraction who prefers work in the theater to film.

Q. *I have been told by personal friends of yours that you would like to say in your column that you consider Elizabeth Taylor to be the meanest, ugliest, trashiest overweight actress in America who has ever sold sexual favors in exchange for stardom, but that you fear legal reprisals and so remain silent. Is this true?* —Name Withheld.
A. Elizabeth Warner, as she is now known, is currently enjoying her role as wife of the candidate for governor of Virginia. Her husband, John Warner, considers her "the best campaigner I've ever met."

Q. *I'm confused. Is Farrah Fawcett-Majors really the illegitimate daughter of Princess Grace (Kelly) of Monaco and the late reclusive millionaire Howard Hughes? Please help.* —Lily Marcus, Bronx, N.Y.
A. Farrah is a talented and beautiful actress who rose to fame on the television series *Charlie's Angels.* She is at present living in Los Angeles with her actor husband, Lee *(The Six Million Dollar Man)* Majors. As of this writing, she is not the illegitimate daughter of Joan Crawford and Marlon ("Bud") Brando.

FARRAH FAWCETT-MAJORS   **THE LATE HOWARD HUGHES**

Q. *Is it true that people in Russia often have nothing to eat for dinner except Brussels sprouts and sour cream?* —Jack Clancy, Boston, Mass.
A. Russia, which calls itself "the Union of Soviet Socialist Republics," is a vast land of tundra and steppes located between Asia and Europe. It was formerly ruled by czars, until the Communist revolution resulted in a bloodbath of social upheaval. Today, many Russians live in igloos, work in salt or coal mines 13 hours a day, and often do eat nothing but Brussels sprouts and weak tea, although thin gruel is also a staple of the diet. Russian leaders drive around in large American-made limousines and eat caviar all the time.

RUSSIA   **BRUSSELS SPROUTS**

Q. *What is the theory of relativity? Please explain.* —Julia M., Niles, Ohio.
A. The theory of relativity states that everything is relative.

Q. *What is the real truth about Rosalind Russell?* —Bill Pechere, San Jose, Cal.
A. Rosalind Russell, or "Roz," as her friends called her, was a fine, fine lady, a talented actress, and wonderful human being, and a very, very great woman. She was marvelous—both as a lady and as a woman, as well as being a talented actress and a warm human person. She triumphed over a life of poverty, friends, career, fame, wealth, family, close and adoring colleagues, wonderful people from all over the world, and that special something which "guts" or "talent" or just plain old magic.

Q. *What did Tammy Grimes, who recently appeared in the N.Y. production of Tartuffe, buy in Zabar's, a prominent delicatessen, last week?* —E.E., Newark, N.J.
A. Tammy, currently the daughter of Boston Philharmonic maestro Seiji Ozawa and Commerce Secretary Juanita Kreps, bought a pound of pastrami, two pounds of coffee, a half-pound of muenster, and three well-done pickles.

Q. *Were Walt Disney and Roy Rogers really the same person? My husband says no, but I want to be sure.* —Jo Anders, Hat, Utah
A. Walt Disney and Roy Rogers were actually very close friends, but were not the same person. Walt was cremated after his death. There was a rumor circulating around Hollywood that Roy wanted to have Walt's ashes stuffed by one of Hollywood's foremost taxidermists, but this was not ever substantiated. It is true, however, that for several years Roy Rogers and operatic prima donna Maria Callas—once wife of Greek shipping magnate Aristotle Onassis—were the same person.

THE LATE WALT DISNEY   **ROY ROGERS**

Q. *Why did the South go to war against the North in the Civil War?* —Mrs. R.T., Ames, Ia.
A. The South wanted slaves and hated the North because they didn't like slavery, and there were other reasons such as industry and agriculture.

© SIR WALTER SCOTT 1978

pomade

THE SUNDAY NEWSPAPER MAGAZINE ROTOGRAVURE THING

FEBRUARY 12, 1978

chairman of the board, **DANNY ABELSON**   president, **ELLIS WEINER**
editor, **PENROSE N. PAPER**   publisher, **ARIF PEDESTRIAN**   assistant publisher, **CIELITO LINDA JONES**
editor at large, **CHARLES FOSTER CANDY KANE**   editor at extra-large, **COMMODORE PERRY WHITE**
art director, **ARTHUR DIRECTOR**
science director, **BUNSEN J. BURNER**
assistant art director, **ARTHUR DIRECTOR, JR.**   assistants to the assistant art director, **SALLY COOK, LALLY ROOKE, HALLIE BROOK**
assistant to the editor, **LOIS PENNY LANE**   editor's assistant, **EMILY POST TOASTIES**
giver of assistance to the editors, **MRS. PAUL FISH STICKS**
washington bureau chief, **LANCE PANTS**   washington chest-of-drawers chief, **RANCE DANCE**
washington fire chief, **VANCE "ANTS" CHANCE**

© 1978, Pomade Publications, Inc., 635 Madison Ave., New York, N.Y. 10022. All rights reserved under International, Pan American, and Trans-World Copyright Conventions, held every year at the lovely Hitler-Stalton Hotel, New York's newest and loveliest hospitality facility. Reproduction in whole or in part of any article without permission is up to you to decide, isn't it? POMADE ®, Marco Polo.

Please address editorial contributions to: Articles, Main Incinerator, Department of Sanitation, 12 Bowery, New York, N.Y. 10001. Although reasonable bribes will be taken, Pomade is not responsible for printing unsolicited material.

SAVE 50% ON CURRENT BEST SELLERS AS A MEMBER OF
THE HALF-A-BOOK-OF-THE-MONTH CLUB

These are the current best sellers, the books everyone is talking about. Now, through the Half-A-Book-Of-The-Month Club, you can receive half of a great best seller every month. These books are half as easy to read and half as easy to afford. Why not start your membership today by choosing any 8 half books for just $1.

Are You a Creative Person?

by Edward de Bonbon

How many times has this happened to you: You have a problem—say, how to hang a particular piece of bunting at the church picnic in such a way that it casts no shadow on the speaker's stand. You climb the ladder and try your hand at it. No luck. You climb the tree and try it from there; still no good. You do everything but practically stand on your head to make it work—and then someone comes along, takes one look at the situation and says, "Why, just tie one end to the volleyball pole!" and there's the solution.

How did that person see it in a flash, while you had to climb over everything in sight merely to end up frustrated? The answer is simple: *CREATIVE THINKING.* In the case of the bunting, you probably assumed that you had to tie it to either the tree or the platform support. Your creative friend, meanwhile, saw the problem more *holistically* (a psychologist's term for the ability to think of everything at the same time), and found an innovative solution with the volleyball pole. And if, by tying the bunting to the pole, the volleyball game is hampered? So what? Your job is to hang the bunting! Let the volleyballers think creatively and solve their own problem!

Other uses

But creative thinking has other uses besides problem solving. For example, take two people. Lock each one in a featureless, windowless room, supply them with food and nothing more, and wait three weeks. One person, the noncreative thinker, will slowly go crazy: alternately manic and withdrawn, he or she will rave and scream, or whimper quietly, or sleep for hours on end, or begin to pace ceaselessly around the room. While the creative thinker? Within a mere four or five days, he* will have devised two or three clever games to play with his food; he will invent nonexistent persons or beings (elves, fairies, spirits, or perhaps simply disembodied voices) with which to converse; he will devise a strict regimen of physical exercise to keep himself healthy, such as alternately slapping his hands on the floor and screaming "YAAAH HAH! ME BIG MONKEY MAN!" And, in less than two weeks, he will learn to conduct lengthy and often quite detailed conversations with himself out loud, and will be seen sitting cross-legged on the floor, discussing this or that topic with himself—often taking both sides of an argument and doing his darndest to convince himself of the correctness of his position!

No foolproof method

How do you know if *you* are a creative thinker? There is no foolproof method for quantifying

I say "he" because most creative thinkers are men. This is unfortunate if you are a woman, but it doesn't mean you can't try.

Albert Einstein, one of history's most creative thinkers

creativity, although many standardized tests administered to schoolchildren, the armed forces, and other pre-adult level minds often can achieve a rough breakdown of types of creativity. There are also no known ways of teaching creativity; however, there are ways to see if you have a certain outlook or tendency to think creatively—and, if not, to enable you to see where you might have taken the ordinary route instead of the creative one.

Try your hand at this test, and remember: In most cases, the correctness of the answers you arrive at is not as important as the way in which you arrived at the answers themselves.

Edward de Bonbon is a writer who specializes in vague generalities. He is the author of *Creativity and the World and the Universe* and the forthcoming *The Forthcoming.*

Creativity Test

1. Here are five matches. Using two matches, and without picking your pencil up off the paper, can you make these five into seven?

2. Your friend hands you two bags of marbles. One contains eight black marbles, and one contains eight white marbles. The next day he calls you on the phone and says, "Put the marbles into one bag," and

you do so. The next day he calls you and says, "I need three white marbles, please bring them over to my house." How many times must you reach into the bag of black and white marbles before you can be sure of delivering the three white ones he has requested?

4. An old man is sitting under a tree. A man walks up to him and points to another man chopping down a different tree some yards away. The man asks the old man, "Who is that other man chopping down the tree?" The old man smiles and says, "Brothers and sisters have I none, but that man's father's son's the one/Whose brother's sister had some fun/With my grandmother's other son/And when his wife, who hadn't done/What that man's mother told her son/She went and got a Gatling gun/And shot his sister in the bun/ And thus was that man's life begun." Who is the man chopping down the tree?

3. Look at this complex numeral for only three seconds. Now, without looking at it again, recite the numeral correctly.

2747364875894859600558575645534231

5. This sum consists of a series of letters in place of numbers. Can you make sense of it?

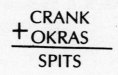

CRANK
+ OKRAS
———
SPITS

6. Tom has three apples. Mary comes along and says, "Say, Tom, why don't you give me one of those apples, and I'll give you one of my oranges?" Tom says, "Wait a minute, Mary. If I give you one of my apples, you'll probably take it to Jim and trade it for one of his pears. Then you'll have a pear and some oranges. I'll have some apples and an orange, and Jim will have one of my apples." Mary says, "So? What's wrong with that? Do you dislike Jim for some reason, Tom?" Tom says, "You bet I do, Mary. Last year my girl friend had an incurable disease, and Jim came over to her house and said, 'If I give you two peaches, will you give one to Tom so he'll give me one of those apples he's expecting to get within the year?'
"So my girl friend said, 'Please leave me alone, Jim, I have an incurable disease.' So Jim left her

house, and shortly thereafter went into a coma, and was unconscious for two weeks. Then suddenly one afternoon she woke up, and told us she had been in a beautiful place full of kind spirits and feelings of pleasantness, and that now that she had come back from this state so close to death itself, she could truly appreciate life and would from now on live each moment to the fullest."

7. Look at this pattern of dots. Can you connect all of the dots with one straight line, without picking your pencil up off the paper?

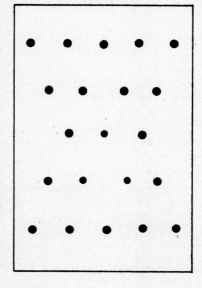

Answers

1. One key element of creativity is in the *definition of the problem.* In this case, there is no rule that says you cannot go out and buy another copy of this magazine, cut out two more matches from the other copy of this test, and place them beside the original five. And if somebody calls you a cheater, you just look them in the eye and say, "Well, I didn't pick my pencil up off the paper, did I?" And you didn't!

2. The answer is none. You're not a creative person. You can't be bothered with the petty demands of so-called "friends" who have nothing better to do than order you about and insist that you serve as their lackey, bringing them marbles of this or that color. You take the whole bag over to this "friend's" house, shove it into his or her hands,

say, "But that is incorrect arithmetic—

You may
15753
+ 24418
————
35789

5. The answer is: 35789

say, "Here. Select your own marbles, pal."

3. If there is one thing creative people know how to do well, it is delegate authority. Thus, in this problem, the creative solution would be to hire somebody to read the numeral back to you—as slowly as necessary, until you are able to repeat it.

4. Obviously the old man is senile, and his entire speech should be discounted. Therefore the matter of who is chopping down the tree is moot, so long as *somebody* is chopping it down.

6. Perhaps the keenest pleasure of being a creative person is the ability to spin forth tiny gems of imaginative fabrication almost at will. It surely has not escaped the reader's notice that I am a fairly creative person myself. Therefore I decided to omit a seventh problem, and instead let my fancy roam free, the result of which is the touching and even meaningful story you have just read.

7. Creative people know when to address problems and when to recognize that a problem may be insoluble, or, at least, not worth the effort.

In sum, then, creativity is elusive and evanescent, yet each of us has the capacity to have it and use it. Today, more than ever, old ways of thinking can be harmful and stifling; more and more our daily lives demand us to be creative. So next time you have a problem, don't just think about it in the old ways. Be creative! And see if it doesn't make a difference.

time and effort it may take to solve it. This particular case is one in which it simply isn't worth the trouble. What do you have to gain by connecting these stupid dots? In such an instance, the truly creative person knows that the best course of action is to go have a beer and watch television.

cally." "Yes, it is, but, from the standpoint of creativity, tough. No one said it had to be arithmetically correct, and anyway stop whining. It isn't creative.

INTELLIGENCE INVESTIGATION

by FLOYD SHNORE

Because of editorial laziness, Pomade regrets that it cannot answer queries concerning this column.

MIRACLE CURE A new medical report claims that impotence can be cured by walking backwards.

According to Dr. Linus Gretsch of the Stanford Institute of Somatic Morphology, impotence among males is particularly severe in cases where the subject has just completed sexual intercourse. "We have found a significant number of men unable to attain or sustain penile erections immediately after intercourse," he said.

"However," he continued, "in many cases, the condition was drastically relieved by subjecting the men to a program of walking backwards around a jogging course for a period of between thirty and sixty minutes. Following this treatment, most subjects were once again able to attain erections and enjoy satisfying sex lives."

CHANGING TIMES Fewer and fewer Americans are wearing underwear, according to a recent survey. The trend seems beyond question, but experts disagree as to its cause.

One sociologist suggests a link between the decline in underwear sales and television. "People watch more television than ever before," he told a recent meeting of experts recently. "They get hypnotized and forget to put on their undergarments."

But other experts disagree. They trace the decline in sales of underpants, panties, undershirts, bras, and even socks to women's lib, fast food chains, and disco music. Notes one expert, "Women want more jobs and equal pay. So they burn their bras. When they get jobs, they send their children to fast food chains for dinner. While the kids are out of the house eating hamburgers, the women go to discos, take off their underwear, and dance the hustle all night. Then they come home, throw away their children's underwear, and indulge in 'swinging parties' until the children come home."

HOST TO HOST Television talk show host Mike Douglas will host a special week of interview talk shows in May in which he'll interview other prominent TV talk show interview hosts.

Douglas will talk to interview hosts Merv Griffin, Johnny Carson, Dick Cavett, Tom Snyder, and Dinah Shore about their interview talk shows. Griffin, et al., have interviewed and talked to the most famous celebrities, stars, and personalities in the world.

The premiere show will feature Douglas hosting a talk with interview and talk show host Dick Cavett. Cavett, who once hosted a talk show on ABC and talks on a hosted interview show on PBS, will show film clips of himself talking to various stars and celebrities about interviews he has done with famous personalities, including one in which he tells former talk show host Jack Paar of interviews which he, Cavett, has had with former talk show interviewer Steve Allen about how witty and stimulating an interviewer, talker, and host he, Cavett, is.

Dear Sally,
I am riting you say hello I hope you having food I am no. Yesterday Jose and Pepito sick sick from having sores on all his skin maybe die soon. Later I look look gutter not find rat or maybe mowse but find man he dead he like my father hit by truck all blodd from mouth is coming out.
Your sponsor child,
Tristana

Dear Tristana,
How thoughtful of you to take the time to write to me about events in your country! Once again, thank you for your delightful letter, and we hope you will feel free to communicate with us in the future, should the need arise.
Sincerely,
Sally Taylor, Vice President,
Investment Division
Intercon

IN THE MIDST OF AFFLUENCE, MILLIONS OF AMERICANS GO TO BED GUILTY

Tristana and Sally have never met, yet they are connected by a bond stronger than friendship. Guilt. Tristana lives in terrible poverty. Each night she sleeps in a filthy hovel in the slums of a South American country too poor to protest against the exploitation of its people and resources.

Sally is the only child of professional parents from a wealthy suburb of Detroit. She holds degrees from Vassar and Wharton, and likes to ski and travel to Europe.

Tristana was a malnourished little girl with nothing to pin even the frailest hopes on. She was desperate. Sally was an attractive woman with everything going for her. She was guilty.

Today, thanks to the Guilty Christians' Fund, all that has changed. We "introduced" Sally and Tristana to one another. Sally's letters are like a beacon of hope shining into the little girl's dark life, showing her that there *is* a better world, a happier world, a world where smiles replace tears and hunger is almost unknown: Sally's world. And Sally sleeps well now, knowing that she has finally *done something* to make a less fortunate person's life a little brighter.

Isn't it time *you* did something to relieve guilt? Your guilt. Sally's guilt. All of our guilt.

For the Love of a Good Night's Sleep

CARTER BONANZA

Things are looking up for the Carters from Plains, Ga. NBC has announced plans for a million-dollar-plus series starring Miz Lillian, the president's mother. The show, probably to be called "Jes' Sittin'," will feature Miz Lillian in a loose interview/entertainment format in which various stars and noteworthy personalities will be invited to interview Miz Lillian about subjects of their choosing. In between talk segments, the grand old lady of Plains will entertain her on-camera guests with songs, impressions, comedy routines, and thought-provoking commentary on the issues of the day. The tab: $100,000 for Miz Lillian, not including merchandizing spin-offs and syndication residuals.

Meanwhile, First Daughter Amy has inked a contract with Random House for a book about what Uncle Billy Carter thinks about kids and dogs. Also sister Ruth Carter Stapleton is reportedly considering offers from International Harvester to lend her name to a line of baling machines. This hot on the heels of brother Billy and his nephew, Jimmy's son Chip, having announced their joint ownership of a chain of dry cleaning-bowling establishments where patrons can roll a game of tenpins while waiting for their suits to be pressed. Between these activities, and First Lady Rosalynn's announcement of her candidacy for the presidency of Belgium, the Carter clan now has more than Jimmy to be proud of.

HERE COME THE ORIGINAL** HITS

Performed by "THE ORIGINAL ARTISTS***"

3889 ì	THIS IS THE MOODY GLUES
MHTA	
25963 POL	CARL SIMON Hotfeet
6932 *	CHICANO IX
64440	POGO The Best of Pogo
23071	ELECTION NIGHT ORCHESTRA A New World Record
70041 *	BUFFALO SPRINGSTEEN
ABC DC	
26855 OLUMBIA	BACHMAN TURNIP Overdub
51462 *	GEORGE BUNSEN Burnin'
26439	INGLENOOK HUMPERDINK Greatest Hits
25505	TOE, KNEE, ORLANDO AND DAWN Throw a Yellow Rope Over a Limb of the Old Oak Tree
2088	THE QUEERS A Night at the Ballet
26850 *	HERB ALPERT AND THE MARIJUANA GRASS Greatest Hits Vol. II
267 * CAPITO	LESLIE FIEDLER AND THE BOSTON POPS The Lone Ranger Overture
24686 IFESON	BERT AND FABIAN BACHARACH
26514 COL	OLIVIA MUTANT JOHN Have You Never Been a Mallomar?

26291 M A	PAUL ANCHOR No Way
6980 †	THE BEST OF NAPKIN COLE
26928 †	RAY GONNIF Send in the Gays
6868 † MBIA	HARRY CHAFIN Songs
69795	LEN CAMPBELL Rhinestone Goatherd
25974 POLYDO	BARRY WHITE Fat Enough to Love You
6876	MORMON TABLENAPKIN CHOIR O Swell Thou Art
26994 †	CAPTAIN CHENILLE Contracts Will Keep Us Together
27196	EMERSON, FAKE AND PALMER On Tour

11 tapes for 29 cents*

(If you agree to buy 129 tapes at the regular price of $8.79 within twelve days)

26353 * ARIST	ROBIN TROWEL Solo
71890 A	DONNY AND MARIE OSMOROID
72153 * MHIA	STEVE E. WONDER Songs in the Key of Hash
27 53 * RSHNE	TUBULAR BALLS
67195 COLUMB	LYNN AMBERSOL Country Hits
23985 OLUMBIA	THE COUNT BASIC ORCHESTRA The Duke of Wellington Songbook
68185 OLUMBI	SIMON GARFUNKEL My Little Bank

*plus shipping charges of $2.99 per selection
** "Original Hits" is a trademark of E-Z Record Club
*** "The Original Artists" are under exclusive contract to E-Z Record Club.

Hors d'oeuvres for a mallow cocktail hour. Just some of the winning combinations possible. On our platter, marshmallows team up with anchovies, cocktail wieners, cheese, mustard, caviar, cocktail onions, and dips.

MARSHMALLOW MAGIC

Whether you're planning a hearty winter meal, a buffet-style spread, or a light summer salad, marshmallows can be your magic wand in creating kitchen sorcery to please and delight your whole family. In the right hands, this versatile foodstuff can make the difference between bland and grand in dozens of different ways. Used in its various forms—full size, cocktail size, miniature, or spread—to help you create delights guaranteed to please the palate as well as the eye.

Marsh-kabob! No need to make the kids wait until after dinner for their favorite cookout treat. Simply place beef cubes, onion, green pepper, and marshmallows on skewer and suspend over fire.

Nifty breakfast or delicious TV treat. Simply add milk and sugar.

Rivalry provides incentive to achieve at weekly sessions called "tests." Points are awarded for correct answers and students are encouraged to compete with each other for the "top mark," meaning the one with the highest "score" number on the "test."

Learning the ABC's of School Reform

by Lawrence Gallump

CHICAGO, ILLINOIS

Donald Bright remembers the April morning two years ago when the idea first came to him. He was bidding a graduating student farewell when he noticed a troubled look on the young man's features. "What's the matter?" the young teacher remembers saying. "Now that you have a diploma, you can look forward to a career and a long happy life." "That's just it, Don," the six-footer replied. "I can't read or write and I don't know how to count. How can I go through with my plans of becoming a doctor?"

The three "R's"

Don Bright's answer to that troubled graduate, and the many others in the school who feel that their courses just don't equip them to compete in today's fast-paced world, was to set up a special prob-

Hard sums for soft drugs at "The Drug Store," which brings the real world into the classroom as students become "dealer" and "client" for an hour each day.

lem at the school based on a theory he calls "The Three R's." "That stands for reading, 'riting, and 'rithmatic," jokes the new director of Experimental Studies at the school,

"and it's based on the perception that Psychic Healing and Inner Volleyball and Vaginal Politics just aren't relevant to our young people today."

Relevant education

At first, the other teachers were resistant to Don's idea, feeling that students could not afford the time spent away from their normal studies. But now that the program is in its second year and starting to show results, Don finds his colleagues are volunteering their own time to help out. "Naturally, it seems strange at first, but the excitement and enthusiasm is infectious, and now even the trustees are beginning to come around," says Don. But for Don, the bottom line is that he is able to help the kids themselves realize that school can be an enjoyable learning experience. "If we can't teach the kids about read-

ing and writing in a way that they can relate to, they'll learn it elsewhere," says Don Bright, educational innovator, who then turns back to the beginning readers who require his attentions.

Sharon, able to read about her country's history for the first time, learns about a British invasion that had nothing to do with the Beatles or the Dave Clarke Five.

10

jest for laughs
by erma bumback

Editor's Note: Housewife and best-selling author Erma Bumback describes herself this way: "You could say I'm just part housewife and part best-selling author." Her chronicles of suburban fads and foibles, notably "Carpools and Crabgrass," "Laundry and Lawns," and "Gravy and Grass" provide a steady stream of hilarious mirth on the subject of suburban life. Here are some of her favorites.

It was one of those days. First the washing machine had gone on strike, the 15-year-old had come home with an injured football helmet, and then I had returned from my dip in the car pool to find Ginger, the beloved family tabby, dead on the kitchen floor. It looked like the poor thing had been hit by a car and come inside to die. Holding back the tears, I hid the kitty behind some bushes for later burial and decided to say nothing to the kids until dinner time.

Naturally, this night my husband was held up and arrived just as the meat loaf was breathing its last. "Dear," I said, as he tucked in, "there's something we have to discuss. The *c-a-t* has been *k-i-l-l-e-d*." "What does that mean?" said nine-year-old Billy, not fooled for a second. "It means, gang," said noble husband coming to the rescue, "that Ginger has gone to sleep for a long time."

"See, Nancy," replied Billy, "I told you they had nine lives. We clubbed the little fucker with a brick and he's just sleeping it off!"

I knew it would happen sooner or later. But after all, I was the one who had insisted on our getting a five-speed, two-toned, chrome-bumpered leaf blower in the first place. It was either that or you-know-who out there with a rake and a very sore back. So we got one, and it was that very same contraption that my husband was putting to use as I conducted an investigation to find out which one of the twins had come up with the delightful idea of making tiny pinholes in Mommy's diaphragm last June.

That out of the way, we climbed into the station wagon, hubby replacing one steering wheel for another, and set off backward down the driveway right into a pile of leaves and the unmistakable and sickening crunch of a small child being run over. "Uh-oh!" I said, "we've just run over one of our children." "No, we haven't dear," said unflappable hubby. "It's the four-year-old from down the block I saw playing in the leaves a few minutes ago. You always expect the worst," and having put Mom in her place, proceeded to set sail for the supermarket.

And then there was the time my husband woke up with an extraordinary plan—he was going to find out just who he was supporting. It was high time, he announced, that the captain of this ship knew the size and condition of his complement, from romper room to attic—even down to details like wives and pets.

After he pried the twins away from the television, with the help of a crowbar and a lot of muscle, and flushed the various inhabitants of our shaky craft from their hiding places, he assembled the entire sleepy crew on the front lawn. "All right, troop," he barked, "is there anyone here who knows of any inhibitants, animal or human, that are not clearly visible on this deck?" "Please, Dad . . . I mean, Captain," ventured our youngest, "what about Mom's pussy?"

"That's not very funny," snapped loyal hubby. "I suspect someone else was feeding it because I haven't seen hide nor hair of it for months."

Collection illustrated is almost actual size

A convenient acquisition plan

As a subscriber to The Great Couples of America, you will receive one medallion per month until your collection is complete. This means, until we have sent you all the medallions you are entitled to. You may not write the Committee and complain that your children, or even you yourself, have inadvertently eaten one or more of the medallions, and request additional medallions of a previous issue merely to update your collection.

You are guaranteed the price of $29.50 per medallion—this, *regardless of market fluctuations in the price of chocolate or gold-like leaf wrapping.*

In addition, you will be sent, at no further charge, a handsome box in which to house your collection. Crafted of the finest balsa, it fits any standard refrigerator shelf for easy preservation of these fine yet edible objects.

Subscription deadline, February 14, 1979

This is a collection you will be proud to own, once you own it. A collection to be displayed, admired, and shared with your children and grand-children, or merely eaten all by yourself late at night when nobody is looking.

To obtain it, simply fill out the application below, and mail it to Nathan Hale Chocolate Mint, Nathan Hale Place, Pennsylvania 19919.

You need send no payment at this time.

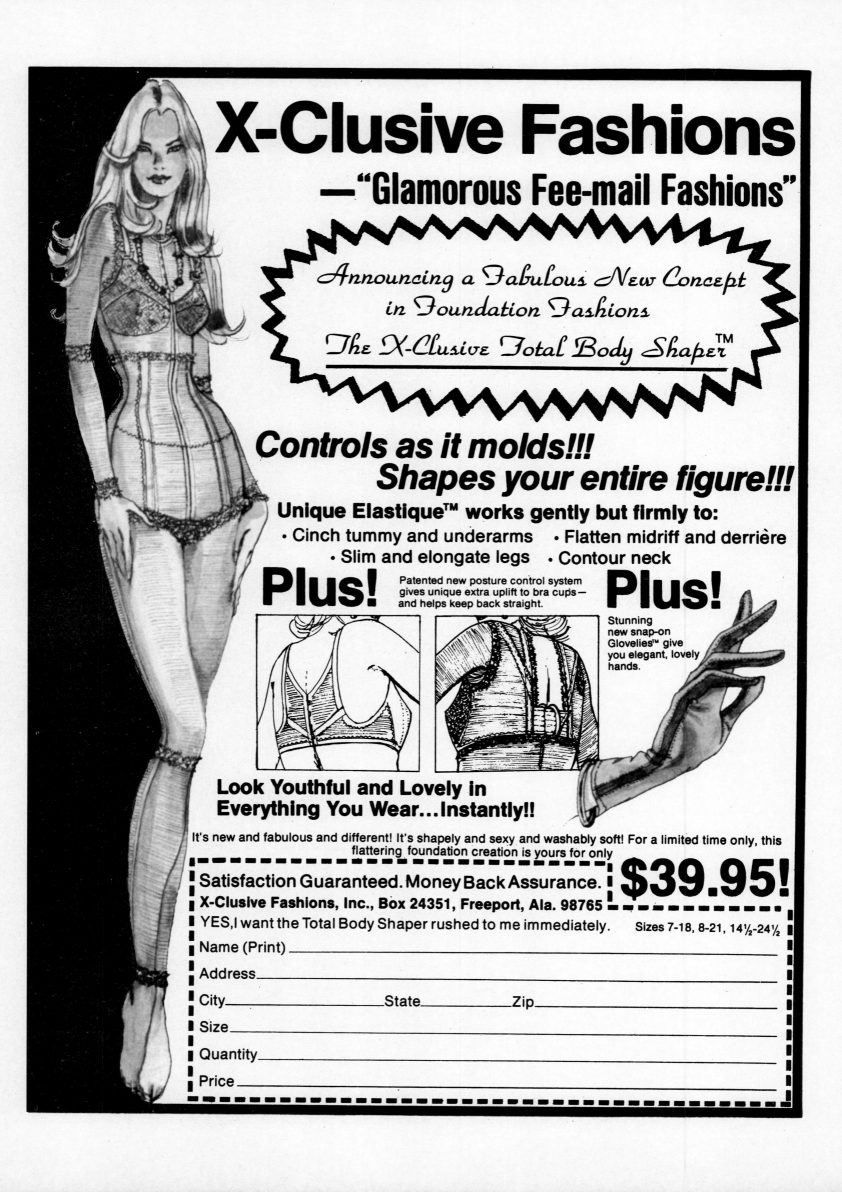

POMADE OF PROGRESS

LOOK AT THESE WONDERFUL NEW INVENTIONS MAKING YOUR LIFE BETTER ■ BY JOHN DRYDEN

END HOT HANDS: You need no longer burn your hands when unscrewing hot light bulbs from one socket to place in another. New bulb turner grasps hot bulb, gently unscrews it, then reverse motor screws it into new socket. Adjustable brackets adapt to almost any size bulb, while sturdy electric motor uses standard outlet power. $19.95 each. *Merchandise Appliances, Inc., 123 Main Street, Your Town, State.*

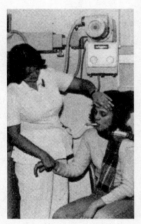

DIGITAL THERMOMETER: Ends ambiguous, hard-to-read temperatures when you or loved one are ill. Digital readout features LED thermocouple, operates on twelve size "D" batteries. Available in oral or rectal models, batteries not included. $49.94. *Commodity Manufacturing Co., 543 Street Road, Chicago, Mississippi.*

CLEANER CLEANER: Now there is a cleaner that cleans dirt, grime, grease, etc., off most household containers of cleaners (cans, bottles etc.). Optional spray attachment gets those hard-to-clean places. Pump-style nozzle is powered by sturdy electric motor, emits no polluting fluorocarbons. $35.00. *Consumer Goods Co., Inc. 508 N. Avenue Boulevard, Los Angeles, Peru.*

Obfuscations

Congress has its way.

We couldn't have said it better. "Learning without thought is labor lost, thought without learning is perilous." Confucius (551-479 B.C.) said that, and he might well have been thinking of the current restrictive policies regarding supertankers and enhanced recovery techniques at the time! In regard to the latter, our engineers are currently working on a means of extracting heavy oil using hot water, carbon dioxide, and a special chemical compound, all piped underground and ignited to help Mother Nature along. Naturally Congress and the ecology lobby would like us to develop and utilize this expensive and dangerous technique without hurting anyone or charging a cent. Confucius would understand.

⊙

Don't say we didn't warn you. Scientific sources report that if EPA standards were strictly enforced, every American citizen could be arrested for violation of air and water quality standards! You see, the human body expels 2.3 pints of liquid and 19 ounces of solid waste per day—way over the proportion allowed for "Mobile Energy Utilizing Vehicles." No one seriously suggests arresting Americans for performing their normal ablutions, but it does give you an idea of the kind of Federal Regulation Monster we have spawned in Washington. Oh, and by the way, you might think twice before breaking wind near one of the 12,347 air quality monitoring devices currently installed throughout the country; if you do, you may find yourself telling the nation what you had for breakfast at one of the televised hearings the EPA is pushing for!

⊙

A Quote We Like. "The very essence of a free government consists of...TRUSTS...bestowed for the good of the country." — John C. Calhoun.

⊙

Ask not what your country can do to you...Did you know that if all the forms printed by the Government Printing Office every year were sorted into 20-lb.stacks, there would be enough stacks to crush 2.5 million innocent babies? Think about it...

Nobil
Presented to the public as a self service by Nobiloil Corporation.

ELECTRIC BOOKMARK: Newly developed device can be inserted in any book, in any page, and instantly records the place you stopped reading. Pleasant light (available in red, blue, or amber) blinks to remind you of unfinished reading matter. *Merchprod, Inc., P.O. Box 2, Slow, Mo.*

LAWN WARMER: New large-size acrylic blanket keeps lawns warm during winter months, protects grass from snow, sleet. Available in several decorator designs and colors; sold by square yard. Doubles as giant picnic blanket during summer months. Sturdy electric motor keeps blanket affixed to ground during wind. $3.75/sq. yd. *Appliance Merchandisers, Inc., 55 Byway Highway, Farmer-in-The, Del.*

REFRIGERATOR BOAT: New multipurpose combination boat-refrigerator. Folds down for easy carrying (weight: 1700 lbs.), then unfolds for sailing. Afterwards, stands on end, plugs into standard outlet, becomes small refrigerator. Sturdy electric motor (10 hp.) cools perishables, propels at speeds up to 8 knots. $430.00. *Products Producers, Inc., P.O. Box 4, Fucktah, Utah.*

Pomade of Progress items are NOT advertising. In some cases, they are NOT items. Write to source or manufacturers if not available in stores. Allow three to four weeks for reply, and if no reply follows, count yourself lucky. We can say this because this is NOT an advertisement, and we do NOT have to worry about loss of revenue from irate advertisers. Manufacturers: POMADE will consider ideas but cannot correspond. We will consider the idea of corresponding, but will not actually correspond.

For People Who Like Books But Don't Like To Read.

THE GREAT BOOK EDGES OF THE WESTERN WORLD

This unique collection of the Great Book Edges of the Western World gives you the expensive look of quality books without the words or paper. These impressive titles are printed on authentic dust cover paper and mounted on a lightweight, wood-like shelf unit that gives any room the look of wealth and taste instantly! With the Great Book Edges of the Western World you can look well-read without opening a book!

Indeed. Imagine, by means of the following example, how our fabulous collection works. Plato's Republic contains hundreds of pages of the popular Greek philosopher's detailed and highly complicated logical argument; unquestionably one of the greatest treasuries of pure thought in the history of mankind, yet wholly devoid of appeal or entertainment by modern standards. Our research shows that a person of average intelligence and reading skills would, unless specially involved or versed in philosophy, conservatively require a minimum of 1,350 hours to complete the book. At an hour an evening, every evening, the total time expenditure computes to a little over three and one half years.

Not only would such a long period limit an adult with a normal life expectancy to an approximate life-total of 15 such works, a patently meager sum to be sure; but in addition, the typical individual may encounter some difficulty in effectively recalling portions of the book read during the first year when he or she has progressed to the second or third year. How many times have you asked yourself toward the end of a 90-minute film drama, "Was that the woman he met in the restaurant at the beginning of the story?" Now, simply transfer that sort of inquiry to a three-and-one-half-year book that consists primarily of two characters extemporizing with one another.

"Did Socrates conclude that a state can exist without agriculture?" is a question you might be asking yourself in 1980, without so much as a clue as to the point in your previous years of reading where the passage appeared. Suddenly, factoring the highly probable element of fuzzy and forgotten links in the discourse, the projected total of 15 books dwindles to an oppressively laborious and tragically deficient one or two. Imagine yourself on your deathbed, flanked by your pair of books. How impressive! Empty walls, empty shelves, and empty space to squarely exhibit an empty, illiterate life.

Now, you have the opportunity to fill those walls, shelves, and spaces with a formidable collection of the Western World's finest written titles, telegraphing for all to see the rich and illuminated texture of your existence. Great Book Edges of the Western World frees you to do the things you can do, while yet securing for you the reward for something you would like to do, but cannot, ever.

We also feature The Great Book Edges of the Mid-Western World, Great Medical Book Edges, Great Legal Book Edges, and for the youngsters, The Great Children's Classic Book Edges.

Spend a "WEEK" in Dacron this Sunday!

DACRON
Republican-Democrat
Sunday Week

Sunday, February 12, 1978

Bunny Gillespie
MISS TEEN-AGE DACRON 1978

MISS WEST DACRON

CALL 555-0831

MISS NORTH DACRON

DACRON'S ILLEGAL ALIENS
Will They Both Be Deported?

A MOUTHFUL OF COURAGE
One Woman's Battle with
Breath Cancer

WINTER ADVENTURE
Excitement and Danger Mark
Excursion into Ohio's Wild
Cleveland Region

Write Your Mind

Letters to the *Sunday Week*
from *Sunday Week* Readers

Please attach your name and address to all WRITE YOUR MIND letters. We will delete them and parts of your letter, too, if you please, Enclose a stamped, self-addressed envelope if you wish your letter returned or do not if you don't.

Dear Sunday Week,

I read with enjoyment an article in your last week's—an essay of a humorous nature about how roast pork was invented, by Barry Deakin. But I was very much surprised to find when looking through my son's grade twelve English text almost the same story written by a fellow called Lamb. Has Mr. Lamb taken Dr. Deakin's story, and, if so, did he have permission?

Mr. Stosh Tadpulski
1171 N. Longfellow

Mr. Deakin, a free-lance contributor, seems to have gotten the idea for his piece from Mr. Lamb, but we feel that, since it was published so long ago and in England, and that since Deakin took a completely different tack with his piece, it's o.k.

Dear Sunday Week,

I was glad to read Miss Plant's article in your last issue unmasking pet store owners who feed small guppies to their larger fish. It is high time this practice was put a stop to by someone. The plight of a tiny helpless guppy trapped in a tank with an Oscar or such is enough to break anyone's heart and I fully agree with the anonymous pet store customer who says she wants to break the aquariums with her camera and let all the Oscars die for being such beasts. Imagine how you would feel trapped in the whirlpool bath at the health spa with a cannibal as big as a deep freeze with six-foot-long molars chasing you around. More of these articles and hoorah for Miss Plant.

Gladys Howkers
Dacron Dells

Dear Sunday Week,

As president of the Dacron council of used car dealers, I must take an offense at your "journalist's" suggestions that we car dealers sometimes resort to deceptive practices in our attempts to sell cars. I can only say that your "journalists" have resorted to the same practices in their attempts to sell articles to your magazine, and when they talk about dealers "winding back the odometers" they are not only winding back the clock to another more corrupt period but they've also got their geography mixed for this has never happened except years ago in Muncie when the owner of the dealership was away. The people who have been sold junk are not the car buyers of Dacron but the readers of this magazine.

Herb Wiesenhimer
President, Dacron Council
of New and Used Car Dealers

Mail all WRITE YOUR MIND mail to:
WRITE YOUR MIND c/o *Sunday Week*
The *Dacron Republican-Democrat* Weekly Magazine
c/o The *Dacron Republican-Democrat*
100 Polk Street   Dacron, Ohio 43701

Dacron Republican-Democrat
Sunday Week

MAGAZINE EDITOR *Edward Mann* **ASSOCIATE EDITORS** *Donovan Groat,*
Dotty Schwimmer **SPORTS EDITOR** *Sandy "Snapper" Trudge* **TRAVEL EDITOR**
Nora Bugbaum **PHOTO EDITOR** *Vince Blum* **FOREIGN EDITOR** *Brian Torst*
ART DIRECTOR *Newton Drige* **WRITERS** *Larry Mickle, Jerry Burger, Lyn Ellbown*

OUR COVER
*Darlene Sputzy, 28, is named the 1978 MISS TEEN-AGE DACRON by Dacron's
Rotary Club Officers who acted as judges in yesterday's 10th annual Miss
Teen-age Dacron Pageant. Miss Sputzy received a $100 scholarship to the
college of her choice and a gold charm bracelet with a charm inscribed "Miss
Teen-age Dacron 1978" in addition to her beautiful trophy. She will now
travel to Columbus to compete in next month's Miss Teen-age Ohio contest
whose winner will be a contestant in this spring's Miss Teen-age Great Lakes
Pageant at Cedar Point Amusement Park in Sandusky.
Miss Betty Cordell, 17, of West Dacron and Miss Angelica Hotten, 18, of North
Dacron, were 2d and 3d place.*

© all contents copyright S.C.O.C.G.E.T.& T. Communications Group 1978

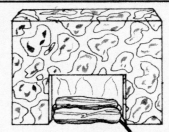
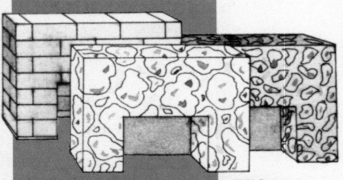

St. Valentine

Patron Saint of "Honeys," "Sweeties," "Hug-a-Bunnies," "Snookums," and "Tootsie-Wootsies"

The wonderful legend of St. Valentine as represented in art by talented local painter and guitar player Faun Rosenberg.

by PATRICIA PLANT

February 14, the day traditionally celebrated by Americans with chocolates and brightly colored cards covered with romantic verses and hearts that look big enough and strong enough to power a 747-sized homing pigeon or, if they are looked upon as symbols of love—which they are—to power a long marriage.

February 14, the day the British serfs, or servants, believed that molting doves chose their mates for life.

February 14, the day Bugs Moron and Al Caper were mugged out in a garage that came to the Dacron fair last year and bullet holes from which were sold by mail-order to Dacronians until Assistant Chief of Police Carl Leper discovered a fraud upon opening his envelope.

February 14 is Saint Valentine's Day, the day we tell each other how much we like each other. How many of us know who St. Valentine was, though? Don't most of us just say, "Oh, he was a saint and very pious" and go on our way more interested in the third class mailing rate for our greeting cards or finding out whether Tad's Carmel Fudg-E-Grams are delivered to friends in Muncie?

Father Liam O'Bottle, a priest from New York staying with relatives in Dacron, says that St. Valentine is a saint surrounded by mysteries because there were seven of him who flourished at various times in Italy, France, Belgium, Spain, and North Africa, although people should not confuse him with a Negro even though he flourished in Africa because it was in the time of Emperor Claudius, and before Negroes could be saints.

Father O'Bottle is an impish man who looks sort of like a cocktail cigarette all dressed up in black with a white collar and a pink face like a coal.

"The *Acta Sanctorum*," he says, "the treatise which chronicles the doughty deeds of the Saints, tells precious little about the Valentines. However, it would appear that the two whose day falls upon the fourteenth of February were Italian orators; one a priest of Rome, the other Bishop of Terni. Both died on the same day and were buried on the Via Flamina. It is because of the striking mysterious inexplicability of the aforementioned circumstances that many have concluded that St. Valentine was a Siamese twin. One of him a distinguished bishop, the other a humble parish priest."

Father O'Bottle went on to say that some heretics and schismatics believe that Valentine's Day was a descendent of an old Roman feast called Lupercalia which Father O'Bottle says was nothing but a big blow-out like the country club "Spring Thing."

He said instead of giving the woman chocolates or flowers, however, the men slaughtered the family dog, cut a strip called a *februa* from its back, and gave the girls a fierce lashing which was supposed to promote fertility but only promoted abandonment and wantonness right on the floor.

"I myself believe," said the Father, "that this saint's day, first celebrated by the English, was simply an attempt by Britishers to arrogate the old Latin practice of lashing to themselves for sinful purposes."

It is strange to think that with all our modern politeness and civilization, we might still be celebrating the martyrdom of a double-headed saint and the wild naked festival of raw crudity of the Romans under Claudius. It is strange to think, too, that the two Valentines might have had a wonderful life as priests saying Masses to each other and calling responses or hearing each other's confession and granting absolution—a very strange idea, or it would be if it were true.

Father O'Bottle is in town till Tuesday and will say a guest Mass at St. Betty's today.

ASPHALT THROUGH THE AGES:
PART I

Man's imagination has been captured by asphalt almost since the dawn of time.

Stone Age men were familiar with "nature's own asphalt" in the plentiful tar pits of their prehistoric period.

Tar pits were a source of many important resources for early man.

They provided him with tar, pits, and large pits full of tar.

They trapped large animals so that he could see them up close and also trapped smaller animals and even birds.

Thus began mankind's age-old romance with asphalt.

Dacron's "Gay" Scene

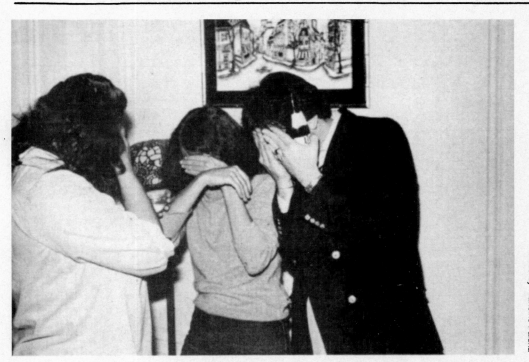

Dacron's gay community at a Gay Awareness meeting. They are each aware that the others are gay.

Photos by Francine Paluka

This woman was not at all in touch with the gayness that psychiatrists say we all have inside us and in fact got real mad when asked if she was.

Dacron gays are often forced to meet in places like this.

by FRANCINE PALUKA

Gays in Dacron, and there are some, all believe that what two or three adult people want to do at home with their own private sex lives is a private matter. For this reason, most are reticent about giving their real names, preferring to call themselves "Binky" or "the Countess" and to give only a phone number until they have seen your photograph.

I spoke with a gay woman who asked to remain anonymous for fear she would be discriminated against.

"Of course we don't know for sure we would be discriminated against, as no one knows our names—but it's as sure as anything, no one at all's going to discriminate *for* us. So, we just lie low."

Many gays do feel they would be discriminated against if their life-styles were lived openly.

"We feel very much a minority. Well, gosh, we *are* one. But having to be so secretive is really an obstacle to us enjoying all our happiness that we have."

Assistant Police Chief Carl Leper sums it up this way, saying, "As long as they don't go round bothering anyone, I won't crack down on them and see they get their name in the paper and their a---- in jail."

To a Dacron gay, not "bothering" anyone is a direct interference in their methods of finding new friends. Which interference could be construed as a violation of their human rights.

Many of the young Dacronians I talked to about gay rights revealed an appalling lack of understanding of what homosexuality was and what gayness meant. Some showed a lack of interest or even a contempt of gay persons or for the gay part of themselves which everybody has according to all psychiatrists.

These young Dacronians, unless they are exposed to gayness when they are young, will grow up to be as oppressive as all previous generations have been of gay people.

Gays have been oppressed for generations, though of course this current generation of gays has only been oppressed for one generation as they have only been alive that long. It is time to stop this cycle through awareness of ourselves and each other's needs. For these problems affect the whole community or at least certain blocks on 6th Street of it and it is up to us to do something about this.

While writing this article, I have had much trouble with my conscience which wanted to make it longer and more in depth and my editor who wanted to cut it out or make it shorter. We reached a compromise and he had his way. People interested in becoming involved in gay struggles can do so at Popper's on 6th Street (men) or at the Whippersnappers Disco (men and women) on the East Side.

Francine Paluka is a practical nurse who works part-time as a high school girl's gym teacher. She lives with her friend Marylin Armbruster who is also a gym teacher and Co-chairperson of the Dacron Chapter of the National Organization of Women People.

Editor's Note: In keeping with the tradition of free speech, we have published Ms. Palooka's article taking out only those pages deemed offensive. The editors and publisher of the Republican-Democrat do not in any way agree with her at all but had no time to assign another article. You are invited to exercise your free speech and tell us not to do it again.

Little Canada

A touch of "up there" right over here

by LARRY MICKLE   **Photographs by "Mac" MacKenzie**

Dacron's "Little Canada," down on Hacknut Street between Irving and Hawthorne.

Down on Hacknut Street between Irving and Hawthorne, not far from the river, the tiny enclave that is "Little Canada" is set into the asphalt skin of Dacron like an icicle dropped in the snow. Dacron's Canadian community has lived and worked in this area for as long as they have been there, and restaurants like "Eat" and stores like "MacKenzie's Hardware" cater to customs shaped by a climate and society a number of miles to the north.

There is much to discover in "Little Canada," shops to service the needs of people who need things like cheddar cheese or wool clothes or a saw. "Eat" can provide the light or heavy eater with a wide selection of hamburgs, including cheese and onion flavored varieties, as well as a hearty stew, the steam from which fogs the windows of the cafe and the glasses of the customers in that same "short order" with which the food appears.

If you really wish to know "Little Canada" though, you must know the people. You must be ready to partake in their easy banter which can start at any minute though usually not for the first fifteen or so. And once you have been accepted by a Canadian, you must be prepared to bear the full force of his hospitality—an invitation to purchase a drink or to walk to the mail box for instance, or you may even find yourself invited to a Canadian home. There you will see fascinating handicrafts, such as sand cast candles with three to seven legs, multi-handled clay beer steins that will not stand and must perforce be drained at a draught and strange knitted hanging things that look like "jolly jumpers" for children but are actually "jolly jumpers" manufactured under license in Canada and called "happy jumpers."

Note also on your visit (and, by the way, if you forget your host's name, refer to him as "Sarge." This is good

If Canadians had a national dish, it would probably be stew.

Home will always be Canada for Canadians, say some of them.

Tradition abounds in the homes of America's trans – planted North Americans.

Canadian cheddar cheese is found in almost every icebox in "Little Canada." Similar to American cheddar cheese (right), Canadians say you have to be born there to tell the difference.

Even Canadians who've lived "down here" for most of their lives still sport the distinctive headgear of their homeland.

Canadian manners, like "Mate" in England) the great quaint grey-painted radio with the shake roof sitting upon the kitchen table. This is the Canadian's link with his homeland. Set at the factory to receive but one channel, the CBC, at only one volume, loud, it brings news of home to Canadians as far away as Indiana. From this "wireless" you'll hear Canadian music, all seemingly performed on the ocarina, and their news, which is much like our news but smaller. But perhaps it won't be on and your host will take out an old oilskin and unwrap a well-worn deck of cards which he will throw on the floor and invite you to pick up while he times you on his pocket watch. This game is played in Canada to help sharpen skills such as gathering, picking up and stacking into

Continued on Page 24

Canada is a bi-cultural country, being both French and like us.

The Lighter Side of Stuff by BIFF LIGHTER

Biff Lighter is the humour columnist for the Republican-Democrat and has had several paragraphs published in the Reader's Digest. His play, The Sun Looks Like an Orange, was produced by the Dacron Little Catholic Players League and got many reviews.

A Conversation with Mark Twain

You know, I often find as I grow older that the mind is a tricky thing. Like an old engine, say, or a 1934 Willys Overland, it has its own quirks and you have to allow for them when you're making use of it. It works at its own speed and it doesn't do to try and hurry it along as I found to my chagrin the other day when dashing out to a Rotary meeting. I returned home to find the pot roast I had been planning to eat halfway through the spin cycle in the washer-dryer and a crock pot full of golf socks simmering nicely on the stove. Well, of course the roast was ruined and I had to get professionals in to clean the sock steam off my kitchen windows.

People often ask me what I think of today's young humorists—how do they compare to the humorists of my day? Well, I told you the mind is a tricky thing and I seem to remember talking about that very matter with Mark Twain on the deck of a riverboat several weeks ago. "Mr. Twain, what do you think of all this so-called humor that's going around now on the TV and newsstands?" I said. Old Sam Clemens looked up at me and I could see he was of a mind to speak on the matter.

"Biff," he said, "there's two kinds of humorists; humorists who say there are two kinds of humorists and others who do not. It's these latter kind that seem so prevalent in your modern times, the most glorious and prosperous times in the world.

"They seems to believe that contempt of government is funny, and that flouting laws against marijuana in public is smart—they forget the fact that their rights are privileges that may be taken away. You see, Biff, society is like a parent—it has its little peculiarities—but it also has a parental type authority; it can 'ground' us in a jail, or it can cut our 'allowance' by putting us on a blacklist so we don't get any work. This is done for the benefit of the whole social family, though it is sometimes as hard for us as it is for children to realize society is only looking out for our future.

"That's why we shouldn't be smart alecky or sarcastic about governments any more than we should about our parents, nor should we go around making cruel fun of our brothers and sisters, or fellow citizens, just because they spend good money on fuzzy toilet seat covers, or something.

"Biff, one of the wonderful things about America is that there is room for all different types of people. People who want to jiggy-jig Chilean elections or go to war against Communism. Other people, who prefer to be older, stay home and support those overseas. Some people want to run large multi-national corporations, others prefer to work for these. Some to make laws, some to obey them. There is room in our great country for all these types of people.

"In our country now we have some dissidents. Some are humorists, bitter and lashing out at the world like a drunk in a hall of mirrors. Others are like the bumblebee, which science tells us can't fly. They believe the world has got itself into an argle-bargle of mighty magnitude because they believe it can no longer fly. We don't need them, Biff, we never did. In my day, we wouldn't have stood still for it. 'If you think like that,' I recall one small town mayor saying to a rowdy running against him on the local soft-in-the-head ticket, 'why don't you go be a Mexican?'

"In a lot of ways, it's the fault of your modern book publishers, and moving picture producers, who don't go out and look through the newspapers of heartland America to see what the people really want."

Well, Mr. Twain had his say on the matter, and I woke up in my back yard. There was a bumblebee flying by and I remembered that some people said that was impossible. Then I woke up again and I was in my bed and it was February. Something to think about, isn't it, how the mind plays tricks on us?

Enjoy Biff Lighter's THE LIGHTER SIDE OF STUFF every day during the week except Saturday in the daily Republican-Democrat.

By Hermwood Litmajor   Rep.–Dem. Crossword Puzzle Editor

Clues Across

1. She's not alive, she's_____
5. Out damn_____!
9. Body of water
12. Thick bloody mass
13. Poisonous detergent
14. Ugly wife
15. Favorite black sex attraction
16. End
17. Raw metal
18. What they do to killers
20. Many pounds
21. What women become after 18 years of marriage
24. Second favorite black sex attraction
25. How blacks pronounce "isn't"
26. Disaster, ruin, extinction
27. First two letters of what a wife has for brains
29. Wrath, anger
30. Murder weapon
31. Wildebeest
32. Short French word
33. Hit
34. Disfigure
35. What blacks get on my bedsheets
37. Grouches
38. Celestial body
39. What I would use if I didn't have a knife
40. Gone, past
41. Wife's temperament
42. Stupid, clumsy
43. Where a wandering wife spends eternity
44. Lake where murder weapons are deposited
45. Wicked
46. Name of wife's first love
47. Wife's favorite room in a gas station
48. Wife's favorite crime

DOWN

1. Dead On Arrival
2. A long time
3. Abbr. azure
4. A woman's soul is like a_____
5. What a man does with a knife
6. Pineapple
7. Jigaboos have lots of this under their arms
8. The number of times I've caught my wife fooling around
9. What I'd do if I had a gun
10. To receive for one's work
11. Wife likes coloreds of all_____
19. Who killed the bitch?
20. The delivery boy with the muscles
21. Noise a wounded woman makes
22. Employ
23. Number of lovers God allows a womao
24. Digit
26. How one makes a grave
27. Preposition
28. To cut in short strokes
29. What a colored does when he makes love
31. Danish airline
32. Thirteenth letter of the Greek alphabet
33. Leg (slang)
35. Source of light
36. What I committed
37. People who ruined my life
38. Hereditary material that makes me do these things
39. Sun god
40. Injure by beating
41. What a wife can be in the morning
42. Dried up
43. What knife wounds cause
47. Egg
48. Immerse
49. What a bullfighter says

Answers to last week's Sunday Daily Crossword Puzzle appear on page 22.

DACRON THEN & NOW

Monroe Street between Upton and Bancroft in 1903

Photo courtesy Mrs. Philpot Hugs

Monroe Street between Upton and Bancroft today

75 years ago the land along Monroe Street between Upton and Bancroft in West Dacron was nothing but wasted space.

Today this area is a bustling center of retail trade.

CAMPS & SCHOOLS

But What If This Had Happened on the Street?

The telephone helps make our lives wonderful even when we don't think so. Consider an obscene phone call, for instance. Sure, it's a bother, but what if that mentally disturbed person didn't have a phone? He would have had to be obscene in person. Think how much worse that would be for everyone. Plus, according to a recent study, obscene and annoyance callers use their telephones more than three times as much as the average telephone customer, so their extra message units help keep your phone bills down while still providing the investment income that your telephone company needs to bring you the best in up-to-date service.

**South Central Ohio
Telephone and Telegraph Bell**

Remember... Call Somebody, Anybody, Right Away, and Keep Calling People Up Day and Night!

There Blows Another Big Bottle of BUCK
The Thirst Drencher

When you're really thirsty, drinking an ordinary cola is like tossing a cup of tea down a volcano. Not so with thirst-drenching Buckeye.

Buckeye contains enough of nature's most powerful thirst drencher, H_2O, to drench the most powerful thirst. It also contains plenty of energy-rich sucrose, the one-hundred percent natural sweetener made from tropical shrubs.

Dacron, next time you have a thirst that needs drenching, try a fizzy big bottle of Buckeye: The thirst drencher.

Buckeye Cola and Ruck are registered trademarks of the Buckeye Beverage Company. Dullsville, Ohio.

"It's Health-Licious"

SUNDAY NEWSPAPER PARODY
Conceived and edited by P.J. O'Rourke
Designed and art directed by Skip Johnston

Associate Editor: John Hughes
Writers: P.J. O'Rourke, John Hughes, Ted Mann, Tod Carroll
Swillmart Advertising Supplement written and and illustrated by Bruce McCall
Pomade magazine written and edited by Danny Abelson and Ellis Weiner

Sunday Week magazine edited by Ted Mann
"Keeping up with the Joneses" and "The Eyes Have It" comics written and illustrated by Shary Flenniken
Additional material by Bruce McCall, Douglas C. Kenney, and Denis Boyles
Asst. Art Director: Muney Gurson
Asst. Art Director-Ads: Alan Rose

Copy Editor: Edythe Tomkinson
Associate Copy Editor: Susan Devins
Research: Katrina vanden Heuvel
Editorial Associate: Chuck Bartelt
Special Thanks for Aid, Encouragement, Ideas and Suggestions: to William Attwood, the staff of *Newsday*, Peter Kaminsky, and Seymour Rothman of the Toledo *Blade*
Stock Photos: U.P.I.-Stan Friedman
Additional stock photos from Wide World, Milky Way Productions, Bettmann Archives, and the Memory Shop
Models: Nicholas, Virgina, James, and Christine Paladino as the family on the cover of *Pomade* magazine
Liz Maclowe, Fresca Jasper, and Susan Rosenthal as the beauty contestants on the cover of *Sunday Week* magazine
Arthur Rousmaniere as Bobby MacAdam
Muney Gurson, Elise Cagan, Audry Jaenchen, and Ruth Kabat as *Republican-Democrat* newsboys
Matty Simmons as Rutgers Gullet
Pamela Osowski as the model in the housecoat fashion show
Robert Hopfan, Peter Littell, Bill Donner, and Wayne Spearnak as models in the men's fashion show
Beau Williford as Derrik McChienery and the Human Meataxe
Norman Kremer and Meryl Hopfan as John and Donna Devish
Carol Smith as the girl in the telephone ad
Photo Locations: Gleason's Gym, Oyster Bay Auto Repair, Sparkle Car Care Center, C.W. Post College

Additional Layout and Design: Taurins Design Associates, Al Izen, Kerry Gavin, Clint Brownfield, Ruthanne Hamill, Karen Mastropietro, Sandra E. Popovich
Photographer: Cleveland Storrs
Additional Photography by Skip Johnston, Pedar Ness, Ronald G. Harris, and Susan Rosenthal
Photo Coordinator: Susan Rosenthal
Photo Retouching: Bob Rakita
Cover Artist Andy Lackow
Additional retouching by Bishop Retouching, Inc.
Art Assistants: Ruth Kabat, John Flagg, Rich Puglia, Alan Andresen, Charlene Boyer, Elisabeth Huettermann, Camille Colton, Eliot Bergman, James Cook, Arthur Robinson, Jr., Sophia Laskaris
Contributing Artists: Virginia Hanlon, Enrique Suescun, Frank Springer, Joseph Russo, Al Bates, Bob Larkin, Randy Enos, Warren Sattler, Judy Jackliin, David Pieratt, Skip Wells, Mary Wilshire, Jerry Breen, Herb Dumaresq, Irv Novick, Roger Tomlinson, Karen Mastropietro, Frank Heller, Jane Ziegler, David Air
Comic Artists: Warren Sattler, Frank Springer, John Hughes, John Workman, Chris Browne, Frank Furlong, Randy Enos
Color and Separations: Jack Alder
Typesetting and Film: George Fisher and Charlie Graham at Daystar Graphics, Ltd., TypeArt, and Ready or Camera, Ltd.
Thanks for Production Assistance to: Trans Central Reproductions, Inc., Don Reilly at Hour Hands, Inc., James Ransom at Techni-Force, Inc.

Rugged Land Version
Typesetting, Design, and Restoration: Jay Naughton
Digital Prepress: Jay Naughton and Kim Thompson

www.nationallampoon.com